THE PERILOUS
ST. CROIX RIVER VALLEY
FRONTIER

THE PERILOUS ST. CROIX RIVER VALLEY FRONTIER

KEN MARTENS

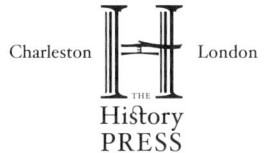

Charleston · London
THE History PRESS

Published by The History Press
Charleston, SC 29403
www.historypress.net

Copyright © 2014 by Ken Martens
All rights reserved

First published 2014

Manufactured in the United States

ISBN 978.1.62619.349.9

Library of Congress CIP data applied for.

Notice: The information in this book is true and complete to the best of our knowledge. It is offered without guarantee on the part of the author or The History Press. The author and The History Press disclaim all liability in connection with the use of this book.

All rights reserved. No part of this book may be reproduced or transmitted in any form whatsoever without prior written permission from the publisher except in the case of brief quotations embodied in critical articles and reviews.

CONTENTS

Acknowledgements	9

Introduction
About the Book	11
Proximity: A New Definition	12
Revenge, Revenge, Revenge: Understanding the Scope of Violence in This Book	13
The Devil's Chair Mystery	13

Part I
An Early History of the St. Croix River Valley	15
Vanished Civilizations: Their Evidence Survives	18
Moon Mounds: Astronomical Earthen Structures	21
Landforms and Mysterious Geology	24
Rattlesnake Effigy, Afton, Minnesota: A Native American Spiritual Site	25
River Life Today	27
Naming the St. Croix River	30
The First Shot: The Dakota and Ojibwe Go to War	31
The Battle of O'-ki-zu Wa-kpa'	34
A Life for a Life: Omigaundib of Rice Lake	36
A River Legend Born from a Warrior's Death on the St. Croix: The Legend of Catfish Bar	37
The Battle of Grave Marker River: The Last Battle of the Fox Indians	38

Contents

Night Fight, 1785: A Dakota Camp Attacked on the Willow River — 41
The War That Almost Was: Zebulon Pike Meets Chief
    White Buzzard — 42

Part II

A Land Dispute Settled by Death: The Battle of Zion Hill — 53
The Last Buffalo East of the Mississippi, 1832 — 56
Massacre at Battle Hollow: Treaties and Warfare on the
    New Frontier — 59
The First Pioneers of the St. Croix Valley: Haskell and Norris
    Raise Wheat — 64
The First Pioneer Women in the St. Croix Valley: Mary Hone
    and Lydia Carli — 68
Life and Death on the New Frontier — 70
Burial Ground Needed: Catfish Bluff, Willow River, Fahlstrom's
    Family Plot — 73
A Bold Ojibwe Attack: Pine Glen, 1842 — 79
A Partnership Made to Farm the Land "Unto Death
    Us Do Part":Educators of the Kaposia Mission — 80
Delivering Winter Supplies to the St. Croix Valley Alive,
    If Possible — 83
Early Marriages of the St. Croix Frontier — 84
A Burial Wish Come True: Silas Snell on Liberty Hill — 85
Stillwater's First Murder Trial, 1847: The Murder of Henry Rust — 86
Murder for Hire: Whiskey Rivalries Become Deadly — 87
White Man's Justice: A Fearsome Thing — 88

Part III

Early Elections in Stillwater, St. Croix County, Wisconsin Territory — 89
Gateway to the Raw Frontier, Stillwater — 90
Whose Baby Is Whose?: Early Socializing in Stillwater — 91
Border Country and Statehood — 92
Black Pioneer Dick: Joel Foster's Indentured Servant — 94
Scalp Dance in Downtown Stillwater: Terror on Broadway — 95
Rats Attacked by Tom the Cat: Terror in Stillwater — 97
Rain, Lightning and Thunderbird: Terror from the Sky — 97
Risky Opportunity in the "Pineries" — 99
Risky Opportunity on the Frontier — 101
Taken from the High Chair: Struggles on the Frontier — 102

Contents

Struggle for Life on the Frontier: Sophia and James Norris Begin a Family — 104
Drowned on the Fourth of July: Martin Atkinson — 104
Diphtheria Attack: The Stouffer Children — 105
Deer Harvested by the Thousands: Grand Hunt on the "Sunrise Prairie" — 106
Afton Water: Electa Getchell — 107
Fear the "Zephyrs" of Spring: The Radinzel Family's Funeral — 108
Under the Ice: Thomas and Anne McDonald — 109
Bodies Found Drifting in the Mississippi — 111
Coroner's Report!: Body Identified — 112
Drowned at the River's Ford! — 112
Body Discovered! — 113
Ann McDonald's Grave — 113
Gone Missing: The Prescott Ferry Operator — 114
Body Found Floating: Value $200 — 114
Disappeared: Four Men in a Skiff — 115
A Failure to Arrive: Brewer Augustus Benz — 115
Travel on the Turbulent Waters: Harry Wheeler — 116
Death Rock: Deadly St. Croix Falls — 116
Traveling on Highways of Water: Steamboat Adventures — 117
Attacking the *Banjo*: Or, We Haven't Any Shingles! — 118

Part IV

A Ship's Carpenter's Luck Runs Out: Thomas Ramsden — 121
Arrival on a Plague Ship: Ambrose Secrest's Pioneer Crisis — 122
The Wreck of the *Equator*: Captain Asa B. Green — 124
How to Survive a Steamboat Wreck: Never Learn to Swim — 126
"This Trail Is Mine," Road Rage Frontier Style: Chief Pinichon versus the Trader — 127
Road Rage, Horse and Buggy Style: Elias McKean versus Dr. Stone — 129
Road Rage, in a One-Horse Open Sleigh: Accident or Manslaughter — 130
Wagon versus Road Builder and a Wild Man!: Constable Able Cudd Is Overturned — 131
Dead on Arrival: The Three Deaths of Dr. Carmin Garlick — 132
The Last Ojibwe Fight with the Dakota, Murphy's Landing — 137
Black Pioneers in Afton: London and Jane Peters — 139

Contents

William Bartlett's Journey to an Icy Demise	140
Winter Couldn't Be Worse, 1860–1861	141
An Old Pioneer, Now a Ghost	142

Part V
Accidental and Cruel News	143
Runaway Team of Gray Horses	144
Runaways Gone Missing	144
The Spring of 1861 Arrives with Serious Events	145
A Virginia Wildcat with a Gun!	146
Civil War Troubles in Afton	147
The Fighting Reverend: Reverend Simon Putnam	148
Stillwater's Panic and Fear of Dakota Attack	151
Fun, Frolics and Fiascos: Ice-Skating on the St. Croix	152
A Confederate in Stillwater: John Colby	153
The Grief of War: John F. Peterson	154
Baseball Amusements in the St. Croix Valley	155
Freedom with a Bang: An African American Community Celebrates at Prescott, Wisconsin	156
Beaten to Death by Accident: RIP James Clegg, Saloon Keeper	157
The Postmaster's Dead Tree	159
"I Danced with Jesse James": Widow Eliza Ross	161
The Questionable Death of Captain Emil Munch	163
Woman of Mystery: Mary Traveler	165

Epilogue
The End of an Era	167
Enter the Modern Era, or "Locked Inside the Bank's Vault"	169
Bibliography	175
Index	179
About the Author	187

ACKNOWLEDGEMENTS

I would like to thank the following historians and individuals for their research, insight and contributions to *The Perilous St. Croix River Valley Frontier*: Hank Sampson, 1930–2008; Willis Miller, 1919–2008; Gary Cran, 1941–2010; Marian Williams Glynn, 1914–2010; Jack Koblas, 1943–2013; Brent Peterson; Pamela Ross Reuvers; Leah Junkert; John Martens; Robin Misswandt; Phil Cudd; Bruce Ramsden; Ted Stout; Rodney M. Nerdahl; and special friends. I would like to mention Sarah Johnson, whose cemetery documentation, preservation and genealogical research contributed to the content of this book. Thanks also go to Vince Barrows, whose Cahokia Mounds and ancient culture expertise played an important role in the writing of this book. A special thank you goes to Mary Divine, a talented writer for the *St. Paul Pioneer Press*, whose skills in reporting historic news events attracted national attention that resulted in the publishing of this book.

HISTORICAL ORGANIZATIONS AND SOCIETY ACKNOWLEDGEMENTS

Afton Historical Museum, Afton, Minnesota
Barnes County Historical Society, Valley City, North Dakota
Cahokia Mounds State Historic Site, Illinois
Hastings Public Library

Acknowledgements

Hudson Public Library
Minnesota Historical Society
National Park Service, St. Croix Riverway Headquarters, St. Croix
    Falls, Wisconsin
Pierce County Historical Society, Prescott, Wisconsin
Stillwater Public Library
Taylors Falls Historical Society, Taylors Falls, Minnesota
Washington County Historical Society, Stillwater, Minnesota
Wisconsin Historical Society

State Park Acknowledgments

Afton State Park, Washington County, Minnesota
Aztalan State Park, Aztalan, Wisconsin
Interstate Park, Taylors Falls, Minnesota and St. Croix Falls, Wisconsin
Kinnickinnic State Park, Pierce County, Wisconsin
St. Croix State Park, Pine County, Minnesota
Wild River State Park, Chisago County, Minnesota
William O'Brien State Park, Marine, Minnesota
Willow River State Park, St. Croix County, Wisconsin

INTRODUCTION

About the Book

This book is intended to be read from the first word through to the last. There are rare bits of information scattered throughout to help the reader comprehend the incomprehensible. Reading this book is like following a thread through the fabric of time. If you happen to skip something, the ensuing interpretive narration might not read as an integrative whole.

There is much about native culture that was nearly lost forever, and tragically, certain things have indeed been lost. One hundred years ago, almost all of this nation's native children were taken from their traditional lodges and sent to boarding schools, where they were taught to forget everything they knew. I'm not sure if this damage can be undone, but I hope to help by sharing what I have collected from a vast array of native people, from whom I have learned a great deal. This has been a rare adventure for me, and now some good might actually come from it.

It's widely known that Christopher Columbus arrived in the western hemisphere by error and misidentified the people here, naming them Indians (for another culture that was halfway around the world). Native people understand that a name is something given to them, yet the truth is that the original people on this continent are just that—people.

This book covers a vast subject matter, although it has its limitations. There just isn't space for a historical work that might lose the reader to minutia and doldrums. The table of contents is meant to serve as an index

Introduction

as well. The real intention is to bring life to a forgotten historical era that inspires one's curiosity to search for more.

Something important to keep in mind as you read this book is that there are no absolutes, and there is an exception to every rule. Anything is possible, and this book, in particular, communicates that history is stranger than fiction. The stories herein are a one-of-a-kind compilation. They are an impartial interpretation (as a collection) of personal and individual accounts set in the broad swath of history. I have used multiple and expansive resources to assemble these true-life tales in a way that has not been done before. My historical advisors have told me that much of this information has never been combined in this way, and if I neglect to write it down, it will never be reconstructed again.

This book is a story of history, about the rise and fall of cultures. Two thousand years ago, a culture of mound-building people existed here who eventually met their demise, to be replaced by another culture and broken into tribal groups of survivalists who lived amid conflict. The enormity and complexity of these stories tied together in this book cast a light on the best of people and the worst of people. Whether this history digs into the adventurous sides of people or their greedy sides, the selfless and heroic or the less than brave sides of history, it always speaks to the resilient nature of the people who have lived in the St. Croix Valley.

Hopefully we might understand ourselves and our era in time a little better after having read this book.

Proximity: A New Definition

In our current era, we live with proximity as an exacting science. We have our legal addresses and GPS, always certain where something, someplace or someone is. Proximity was far different in historic times, where "close to it" was meaning enough.

An extreme example of historic proximity is the story written about the great Ojibwe chief Hole in the Day, whose relative Little Frenchman was killed at the St. Croix River about 1835. The death took place anywhere from 85 to 135 miles from their home adjacent to the Mississippi River. The St. Croix is 164 miles long, so the murder could have happened anyplace, and it's probably too late to ask where.

Introduction

A similar example of historic proximity is the case of a sawmill constructed on the upper St. Croix River by Dr. Carmin Garlick. By historic description, the sawmill's location was to be found at the mouth of the Sunrise River on the St. Croix. The actual mill site was 6.75 miles below the Sunrise River, but the tributary was the closest area landmark by which to identify the mill. This discrepancy in distance would not have hindered the hardy frontier pioneer. A sawmill operation belched so much steam and acrid smoke combined with the powerful odor of pinesap and tar that one would know exactly where to find it.

Historic standards on the frontier were much different from ours of today. Related incidents occurred miles apart. The modern reader should accept greater distances as a relative factor when reading the history contained herein.

Revenge, Revenge, Revenge: Understanding the Scope of Violence in This Book

It might be difficult for some readers to comprehend the early history of intertribal warfare written. To help the reader understand the nature of native warfare, I resourced the oldest history book ever written. In that book, the story is told of Cain's extreme jealousy of his brother, Abel. Acting in a jealous rage, Cain struck his brother down. In judgment for the murder, Cain was banished to a harsh and unforgiving land, where the inhabitants were instructed that no one was to kill him. A ruling was issued that if Cain were killed in reprisal, his death should be avenged sevenfold.

In a second historic account following Cain's tale, Lamech killed a man in self-defense—after being assaulted and wounded. In Lamech's case, a ruling was issued that if he were to be killed for his defensive act, he should be avenged seventy-seven times. Eventually, the revenge ruling was violated and, reprisals becoming the norm, grew exponentially.

This foreknowledge should aid the reader's ability to comprehend the scope of events that took place on the ever-changing frontier.

The Devil's Chair Mystery

The origin of the name "Devil's Chair," given to a majestic rock formation that arose above the west bank of the St. Croix River, is unknown. There is no

Introduction

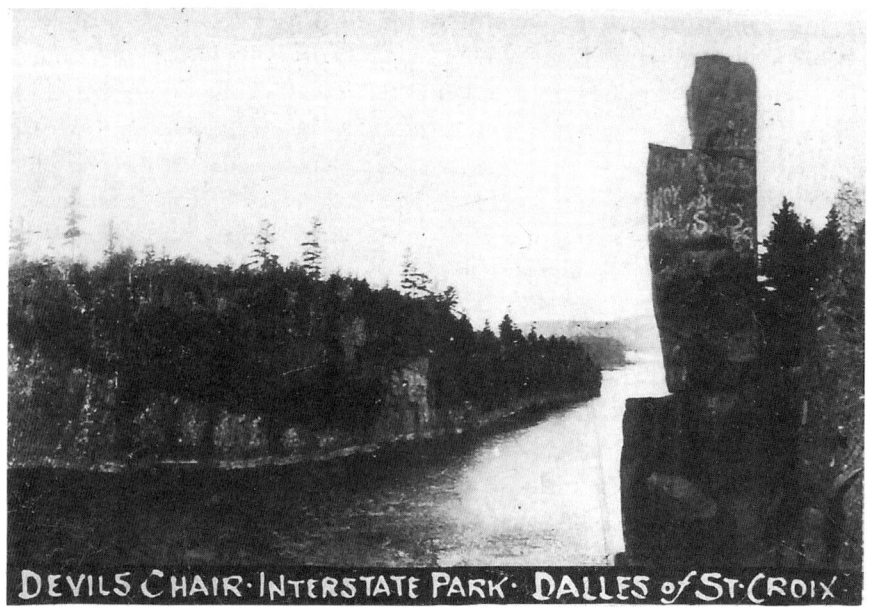

A 1912 Interstate Park souvenir postcard image of the Devil's Chair. The rock formation amazed many for centuries but collapsed in 2005.

known legend of a devil in the Dalles (dallas) of the St. Croix River; it's simply a fictional title for the dramatic columnar shape of basalt. The mystery is how the chair survived the destructive forces of erosion that created the rugged Dalles and Falls of the St. Croix. The crisp edges of the rock show little evidence of age, as if it were created during more recent geologic times.

Huge rewards have been posted for information leading to the arrest of vandals who toppled the Devil's Chair in 2005. No suspects are known. Heavy spring rain, strong winds and lightning strikes have not been ruled out in the loss of the chair. Natural causes are the most reasonable explanation for its ruin, as natural erosion is a constant enemy to nature in the area.

The history of the St. Croix River Valley above and below the historic Devil's Chair is something of special interest. Cultural change and conflict led to the demise of one civilization and the creation of another. The European migration to the area replaced native peoples, who had existed there for centuries. There are many tragic tales surrounding the exit of the native people and many more tales of tragedy concerning the new civilization's struggle to take hold. The question might be asked: was the devil there sitting in the chair?

PART I

AN EARLY HISTORY OF THE ST. CROIX RIVER VALLEY

The St. Croix River Valley was carved out of the terrain by a catastrophic deluge that flowed south out of glacial Lake Superior. Lake Superior is North America's largest body of fresh water, but the great lake lost half its volume when the last ice age ended ten thousand years ago. The glacier that covered this area was thousands of feet high, likely a five-thousand-foot or mile-high mass of ice. This massive sheet of ice melted rapidly as the climate warmed dramatically, causing Lake Superior to overflow its southern shore. Geologists know that the original shoreline of the great lake was six hundred feet higher in elevation than it is today. They also know that the southern shore was similar to a natural earthen dam that retained the body of water, which had once been a solid block of glacial ice. It was this earthen barrier that eroded and broke when the flow of water became more than the dam could hold. The resulting natural disaster ripped out soil and bedrock, creating a new riverbed and valley—20 to 90 miles wide and 120 miles long—that would be named the St. Croix.

There is more evidence of great glacial melt and erosion west of the glacial St. Croix River in central Minnesota. The Mississippi River, the longest river in North America, lies in a twenty-mile-wide valley that was once the glacial River Warren. Today, the mighty Mississippi is merely a trickle compared to the massive waterway, the River Warren, that flowed during the time of cataclysmic melt and runoff.

The Perilous St. Croix River Valley Frontier

Farther west of the glacial River Warren is Brown's Valley, another geological remnant of the glacial age. Prehistoric Lake Agassiz was created by melting glaciers, and it, too, overflowed its southern shore, creating Brown's Valley, which is nearly twenty miles wide. Big Stone Lake is at the head of Brown's Valley, and its source begins at the Traverse Continental Divide. This is a north–south divide from which Big Stone Lake flows to the south and Lake Traverse to the north. It is quite unique in that one can stand on the Traverse Divide and see water on both sides, with each body flowing in opposite directions.

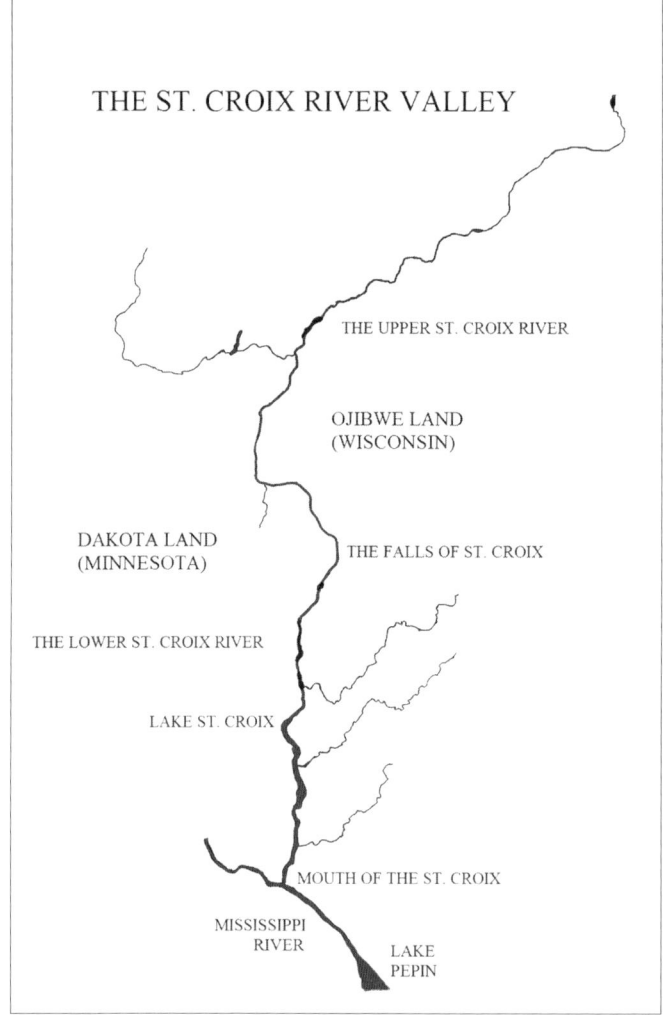

The St. Croix defines the border between Minnesota and Wisconsin. During historic times, the river served as a border between the Dakota and Ojibwe people.

Part I

Once many times larger than Lake Superior, glacial Lake Agassiz is dry today. Canadian Lake Winnipeg is the final remnant from the great glacial Lake Agassiz. The glacial geology of Brown's Valley, the River Warren and glacial St. Croix River spans two hundred miles of land from Wisconsin across Minnesota to the Dakotas. Similarly, the St. Croix River flows south directly from the Northern Divide in Wisconsin. Only two miles north across this continental divide is the source of the Bois Brule River, which flows north into Lake Superior.

During historic times, native people were quite able to travel by canoe from Lake Superior to the Gulf of Mexico, with the exception of a two-mile portage from the Bois Brule to the St. Croix. The St. Croix River, being a tributary of the Mississippi River, makes this incredible journey possible. There once were boulders creating turbulent waters named the Falls of St. Croix. The falls were located at a narrowing of the river called the Dalles (dallas), which would challenge a skilled canoeist, but with a short portage, the journey could be safely done. Located at St. Croix Falls, Wisconsin, and Taylors Falls, Minnesota, are the Dalles of the St. Croix, the most rugged

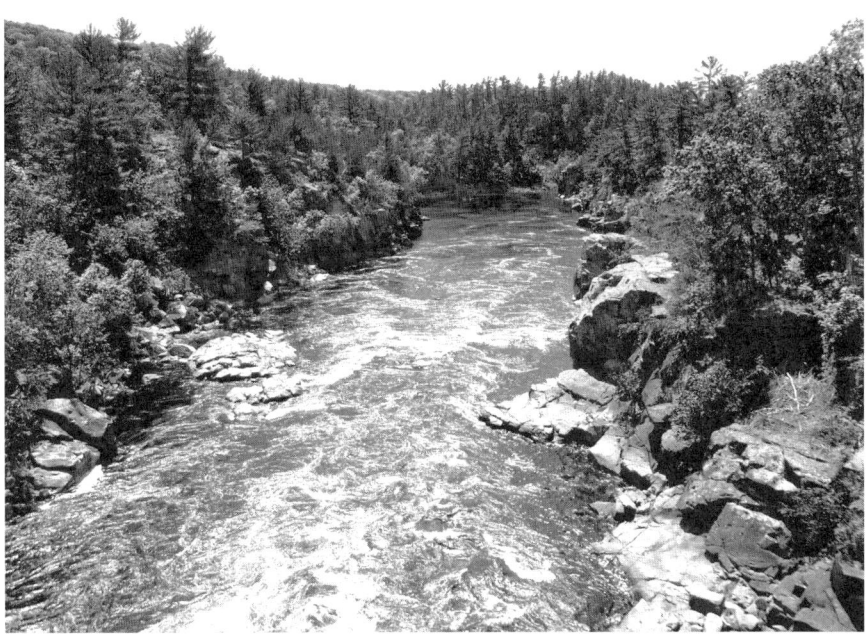

The rugged Dalles of the St. Croix at St. Croix Falls, Wisconsin, and Taylors Falls, Minnesota. Interstate Park is located on both sides of the river for visitors to enjoy.

portion of the river, where the rock formations are jagged and the cliffs are high. Here the evidence is clear that a torrential flow of water ripped out volcanic bedrock with unbelievable force.

Native people who resided on this continent for several thousand years understood that water was the greatest force on earth. They were scientifically correct. It is a law of physics that, of the elements, earth, wind, fire and water, the power of water is the greatest of all. For this reason, native people always respected water. They clearly understood that water could give life or bring death.

Vanished Civilizations: Their Evidence Survives

A great culture of earthen mound–building people populated the St. Croix Valley one thousand years ago. The earth structures that these people constructed are of an immense size and required a demanding amount of labor. The mid-American culture of Hopewell people flourished two thousand years ago and then faded away, to be replaced by the Woodland culture one thousand years ago. Both of these established people constructed mounds of great size from the soil, many of which can be viewed today.

The largest earthen mound group in North America can still be visited in Cahokia, Illinois, near St. Louis, Missouri. About seventy-two of Cahokia's mounds have survived modern development, fifty of them having been destroyed. The greatest mound is Monks Mound, covering thirteen acres in area and reaching a height of one hundred feet. The top of the mound is terraced, with the northern portion being higher than the southern part that overlooks the plaza of the ancient city of earth. The Mississippian culture of people who constructed the metropolis of earth has disappeared, leaving its mysterious monuments behind.

Similarly, the St. Croix River Valley is home to earthen structures of great proportion, having been constructed by mound builders about one thousand years ago. The Woodland people, who are locally referred to as the Oneota, occupied the area until their disappearance about six hundred years ago; they might have been responsible for the immense monuments. The Dakota people of recent history utilized mounds for burial but were not responsible for the St. Croix Valley's mounds, which exceed 150 feet in length.

Mound sites are generally located on water sources to quench the builders' thirst. Mounds located at a distance from water would be difficult

Part I

to construct without a brigade of relief attending to them. These mounds must have been of great importance to the people to put such extreme effort into them.

Equally important would be the location of village sites on rivers or lakes. Most St. Croix River village sites were located on tributaries or springs due to the winter requirement of flowing water. The river ice freezes to a thickness of two feet, which made running streams or creeks the primary source of winter water.

Evidence of the civilizations prior to our current one can be found throughout the river valley and in most of its river towns. It is as if the people of our era have recycled and reused previous occupation sties. One of the largest mounds that can be found is among a group of smaller ones in Stillwater, Minnesota, at Fairview Cemetery. The large mound in the center of the cemetery measures 820 feet long by 350 feet wide, covering six and a half acres of land.

A unique feature of the east–west direction of the mound is that its profile is highest on the east and then slopes gradually to the west. It's possible that the mound is just a random geological landform, or "drumlin," but the first surveyors of Stillwater platted a street outside the cemetery and named it Mound Street. Although the street was designed on paper during the 1880s, the descriptive name was never put into use.

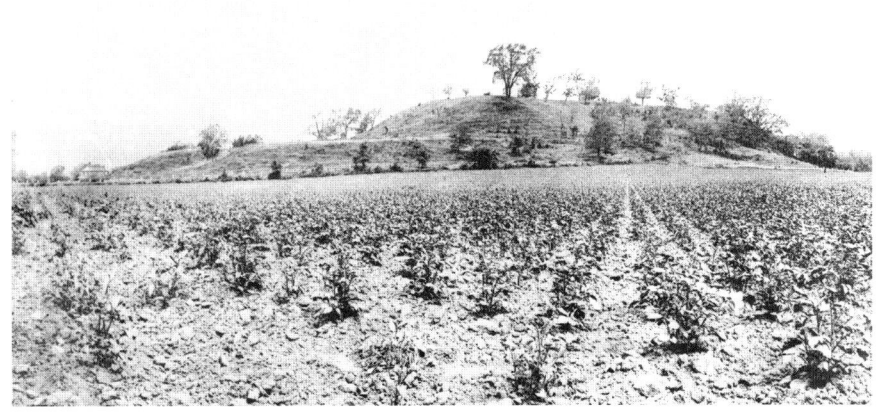

A 1907 photo of Monks Mound at Cahokia, Illinois. The importance of the large earthen structure would have influenced the river people, who lived in proximity to the mighty Mississippi. *Library of Congress, 97505973.*

The Perilous St. Croix River Valley Frontier

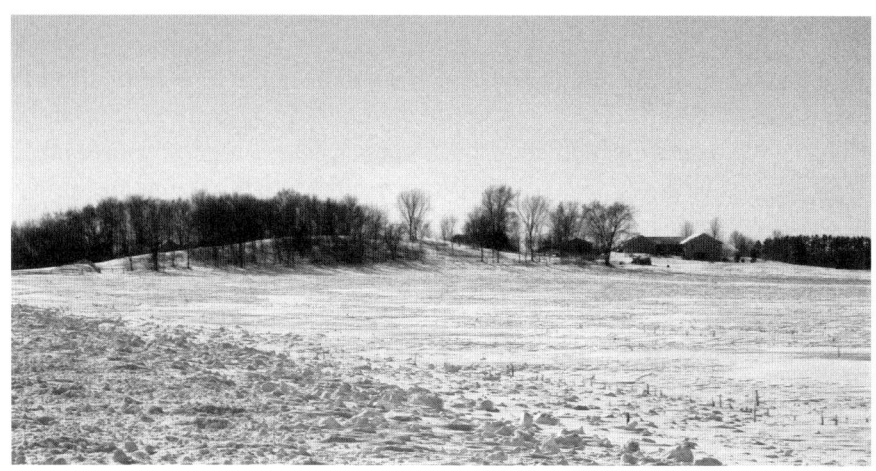

A large mound resembling Cahokia's Monks Mound is located near the entrance to Kinnickinnic State Park. A house has been built on the lower portion of the mound.

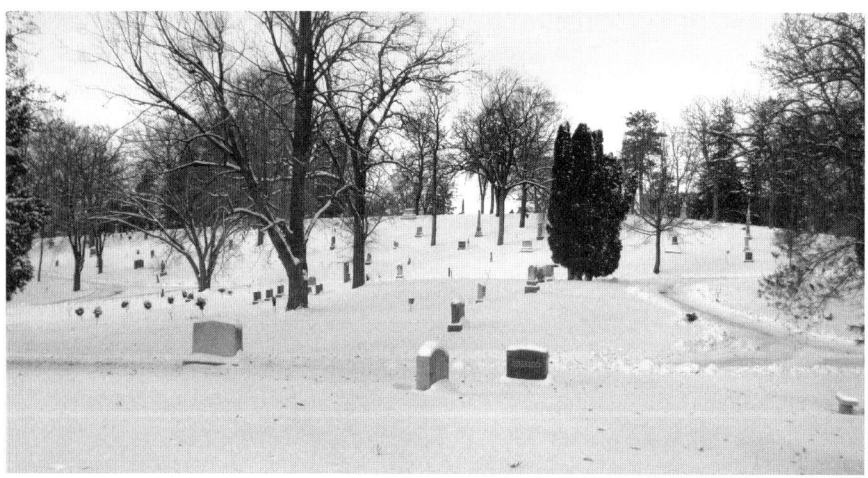

The immense size of the cemetery's mound site suggests it can be considered a burial mortuary. Although the cultures have changed, the use remains much the same. Burial vandalism fines begin at $10,000. Please respect the site.

To add to the mystery of the historic mounds of the St. Croix Valley is a similar mound situated at the confluence of Wisconsin's Kinnickinnic River and the St. Croix River, located fifteen miles below Stillwater. The large mound, located on elevated farmland, measures 830 feet by 355 feet and is oriented east to west, with the highest portion at the east end.

Part I

The two large earthen mounds are of such similar design that it appears as if the same builder constructed both of them using the same units of measure. Also, Monks Mound appears to have been used as the model to create half-scale replica mounds. The rivers, Mississippi and St. Croix, provide a common connection to the communities 550 miles apart, north to south. The historic river people were canoe builders, so much so that theirs was a culture of canoes and water travel. Therefore, the influence from Cahokia to the St. Croix Valley would have been common.

Moon Mounds: Astronomical Earthen Structures

The twin mounds of the lower St. Croix Valley are evidence of intelligent design, as opposed to being random acts of nature. Further evidence exists of calendar mounds constructed to warn the survivalist tribes that the hottest portion of summer was to begin. These elongated directional mounds line up with the summer solstice sunrise in the northeast or the sunset in the northwest. It was crucial to the native people that they remained close to water sources and lakeshore shade trees to prevent irreversible heat exhaustion and death. Likewise, utilizing these specific mounds in reverse gave them a winter solstice calendar that warned of bitter cold weather, for which they needed to prepare in order to survive.

The early calendar science that these forgotten people depended on for survival went beyond solar studies into lunar research as well. A curiosity for the lunar cycle drove a particular mound builder of the St. Croix Valley to construct two mounds that direct one's view to the north-northwest, within thirty degrees of true north. Following the moon to its mid-winter lunar set was permanently documented by an elongated mound in Baytown Township, just outside Bayport, Minnesota.

It would not be a coincidence, then, that an exact duplicate lunar calendar mound can be identified southeast of the first, located across the St. Croix River in Hudson, Wisconsin's Birkmose Park. The twin lunar calendar mounds are five miles apart, yet they both point 330 degrees north by northwest. The only way that could happen is if the same builder used the moonset to orient the linear mounds.

What one could learn from following the lunar rise and set is somewhat of a mystery. Following the draconic cycle of the moon, combined with

The Perilous St. Croix River Valley Frontier

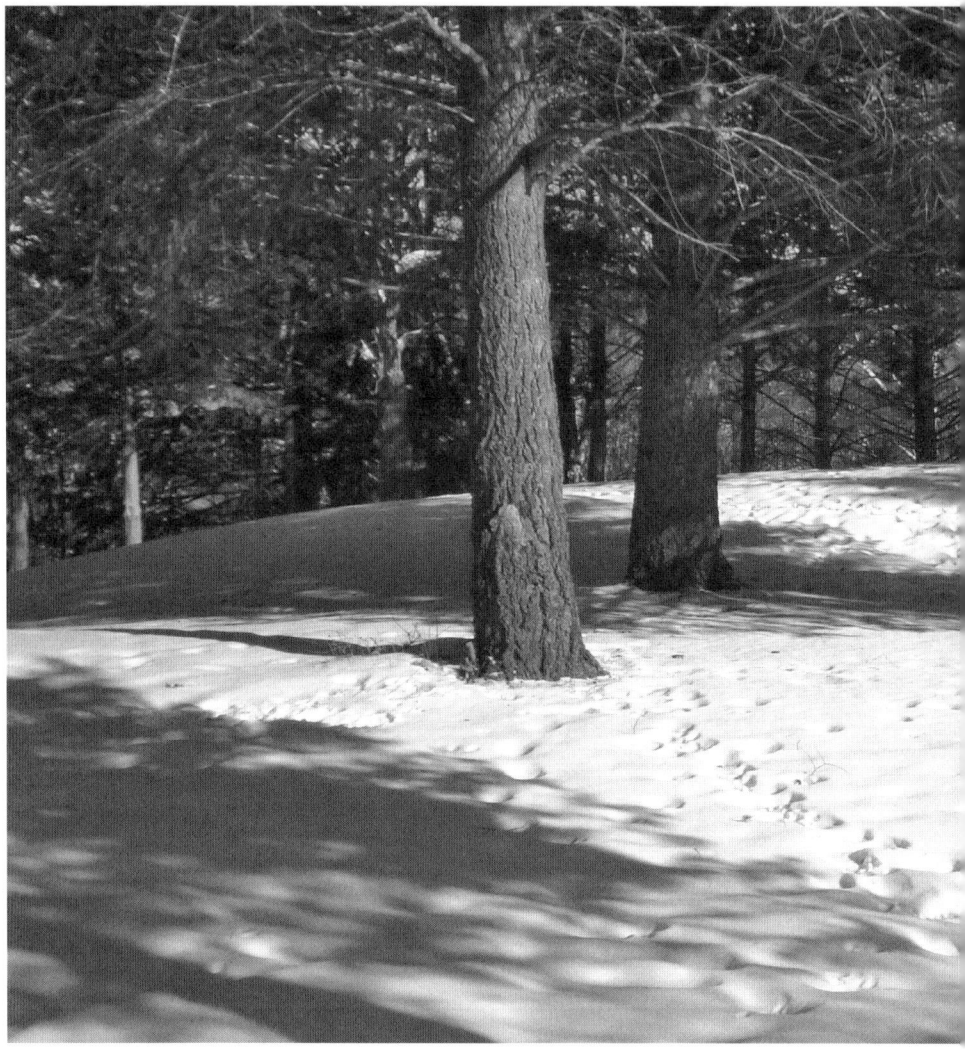

There are ten mounds at Birkmose Park. This linear mound lines up with the moon set. A clear view of the moon was possible during the era of vast prairies.

the refraction of light through the atmosphere, was a work in progress, the ultimate lunar determination having been interrupted by the decline and collapse of the civilization.

"People of the Moon" might be a title by which we could identify them. Alternatively, many assume that they worshipped the sun. Not so. Respect for the sun is what the people had; most spiritual Native Americans today

Part I

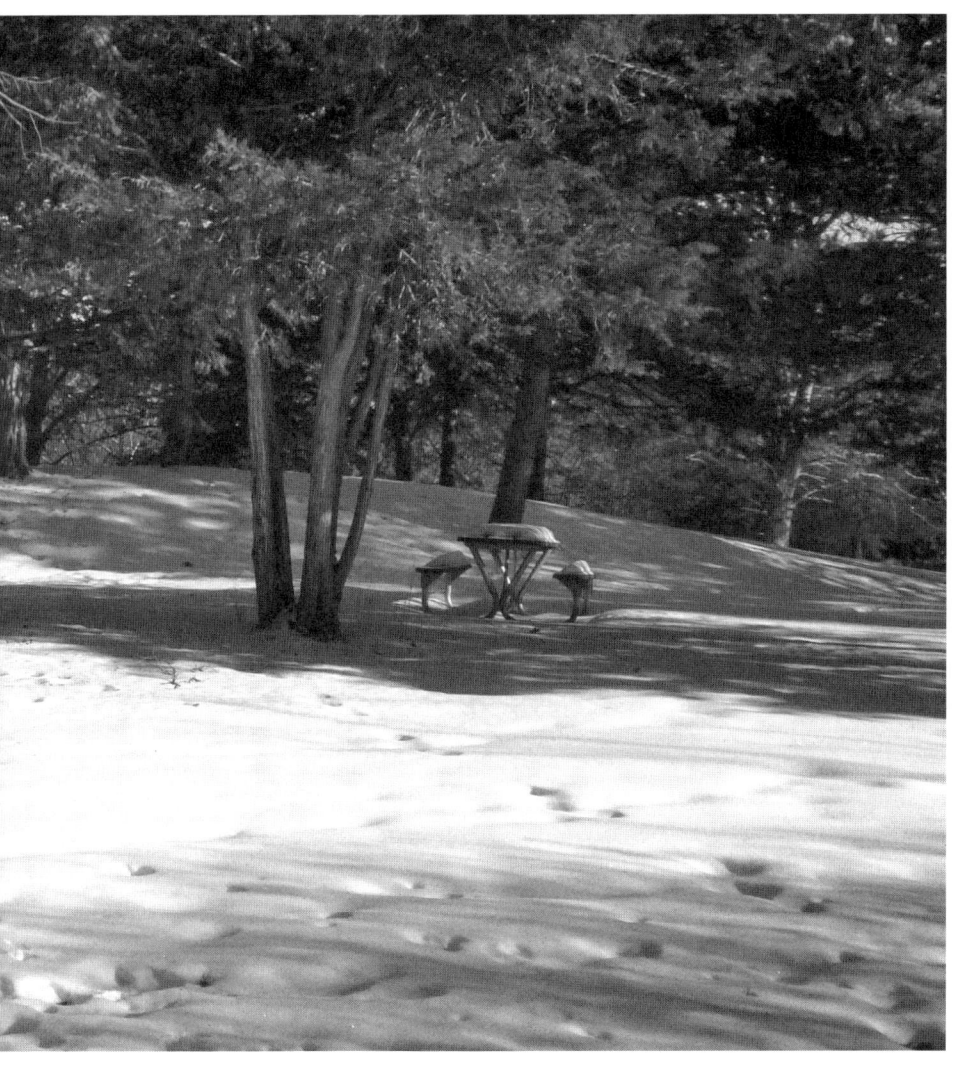

continue to pray to the Great Spirit that the sun shall not be too hot for their people to survive.

Where did the historic native population disappear to? Something of catastrophic proportion must be considered in the loss of an advanced culture. Weather factors of drought or cold temperatures could have contributed to the depletion of food resources. Historic earthquakes or volcanic eruptions would have increased the difficulty of harvesting food or animals, leading to starvation. Disease enters the formula for human disaster during the harshest of times. If warfare were to be introduced into the scope of this era, the civilization would have collapsed quite rapidly. Yet we are left to wonder: who were these mysterious people who lived here centuries before us?

Landforms and Mysterious Geology

There is a geological landform of unusual nature located in Minnesota's Afton State Park. It is a terrace of uniform proportion, 175 feet high on the bluff above the west bank of the St. Croix River. The terrace, with its growth of mature oaks, isn't obvious to the untrained eye. To the curious observer, the point of land appears to have been sculpted in four separate levels, dropping 100 feet in elevation over a distance of 600 feet. It's like a giant set of stairs created in mathematical proportion that suggests intelligent design.

It is possible that the terrace is a result of fluvial erosion that caused a down cutting of the soil as floodwaters receded by dropping in thirty- to twenty- to ten- to one-foot increments. This theory implies that a great flood occurred several thousand years ago, just as Minnesota geologists have speculated. Yet the Afton State Park's "terrace" has the appearance of being man made—a uniform sculpture of the land.

Many of the great mounds and landforms appear to be man made, created by intelligent design. Likely, the largest landforms were natural geological formations but were altered or enhanced by prehistoric people, creating works of art from the geology. At one time, archaeologists of Aztalan in

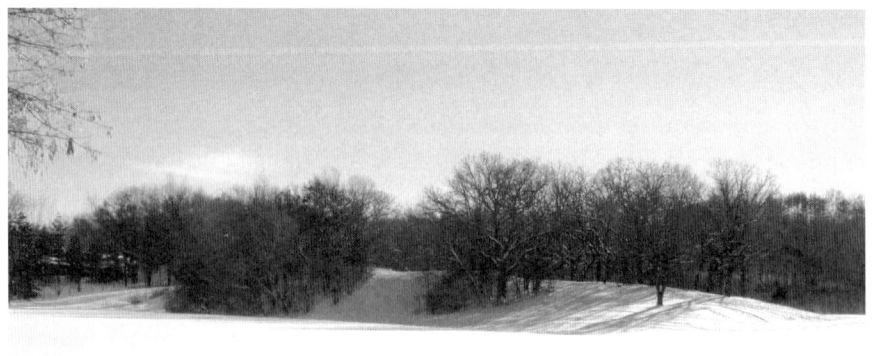

A mound 350 feet in length at Bayport Minnesota's Barker's Alps Park. Two Dakota burial mounds can be found on the top of the ancient earthwork. Once utilized as a calendar mound and cemetery, it continues to serve the public as a recreational sledding hill.

Part I

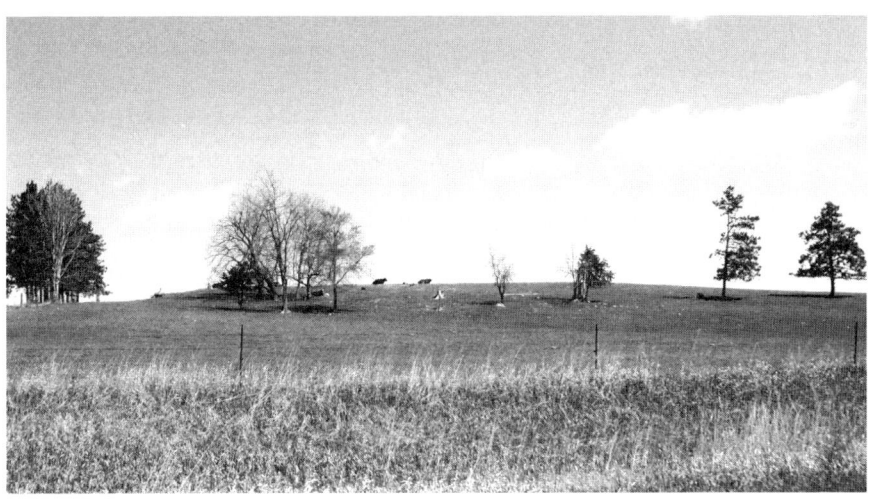

This hilltop cattle pasture at Franconia, Minnesota, above the St. Croix, resembles a pyramid. Other similar sites can be found in the state. Early archaeologists suspected an Aztec influence in the area. Today, a "Cahokian" influence is considered more likely.

eastern Wisconsin once speculated that the Aztecs were here 1,600 years ago. A reassessment of some of the largest, "suspect" landforms adds credence to the ideas of archaeologists of the late 1800s, whose opinions of Aztec influence in Minnesota and Wisconsin might have been valid. The mystery for us is: if the Aztecs were here, why did they leave?

Rattlesnake Effigy, Afton, Minnesota: A Native American Spiritual Site

Effigy mounds are rarely found in the St. Croix Valley. The small village of Afton, Minnesota, was host to a rattlesnake effigy mound that was discovered by pioneer Joseph Dernally. Dernally was a well digger in Afton who had planted corn in a field across the road from his home. In the process of plowing under the prairie sod, he discovered a shape in the soil that was unusual. The lengthy form had a head and a unique tail that resembled that of a rattlesnake.

Afton is located on a vacated native village site that also qualifies as a spiritual site due to the nature of the effigy. Rattlesnakes were common to the area before bounties were placed on them, but to the native people who constructed the mounds, they were a representation of eternal life.

THE PERILOUS ST. CROIX RIVER VALLEY FRONTIER

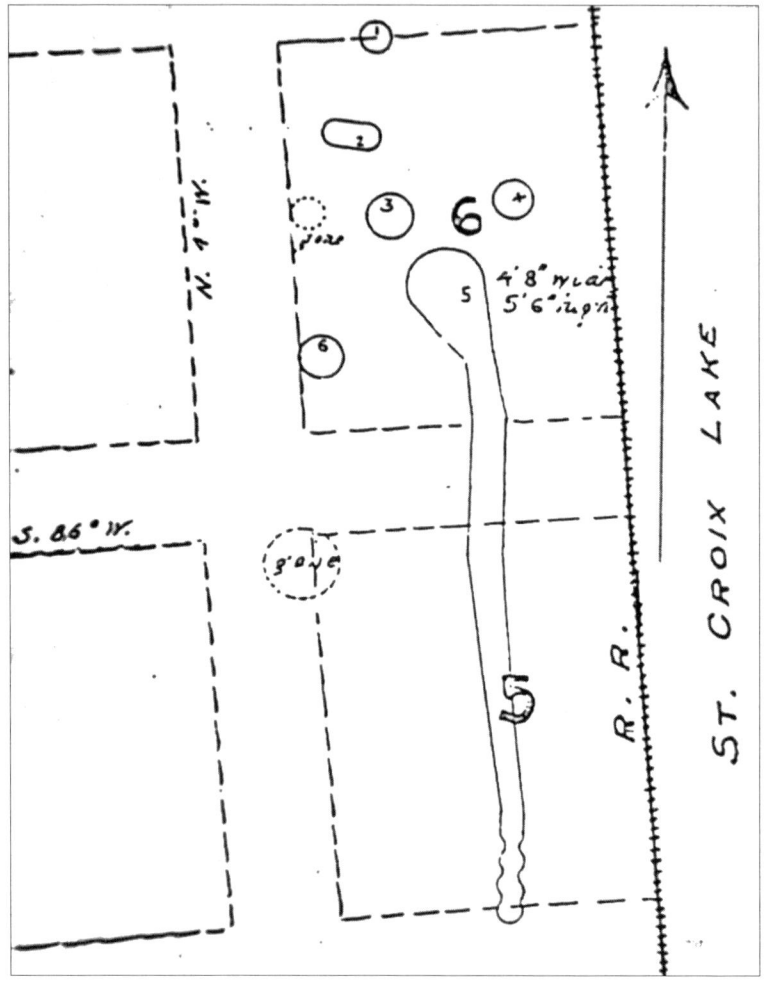

The Afton village mounds were documented in 1888 by J.V. Brower and T.H. Lewis. The rattlesnake measured 534 feet in length. Its body was 2 feet in height, and the head was 5 feet, 6 inches tall. *Image courtesy of Afton Historical Society.*

Snakes regularly shed their skin, leaving an old shell behind as a biological curiosity. A snake with fresh skin continues on its merry way looking glossy and new. Native people marveled at the snake's transformation from "dead" (skin) to new life, thus reinforcing their oral history of the biblical teaching that life is eternal.

As the native people migrated from the winter campsite to the summer campsite, they burned off the tall prairie grass prior to setting up their

Part I

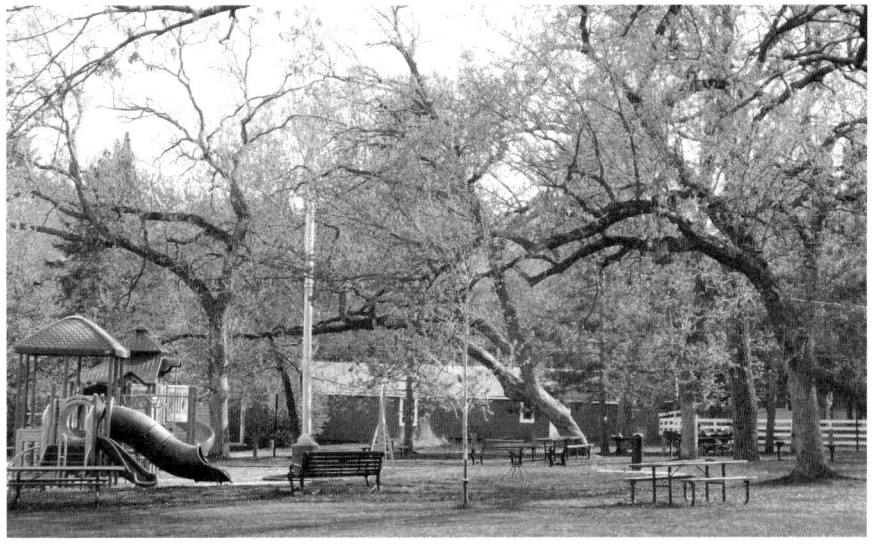

Nothing of Afton's mound site was preserved, but the marker trees, altered by native villagers, still point to the location where the rattlesnake mound could be located below the tall prairie grass.

lodges. Oak marker trees, resilient to prairie fire, were used by the people to assist in relocating the lodge sites and to mark the burials of family members they left behind. The Afton village site was wisely located below tall bluffs that provided protection from high winds and westerly zephyrs.

Raising children was no simple task, and as a safety measure, much of the tall prairie grass was burned off. Children could work, learn and play without becoming lost in the tall grass, never to be seen again. As a result of maintaining the prairies with fire, only the oak trees survive. The other, weaker stands of trees were kept clear of the prairie, aiding in the hunt for herds of wild game. Not a single conifer tree was in the thirty-five-square-mile township of Afton when the first pioneers arrived.

River Life Today

Within the last one hundred years, the deadly plague of cholera among pioneers ended. The fearsome intestinal disease was mitigated by the creation of sewage systems that processed human bacteria, placing it at a distance from

The Perilous St. Croix River Valley Frontier

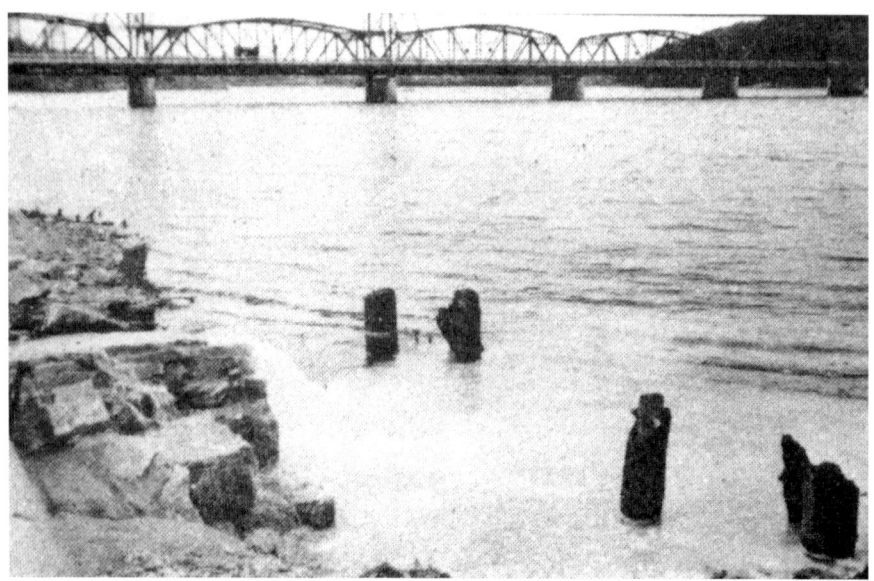

Stillwater City sewage flows directly into the St. Croix River in 1935, as in all of the valley's cities. Modern sewage treatment facilities have corrected the pollution problem.

where people lived. On the farms, the outhouses were located at a greater distance from wells and water sources; later, these outbuildings were replaced with septic tanks. In the cities, sewage drains would be connected to every home. The earliest city sewage systems in the St. Croix Valley terminated by directing the toxic flow straight into the river, dispersing it into the water. By the middle of the twentieth century, the St. Croix River was quite polluted. Also, during periodic times of drought, the St. Croix River was low enough in places to walk across. These low-water events exposed the river bottom, revealing the debris that had been dumped years before. Not only was the St. Croix River a garbage dump, but it was a sewer system as well.

In 1935, serious action was taken to identify the St. Croix as severely polluted in order to create a permanent solution to clean and preserve the great waterway. This action was reported by the Minnesota State Board of Health, the Wisconsin Board of Health and the Minnesota Department of Conservation. It would take several decades of intense action before the St. Croix would be restored to its earlier glory. Chamber pots and outhouses were replaced with modern septic systems, and city sewage treatment plants replaced the river drains. As of the mid-1960s, pleasure boaters with direct-flush toilets were required to install holding tanks onboard. The

Part I

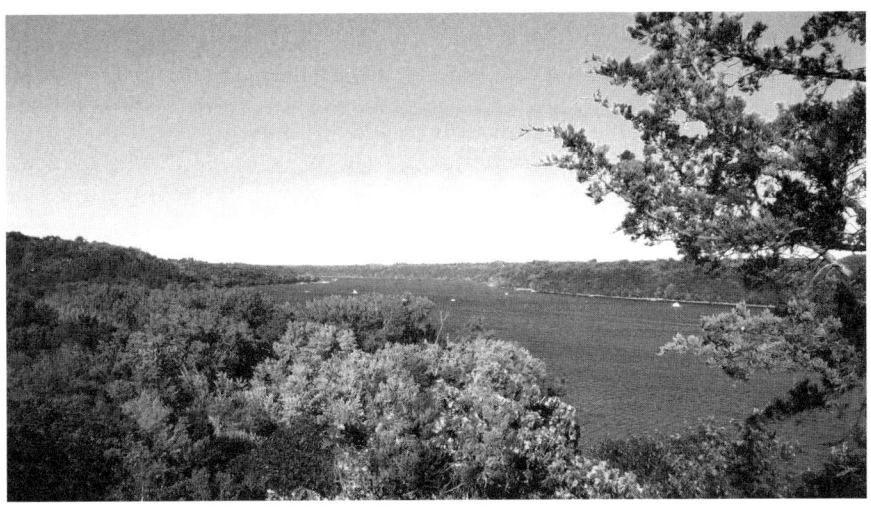

Lake St. Croix's natural beauty, preserved by the federal Wild and Scenic River Act of 1968.

river regenerated itself from its source and from its springs as it continued downstream, terminating in the mighty Mississippi.

The Mississippi River was no example of cleanliness either; in fact, it was quite the opposite. While people always found St. Croix River beaches a pleasure to bathe in, no one in his right mind would step into the polluted Mississippi. The St. Croix River ultimately went into a permanent state of preservation in 1968 with the passage of the Wild and Scenic River Act. The upper St. Croix River, from Taylors Falls, Minnesota, to its source at Solon Springs, Wisconsin, was designated a National Scenic Riverway and placed under the protection of the National Park Service. By 1971, bathers were safely using the Mississippi River below the St. Croix, a result of improving conditions on both rivers.

The lower St. Croix River, from Taylors Falls, Minnesota, to its confluence with the Mississippi River at Prescott, Wisconsin, grows broader and deeper than the upper St. Croix. The lower portion of the river was placed under the protection and management of the Minnesota Department of Natural Resources in 1972. The entire St. Croix River, 164 miles long, was now designated a National Scenic and Wild River and proclaimed the cleanest river in America. As a National Scenic and Wild River, both the upper and lower St. Croix portions have been placed in a permanent state of preservation for residents, visitors, sportsmen and pleasure boaters. The future of the St. Croix River is now protected from exploitive residential and commercial development, maintaining its natural beauty to this day.

The Perilous St. Croix River Valley Frontier

Naming the St. Croix River

The St. Croix River has gone by a variety of native names over the last several centuries. Each tribal people occupying the valley tied their own descriptions to the river. One native translation of the waterway was the "Fish River." This name fit logically due to the large size and numbers of catfish, prehistoric sturgeon and paddlefish that were unique to the broad, deep waters of the lower valley. "Rice Water River" and "Wild Rice River" are other historic variations used to identify the water. The northernmost region of the waterway flowed adjacent to marshes of wild rice (grain from marsh grass), a major staple of the native people.

In recent history, the naming of the St. Croix (kroy) River by European explorers is less clear. There appears to be several disputed reasons for naming the river the St. Croix. One of the earliest claims of naming the river was the discovery of an Indian's grave marked with a cross. The Indian had died from a rattlesnake bite on the river's shore near the confluence of the Mississippi River. Also, the way the river flows into the Mississippi is distinctly perpendicular, as if the two rivers form the shape of a cross. The phrase *St. Croix* is French, meaning "Holy Cross," so in this way, the first French missionaries traveling with explorers and traders labeled the waterway. One early rumor exists that a French trader named St. Croix capsized his canoe and drowned at the mouth of the river, so it was labeled for the incident that occurred there.

The most reliable or plausible reason for the river's name is the drowning of a French missionary at the mouth of the river. It's true that French explorer Daniel Greysolon, Sieur du Lhut (or Duluth), traveled down the river from Lake Superior in 1680. Greysolon had been in trade negotiations and creating alliances when he was made aware that a French Catholic priest was being held captive by a war party of Dakota farther to the south. Sieur Duluth, with his entourage of voyagers, made a canoe trip down the river, successfully locating Father Louis Hennepin and rescuing him from his captors. Apparently, an incident occurred about this time involving the loss of life of another missionary, a holy man who drowned where two rivers form a cross. Whether legend or fact, this is the most likely reason for naming the St. Croix River.

Part I

The First Shot:
The Dakota and Ojibwe Go to War

Many indigenous cultures have occupied the St. Croix River Valley over the last several thousand years. Unfortunately, none of these prior civilizations lasted much longer than a handful of centuries. The Hopewell culture of mound builders was active here two thousand years ago, leaving their large earthen monuments as faint reminders to curious onlookers today. Similarly, one thousand years later, the Woodland culture of mound builders continued where the previous culture left off. Eight hundred years ago, the Oneota people simply existed here, fishing, hunting and foraging for food. It would take an archaeological dig to locate fragmented evidence left here by the Oneota.

Dakota (Sioux) people are known to be the most recent indigenous occupants of this land, although that would be disputed by eastern arrivals, the Ojibwe (Chippewa). If you were to listen to the wisest of Dakota elders, they would tell you that Cheyenne people lived in the St. Croix Valley before the Dakota, five hundred years ago. Although quite rare, Cheyenne artifacts have been found in the St. Croix Valley.

Five centuries ago, the Dakota were a woodland people who were living on and fishing out of Lake Michigan, three hundred miles east of the St. Croix Valley. Once the Europeans arrived in the western hemisphere and began populating this continent, the native peoples felt the pressure to move from their traditional homelands. As each tribe moved farther west of the European populace, the next tribe felt compelled to move west as well. Native peoples were now shifting their homelands farther and farther to the west.

A river located in what is now west-central Wisconsin was named the Chippewa because it delineated a new border between Ojibwe land and Dakota land. Defining borders among tribes was important due to the preservation of their respective hunting grounds. Each tribe maintained a specific area on which to hunt wild game, allowing for the prosperity of small game and large herds.

Hunting grounds of the Dakota were generally woodland and prairie, while traditional Ojibwe hunting lands were forested. The Ojibwe subsisted on small game animals as a rule but were also skilled in taking deer and trapping live black bear. The Dakota were adept deer, elk and bison hunters, occasionally taking black bear. The western band of Dakota people, the Lakota, were expert elk and bison hunters of the prairies.

If someone unfamiliar with tribal hunting grounds were to trespass on them, the consequences could be dire. The seriousness of an uninvited trespasser discovered on native hunting land likely meant his demise. Inadvertently dispersing the game or animal herds meant that hunters might return empty-handed to their families and their tribe. To the hunter, whose hungry family depended on him, returning without food was an embarrassment worse than death.

The arrival of the French and British to this continent also resulted in the expansion of their traditional rivalries and hostilities to this land. Periodically, these two world powers engaged in continental warfare that would destabilize Indian nations, whose relations were generally more peaceful than not. The result of these British, French and Indian wars meant that territorial lines would be redrawn but at an economic expense that was self-defeating. Similarly, the large population of Ojibwe people living in Ontario and Michigan was receiving pressure from eastern European expansion to migrate farther west.

There was a peaceful time of relations between the Ojibwe and Dakota peoples when intermarriage and exchange between the two were natural. Each understood the need to "strengthen their blood" by introducing others into the tribe. Each tribe was divided into clans that were identified as such to prevent cousins from marrying cousins, resulting in a weakening of their blood. Likewise, certain clans were permitted to marry into one another. Ultimately, they knew that they were wise to introduce completely new blood into their people. It made scientific sense for them to marry across tribal lines. There was a trading partnership that served a useful purpose between the tribes, as well. These trades simplified access to necessary goods and supplies, making a life of pure survival a little easier. During this time period, the St. Croix River was commonly used by both Ojibwe and Dakota peoples.

The peaceful era between these two tribes was back in the time of arrows, spears, war clubs and stone knives. Theirs was a warrior culture that included hunting and foraging. Each man was a skilled warrior for the purpose of protecting his family from attack or for the necessity of a prolonged war. It would take a hunter's attitude of raw courage to take down a black bear in the forest or a bison on the prairie. Both of these great animals were aggressive and deadly when being stalked as prey by a hunter. If one did not possess a hunter's courage, what good was he to his hungry people?

Between the Dakota and Ojibwe, it would be the Ojibwe who would come into contact with the French fur trade first. This encounter with European culture, which possessed metal and iron tools, would forever change the Ojibwe. With access to what was thought to be an unlimited supply of animal skins and hides, the French would be able to export this treasured resource

Part I

to its transatlantic nation. The French were obliged to the Ojibwe, with the exchange of their furs and hides for iron pots, tin ware, wool blankets and flintlock muskets.

Possessing the musket changed the dynamic of hunting by providing the skilled hunter an additional edge in harvesting prey. Although these native hunters were experts in the use of the bow and arrow, the increased range of the musket allowed for the taking of game at a greater distance. Armed with the musket, the Ojibwe were effectively able to deliver even more hides to their French buyers. The Ojibwe had become fur traders.

The Dakota had been exposed to the French fur trade directly and indirectly. A few traders had approached deep enough into Indian lands to make contact with the Dakota. Indirectly, the Dakota were exchanging their furs for goods with their friends the Ojibwe. In this way, the Dakota participated in the fur trade. Very soon, animal hides that they traditionally would have worn were exchanged for cloth.

One particular gathering of the Dakota and Ojibwe for the purpose of trade took place at a site west of the source of the St. Croix River. This is a unique area where forests of pine, woodlands of oak and prairie marshes of wild rice merge. The meeting was a large one, even though the exact location is uncertain. The fur trade, by nature, was mobile in a way that its posts were rarely stationary, often shifting to new locations every two to four years. This tribal meeting is said to have happened in 1723, when Dakota hunters of the west traveled quite far to participate. As it happened, the Ojibwe were armed with their trade muskets, and many of the western bands of Dakota had not seen or been exposed to firearms before.

It has been said that a curious Dakota hunter asked an Ojibwe (armed with a musket) about the strange stick that he had with him. The Ojibwe hunter replied that he killed with the stick. The Dakota said to the Ojibwe that it was not possible to kill with a stick, to which the Ojibwe replied that it was possible with this stick. The reply angered the Dakota hunter greatly, and he insisted that it was impossible for him to kill with that stick. The Ojibwe was quite perturbed by the anger of the Dakota hunter, so he leveled his musket in the direction of the offended Dakota and pulled the trigger. The flintlock musket discharged with a flash, a loud report and a cloud of smoke, the result of which the Dakota hunter fell dead.

This action caused intense commotion among the other Ojibwe and Dakota, all of whom wondered what had just transpired. Was this a legitimate argument or simply an outright murder that should be settled by death. Certainly, the two tribes were in a state of confusion and uncertain how to settle this matter, "blood for blood" being the rule of law among native people. Retaliation against the offender would be in order, and the issue could be settled, but many times there occurred revenge for retaliation, and events spiraled out of control. It's likely that other tragic events followed similarly. The scope of these events would spiral beyond control, and by 1736, every allied tie between the Ojibwe and Dakota tribes had been severed. An all-out state of war existed from then on.

European expansion on the continent from the east caused the western migration of native populations. The Ojibwe people of Michigan eventually occupied central Wisconsin lands up to the Chippewa River, which served as a new border between the two tribes.

It would be competition between the Hudson Bay Company and the North West Company that added to rivalries among native hunters, creating tension that had not existed before. The westward movement of the Ojibwe people soon crossed over the Chippewa River, spreading deep into Dakota country. Ojibwe warriors would travel more than one hundred miles to attack Dakota villages. In retribution, Dakota warriors would respond with similar attacks. Unfortunately, the Chippewa River had served as a border between the two tribes for only a short time.

The Battle of O'-ki-zu Wa-kpa'

At the mouth of the St. Croix River and confluence of the Mississippi River once stood a great Dakota village of one thousand people named O'-ki-zu Wa-kpa'. In 1755, the large village was attacked by one thousand Ojibwe warriors who had assembled from two hundred miles away. Stealth and surprise were common tactics of warfare, and the Dakota villagers were taken unaware. As the Ojibwe attack began, women and children scrambled from their lodges down to the shore of the Mississippi River, where their canoes were beached. As fast as they could, they clambered into the canoes and shoved off into the Mississippi, but without having grabbed any of the paddles. At the time, the current was such that whirlpools near shore caught the canoes, causing them to swirl in circles. The Ojibwe warriors rushed directly into the shallows, retrieved the canoes and killed all of the occupants.

Dakota warriors had their work cut out defeating the Ojibwe attackers. It seemed possible that the Dakota defenders would prevail in defending their village and drive off their blood enemy. This was a battle where

Part I

flintlock muskets would be fired and then swung like clubs. With little time to reload muskets, war hammers would become the primary weapon in hand-to-hand fighting, dealing blunt-force trauma with strategically aimed blows at the skull.

Unfortunately for the Dakota, there was a second wave of Ojibwe warriors that had not yet engaged in the desperate battle. During the confusion, the enemy was seen approaching, but not by any of the Dakota; rather, it was viewed by an Ojibwe man who was being held captive in the Dakota camp. He had been among his captors long enough to learn some of their language, so he cleverly yelled out in Dakota, "Dakota warriors are coming to help defeat the Ojibwe!" The ploy worked successfully, creating a false sense of victory among the Dakota.

The Dakota warriors who were gaining the advantage in the battle looked to their rear to see the advancing group of warriors, who were charging, and assumed that the day would be saved. With their guard down, the advancing group of fresh Ojibwe took the exhausted Dakota from the rear by surprise and with devastating effect. Outnumbered by far, the last of the Dakota took refuge along the cliff base, and all of these Dakota were killed but one.

The sole surviving Dakota warrior leapt from his concealed position, took off at a dead run for the Mississippi River and dove in. The last of the Dakota began swimming to the opposite shore while the Ojibwe reloaded their muskets and fired. Diving below the water to avoid the musket balls was effective, but every time the Dakota rose to the surface for air, he was welcomed with a hail of lead. The last Dakota warrior made shore a half mile away, rose from the water and let out a shrill war whoop of success, to which the victorious Ojibwe warriors replied equally well.

It's likely that many of the Dakota villagers escaped with their lives using stealth and speed in the confusion of battle and musket smoke. Tragically, 335 of the Dakota had been killed, equaling one-third of their population. Comparatively, only a fraction of that number were Ojibwe casualties, and it's certain that many more belonging to both sides sustained serious injuries.

Word of the catastrophe that had taken place at the mouth of the St. Croix would spread quickly among the other bands of Dakota. Retaliation attacks would be carried out against the Ojibwe. The Dakota took their revenge battle to the Ojibwe maple sugar camp, fifty miles to the northeast on the Apple River; thus, the grief and suffering was equal.

The Perilous St. Croix River Valley Frontier

A Life for a Life: Omigaundib of Rice Lake

A Dakota war party proceeded to Rice Lake on the Red Cedar River and killed three children playing along the shore. One of the dead was Omigaundib's daughter. Rather than call for a war party and vengeance, Omigaundib placed his slain child in a canoe, covered her body in the black paint of mourning and traveled to the mouth of the St. Croix River. Omigaundib's destination was the Dakota village of O'-ki-zu Wa-kpa', from where the raiding party had come.

The great trek of Omigaundib was one of deep grieving for his lost daughter. Although blood for blood was their rule of law, each life was equal in the law as well. The life of a child was no different from that of an adult, as was an infant's life equal to a chief's. All life was valued the same. Omigaundib, beset with grief, was acting as if he could not live without this child and set his mind to confronting the Dakota, who were responsible for the killing, in an extreme way.

An Ojibwe arriving on the shores of a Dakota village was likely suicide. This created quite a stir, and the entire village gathered to witness the sacrifice of this grief-stricken father. Omigaundib picked up his deceased child from the canoe and approached his blood enemy with the limp body in his arms. The crowd of villagers expected Omigaundib's anger but was confronted with tears of anguish.

It was a bold act of bravery to confront one's enemy without a sign of fear, and this is what the Dakota villagers witnessed. Bravery such as this was respected in a way that the desire to kill someone so fearless would not be acted upon. Omigaundib, earning their respect, would be allowed to live and have his say among the circle of villagers. The bereaved Omigaundib lamented his loss to the gathered Dakota and begged for them to kill him, for he could no longer live without her. The camp's chief had come forward, listening to the wailing father while sorrow began to overtake the crowd. Mournful cries of Omigaundib's heartbreak filled the Dakota camp, and the chief spoke to the wailing father, asking him to stay for a moment; he would return shortly.

The chief came from his lodge through the crowd with one of his daughters at his side. The chief said that Omigaundib's brave act to confront his enemy was recognized and the depth of his loss was felt. The Dakota would not kill Omigaundib, as he had pleaded, but would make a gift of a child to take the place of the murdered girl. The chief escorted his daughter to Omigaundib's canoe, placed her inside and gently explained that from this time forward she would be his daughter.

Part I

Omigaundib realized that the chief was making a great personal sacrifice by giving up this daughter. The equitable gift of the chief's child was quietly accepted, and together the two paddled away.

A River Legend Born from a Warrior's Death on the St. Croix: The Legend of Catfish Bar

There were many incidents of warfare among the Dakota and Ojibwe as tribal lands progressed farther west. One of the Dakota victories occurred at Red Wing's Village on the Mississippi River, sending many Ojibwe warriors home a great distance in disgrace. It was tradition for the surviving Ojibwe to make their return journey hungry for food, without eating until they arrived in their native encampment. Part of a warrior's grieving process was to deny himself sustenance.

Two of the defeated Ojibwe warriors happened to be returning together along the shores of the St. Croix, making their northward trek home. Darkness came, and the two exhausted warriors stopped to rest for the night on an eastern beach of the wide portion of the river, Lake St. Croix. As they lay back to sleep, one starving warrior spied a raccoon in a tree branch holding a large catfish. The warrior exclaimed that he must have that catfish for he could no longer bear his hunger.

The second warrior strongly advised the starving one not to break the warrior tradition, barring the meal until they returned home with their news of loss and grief. The warning was heard, but temptation was too strong for the famished warrior, so he captured the catfish from the raccoon and ate it.

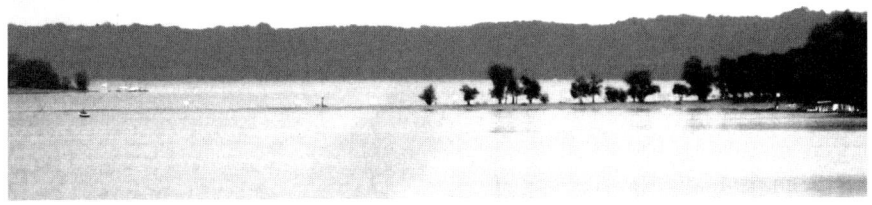

Wisconsin's Catfish Bar on Lake St. Croix of the lower St. Croix River. This landmark is located across from Afton, Minnesota.

Morning came, and the warrior loyal to tradition woke to discover that the famished warrior lying next to him had turned into a huge catfish. The waters of Lake St. Croix were merciful to the sight of the transformed warrior's grotesque body, gradually covering it with sediment and sand. Now removed from man's curious gaze, sand covering the body of the giant catfish is how Lake St. Croix's Catfish Bar was made.

THE BATTLE OF GRAVE MARKER RIVER: THE LAST BATTLE OF THE FOX INDIANS

The Odugamie, more commonly known as the Fox Indians or the Fox, were an aggressive people who occupied the eastern half of Wisconsin. They lived in conflict with many native traders who were doing business with the French. French fur trader Nicholas Perrot attempted to create trade beyond the territory of the Ojibwe, extending west of the Mississippi River, with the Dakota people. This act infuriated the Fox people, who had been trading with the British and then with the Dakota. Perrot had been guilty of squelching British fur trade by instigating Indian wars against them. Now that Perrot was pursuing trade with the Dakota, the Fox, who were allied with the Dakota, went to war with the Ojibwe, who traded with Perrot. The Ojibwe and Fox had been traditional enemies, but the recent frustrations with Perrot had launched the Fox into an all-out state of war.

The British fur trade was bringing better-quality goods to the native people at lower prices than the French. Adversely, the British were guilty of sweetening the trades with alcohol, so much so that trading with the British was destroying the Indian people. Eliminating native people via the negative effects of liquor had become a European tactic early on. Unfortunately, this would be true for the Fox. Losses were already staggering for the Fox as they waged war against the Ojibwe, and they were ultimately driven from their lands west to the Mississippi.

Since the year 1742, the Fox people had occupied land among their friends the Sauk and their allies the Dakota. In a few decades, the reinvigorated Fox people wished to retake land back from the Ojibwe. Recovered from the prior war with the Ojibwe, the Fox were confident of a victory, fighting just one great battle with their traditional enemy. About the year 1770, the Fox reorganized their forces and invited the Dakota to come witness a victory over their mutual foe. In a flotilla of dugout canoes made of sturdy

Part I

cottonwood, the two bands of warriors departed the Mississippi on an upstream excursion of the St. Croix River. Needless to say, it was slow going, but they were certainly up to the challenge.

The Ojibwe people were now able to populate western lands with less restraint. Young Chief Waub-o-jeeg of the Lake Superior band of Ojibwe was heading south on a similar excursion with three hundred of his warriors in search of any enemy he might encounter. Waub-o-jeeg was a young chieftain who had inherited his position at a youthful age. He was merely twenty-three while leading these great numbers of warriors.

It's likely that open territory discovered by Waub-o-jeeg on this venture would lead to the establishment of new campsites and villages for his people. Although in his early twenties, Waub-o-jeeg was wise enough to request the attendance of sixty more warriors from a northwestern camp of Ojibwe. The invited Ojibwe had yet to arrive at the preplanned meeting point, the Falls of the St. Croix.

As fate seemed to have it, the well-armed Fox warriors and their Dakota allies arrived below the Falls of the St. Croix at the same time that Waub-o-jeeg's forces arrived above. Both tribes of oar men were prepared to make the canoe portage across the rocky terrain at the narrows of the river alongside the raging rush of waters. Instead, preparations were being made for battle now that each had spotted the other among the cliffs and trees. Clothing was stripped off, and war paint went on. Only medicine pouches, arms and ammunition would be carried into the fierce battle to come.

The Fox, having seen the number of Ojibwe warriors, were now confident that they held the advantage and victory would soon be theirs. They requested that the Dakota warriors wait and witness the destruction of their mutual enemy. The overconfident Fox warriors did not have to search for concealed Ojibwe among the cliffs, cracks and crevices of rock. The enemy was found at the midpoint of the portage, where a classic confrontation presented itself with an explosion of musketry from both sides.

The resounding engagement carried on amidst the roar of the St. Croix's flow around and over the stones and boulders of the falls. The Fox pressed into the Ojibwe with early success, defeating their foe and taking their scalps. Waub-o-jeeg had directed certain warriors into adjacent woods, which effectively prevented the Fox from broadening their attack. The battlefield was now contained in the Dalles of the St. Croix, the narrowest and most rugged portion of the river. The warriors, locked in combat, were boxed in between the cliffs of the Dalles at the Falls of the St. Croix. Retreat was no longer an option for either side.

The Perilous St. Croix River Valley Frontier

Early in the day, the battle went in favor of the Fox, who were later confronted with desperation. The tide changed for the Ojibwe, and the Fox warriors were losing ground, retreating in chaos. The Ojibwe pursued the Fox warriors across the treacherous boulders of the falls, over which dead Ojibwe had previously been swept. It was now the weary Fox who were the victims of the Ojibwe, flowing over the falls that streamed with blood.

The Dakota, who had been quite relaxed from their position of observation, now saw the critical situation that the Fox were in. They realized that without intervention, the Fox would be annihilated. It was at this desperate juncture that the Dakota warriors engaged in battle with the Ojibwe with great success. The Dakota warriors' participation freed the embattled Fox to withdraw from the falls, which were littered with the dead of both sides. The Dakota would be robbed of their victory, though, as the sixty warriors Waub-o-jeeg had arranged for made their late arrival to the struggle.

With resounding success, the freshly armed Ojibwe warriors plunged into their foe. Now it was the Dakota who were taking casualties in the chasm. Dakota bodies began to flow over the falls, the survivors making their retreat

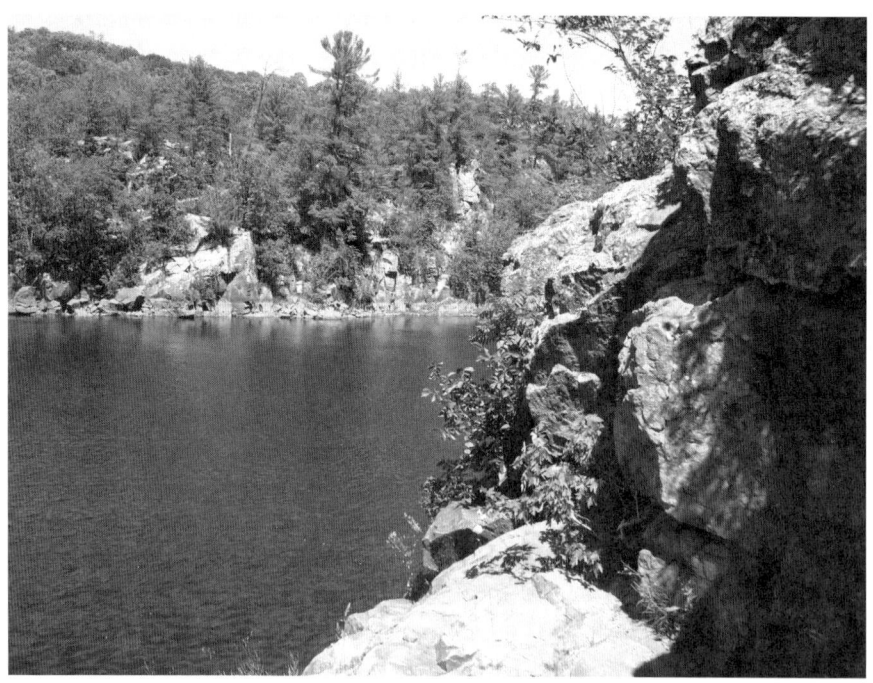

The rock cliffs of the Dalles bitterly fought over by three tribes in 1770. A hydroelectric dam was built in 1907, obscuring the boulders of the historic falls.

downstream. Exhausted warriors were capsizing their own canoes in a futile effort to escape. Bodies drifted downstream from the falls. The dead and the wounded could be found in nearly every crevice of the gorge.

Greatly reduced in numbers, only a few of the Fox and Dakota canoes made the return trip down the St. Croix to the Mississippi Valley. The Fox were saved from annihilation by the Dakota, but by only a thread. No more than fifteen Fox tribal lodges could be counted. Fox warriors surviving the battle of the Dalles numbered forty-one. So many dead warriors littered the *Menominikeshi Zibi*, the Ojibwe name for the St. Croix, that the victors renamed the river the "river of graves," or "Grave Marker River."

Young Chief Waub-o-jeeg, surviving with three bloody wounds, had established himself as a great leader among his people. The resounding victory at the falls permitted the expansion of the Ojibwe nation to the west to Grave Marker River, or the lower St. Croix River, as we know it.

The surviving Fox and Dakota paddled downstream away from their inglorious defeat. Upon their arrival home, the Fox warriors made a sincere plea to their friends the Sauk to be taken in as permanent family for the sake of their people's survival. The Sauk agreed to this, and today they live together as the Sac and Fox Nation.

Night Fight, 1785: A Dakota Camp Attacked on the Willow River

Building campsites on shores of the St. Croix River was less common than one might imagine. Living along the St. Croix did occur, but generally the camps were built adjacent to streams and creeks that flowed into the river. These rapidly flowing tributaries of the St. Croix provided a precious resource—water—during the winters while the St. Croix's surface was frozen two feet thick. One such camp of Dakota was located at the mouth of the Willow River.

Many times, the Dakota and Ojibwe attempted peace by smoking the pipe together in the autumn of the year. Hunting during winter was difficult enough on its own without the risk of enemy attack. Peaceful winters were likely, but renewed hostilities with spring's arrival could be expected.

There would be casualties from these raids and battles that native oral history would record. Traders located near the action would document some of the incidents as well. Trading companies were in business to sell goods to the native people and manage the accounting of such. Many times, a trading company kept notes of the native population's increase and decline. One Ojibwe attack at a Dakota camp on the Willow River took nine lives—women, children and one old man—with five Dakota being wounded.

    The spring of 1785 began as the others with a raid on an enemy camp. This time, the Ojibwe approached the Dakota camp at the mouth of the Willow at night. Each warrior posted silently at a Dakota lodge in the pitch black. At a given signal, the Ojibwe band of warriors fired into Dakota lodges, causing injuries at random. Reloading in the dark, they fired into lodges again, but this time the alarmed Dakota warriors responded with a discharge of their muskets into the night that illuminated their enemy with every bright flash.

    The Ojibwe were now outnumbered by a swarm of Dakota warriors who were well prepared for a fight. The night battle raged, flash for flash, with the Dakota advancing rapidly into their enemy. Some of the Dakota spirited their approach through the dark until they met their foe face to face, dispatching them with a blast of the musket. The battle finally ended when the aggressive Dakota met one another in the darkness with devastating musket fire. They rapidly recognized that they were responsible for many of their own casualties, thus ending the fight.

The War That Almost Was: Zebulon Pike Meets Chief White Buzzard

It was an age of discovery. America had doubled in size overnight with the stroke of a pen. Approximately 880,000 square miles of French Louisiana had been purchased for slightly less than $0.03 per acre but was worth fifty times more. The United States now owned this vast land, all of it west of the Mississippi River up to the Rocky Mountains. For decades to come, the federal government would finance itself by selling off acreage to pioneers for $1.25 an acre.

    Captain Meriwether Lewis and Second Lieutenant William Clark, with a team of army explorers, were commissioned to map the northwestern portion of the territory. They were to navigate the Missouri River from St. Louis to its source and possibly locate the mythical Northwest Passage to the Pacific Ocean. In the minds of many Americans, the Lewis and Clark expedition headed into the great unknown, likely never to return. Some

Part I

thought the trek was impossible, that they might as well be going to the moon and back. The gallant explorers left St. Louis in May 1804.

The Lewis and Clark expedition was assumed lost, having not returned by the end of the next year. The explorers were still missing two years after their departure, and all hope was given up for their return. Miraculously, the expedition arrived in St. Louis in late September 1806 with a vast knowledge of the great Northwest. Although a northwest passage was not found, the undertaking was an astounding success.

A similar and lesser-known expedition was made north to the source of the Mississippi River a year after Lewis and Clark's departure. Twenty-six-year-old army cadet school graduate Lieutenant Zebulon Pike was selected by General Wilkinson to make known to the residents of French Louisiana about the creation of the new Louisiana Territory. The occupants of the purchased land west of the Mississippi were now under the control of the United States government. Lieutenant Pike was held in high esteem, having numerous commendations from his commanders. He was also known for his strength of character, resourcefulness, boldness and fitness to command men. Many historians disagree with Lieutenant Pike's accomplishments to the point that he would not be remembered well.

Pike kept a diary of the Mississippi River expedition that included the French spelling of the native chiefs' names. Pike's French was not known to be accurate, as he recorded the presence of Sac chief Le Becassé (meaning "the Goose") when the correct spelling should have been Bras Cassé, or "Broken Arm." Pike's spelling of Chief Outard Blanche (White Buzzard) could be questioned and translated into "White Goose," but only if he had spelled *outarde* with an *e* at the end. This version of Pike's travels follows his actual spelling of "Chief Outard Blanche."

After his Mississippi River expedition, Zebulon Pike was sent to explore the West, where he attempted to climb a great mountain of the Colorado Rockies. Pike's 1806 expedition would challenge the mountain's slope in mid-November and fail. Today, the mountain retains the name of the man who failed to reach its summit: Pike's Peak.

Shortly afterward, Pike's expeditionary force, heading south and off course, was captured by the Mexican army for a time and held as an involuntary guest. This incident was of great embarrassment to the youthful United States government.

As a result, there have been three different versions written of Pike's history: first, Zebulon Pike was a great explorer and American hero; second, Pike failed in every task set out before him; and third, the truthful version

The Perilous St. Croix River Valley Frontier

that speaks directly to his successes and failures. This particular version of St. Croix Valley history tells it as honestly as it was known to have happened.

The French fur trade days were waning in the central United States. Any remaining trading posts along the upper Mississippi River that were flying British flags were to tear them down and raise the Stars and Stripes. Lieutenant Zebulon Pike was provided with four months' worth of provisions that included bundles of American flags for the task of asserting U.S. authority at every post and village he located. Pike would also meet with leaders of the sovereign nations of native people that dotted the land. The chiefs would be informed of the change in government west of the Mississippi and that their loyalties were now to the United States.

A seventy-foot-long keelboat with oars, mast and sail served as Pike's vessel, along with two corporals and seventeen privates under his command. A supply of ammunition was included for the purpose of hunting for their own meat. Heading upstream on the Mississippi, the explorers left St. Louis at the midpoint of summer, August 9, 1805, with sunlight becoming shorter every day.

The keelboat's sail was generally a hindrance to upstream travel on the Mississippi. The prevailing winds were from the north and west, the same direction from which the great river flowed. On days that the wind changed in favor of the expedition's direction, the explorers could log twenty-four to twenty-six miles. The boat was outfitted with oars and rowed against the current on windless days. Rowing into a sturdy headwind would not work; during these times, the keelboat was pulled upstream by effort of the soldiers slogging along the shore.

Birch canoes were utilized by the expedition as well. These canoes, lightweight by nature and swift in the current, were fragile and subject to cracking and breaking in two. The canoes were quite useful at times but were unable to keep pace with the long and slender keelboat when under oar power or sail.

A mixed-blood river trader by the name of Jack Frazer was traveling by canoe. He caught up with Pike's keelboat and was allowed to board. Frazer joined Pike and accompanied him to the Falls of St. Anthony, the limit of the navigable, or lower, Mississippi. Frazer had a violin, as did Pike, and together they played violin while plying the great waters of the mighty Mississippi.

Part I

Whether on the east or west bank of the Mississippi, Pike visited each native village that was encountered along the shores. He met with their respective chiefs, describing his presence as peaceful and then inquiring about the state of war that existed between the tribes. Pike regularly asked about the Sac, Reynard and Sauteur (Sauk, Fox and Ojibwe) war, of which certain actions were still taking place. Pike was able to communicate through his interpreter, Rosseau, or by speaking French, with which he was somewhat familiar, although Pike's misspelling of French was evident in his daily logs. Rosseau's previous experience traveling the Mississippi would prove invaluable.

Pike was quite intent on ascertaining the current state of war that existed between the Sauteur and the Sioux (Fox and Dakota). He had been told of fifteen Ojibwe who had been killed by the Dakota and of a recent retaliatory raid at the mouth of the St. Peters River (Minnesota River), which resulted in the killing of ten Dakota. Pike assured each chief that his representation of the new government meant that posts would be placed at locations to supply them with necessaries, and agents would attend to their business, but the primary endeavor was to make peace between the Sioux and Sauteur.

On September 2, one day's progress of forty miles was achieved. Again, on September 16, benefitted by a strong south wind, the keelboat sailed north forty miles in a single day. Such success was rarely the case but was greatly appreciated, as the weather was turning cold. The next day, passing twenty-five miles through a broad and deep portion of the Mississippi named Lake Pepin, Pike noted that he met a Dakota chief named Red Wing at a west bank village on the Canoe River. (Later, and of historic note, the Canoe River would be misidentified or misnamed the Cannon River.) Chief Red Wing promised to accompany Pike to the St. Peters River.

Zebulon Pike noted the change in color of the Mississippi's water above Lake Pepin. The river had turned reddish in color, for which the shallow and muddy parts of the river are known. Slightly deeper places on the Mississippi that became as black as ink amazed Pike. Arriving at the St. Croix River on September 19, Pike made specific notice of the blue and clear quality of its water. Further, while examining the shoreline below the St. Croix, he found unburied human remains. The exposed bones were evidence of someone killed in battle. Pike picked up a jawbone and kept it.

Pike took time to eat at the village at the mouth of the St. Croix River. This is likely the Dakota village O'-ki-zu Wa-kpa', where several generations of great Dakota leaders and chieftains originated. At least four great men each named Little Crow traced their lineage to the area. The large village was located on the east bank of the Mississippi and the east side of the mouth of the St. Croix. To Pike, this was an important confluence of rivers, where the shores rise dramatically in elevation, creating a commanding view of both the St. Croix and the great waterway the Mississippi.

Pike foresaw the strategic military importance of a location such as this. There was a broad, open prairie on the western bluff across from the village at the mouth of the St. Croix. The bluff had an appearance suitable for a fortification to serve in the area's long-term protection, whatever the threat might be. Pike was certain that a fort should be built on the site. He set out to purchase the confluence of the St. Croix and Mississippi Rivers from the Dakota chief Le Petit Corbeau (Little Crow). The two leaders befriended each other and agreed to make a land trade.

Pike set up his next camp farther upriver at a vacant lodge site adjacent to a single granite boulder that the Dakota referred to as the Red Medicine Stone. The Dakota thought of the four-foot-long boulder as a sort of mystical rock. Obviously, it was a lone rock near the shore of the river with an expanse of prairie on three sides. With nothing else in the area to compare it to, it became a reference point of notoriety. To emphasize its importance, the Dakota had painted the rock red.

On September 21, the expedition made twenty-four miles' distance to a large island, nearly two miles long, that sat at the mouth of the St. Peters

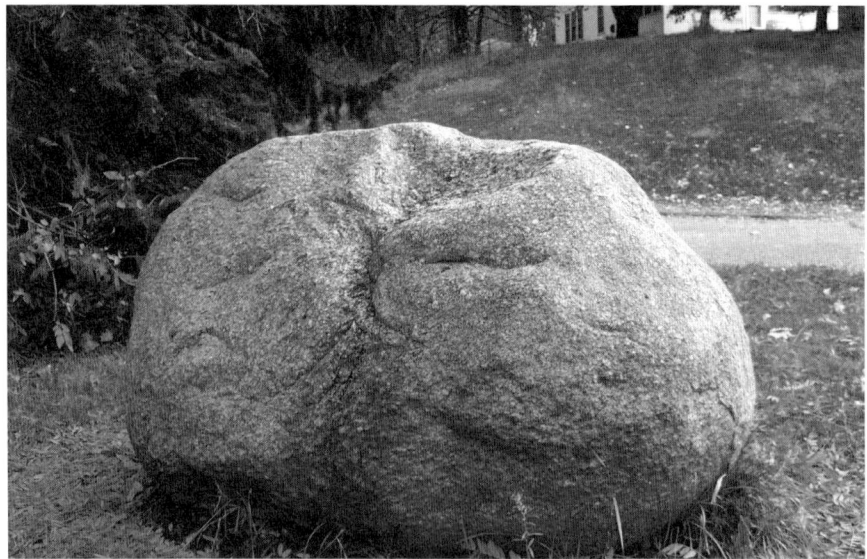

Red Rock was a geologic "erratic," deposited by melting glaciers alone on the prairie banks of the Mississippi River. The lonely rock presented a mystery to the native people of the area, who painted it red. *Photo by Leah Junkert.*

Part I

River. Pike placed his camp at the northeast point of the island and made plans to meet with area bands of Dakota for the purpose of sealing the land acquisition. Similar in nature to the confluence of the St. Croix and Mississippi, the St. Peters River was bordered by bluffs of much higher elevation. A military post located at the prominence here offered even better prospects than that of the St. Croix's.

The day prior to Pike's council with area chieftains, Chief Le Petit Corbeau arrived with 150 well-armed warriors under his command. They fired their guns with a thunderous salute to Lieutenant Pike and changed their present battle plans (pursuing their blood enemy), deciding to camp quietly with Pike and his men on the island.

On September 23, Pike held council with the chiefs on the island's beach under the shade of the keelboat's converted sail. Two Dakota chiefs, two war chiefs and a Sac chief were present to hear Pike's request for 100,000 acres of land from the tribe, equal to 156 square miles of area. Pike asked for land on both sides of the Mississippi River from the confluence of the St. Croix River beyond the confluence of the St. Peters River, up to the Falls of St. Anthony. Pike also requested that the Dakota people make peace with their enemy the Ojibwe.

Pike stated in his own words that the Dakota gave him the land he requested, though he knew its value was $200,000. Pike was assured, by the Dakota, safe passport on the land as well, but the chiefs were quite doubtful of the peace he asked of them. Pike wrote a government promise to pay $2,000 and then made small gifts to the chiefs, totaling $200 in value, including sixty gallons of diluted whiskey.

Pike concluded by asking Le Petit Corbeau, the head chief, to sign his paper, signifying the agreement. This request was refuted by Le Petit Corbeau, who stated that they had granted him the land and that their word of honor was enough. Pike was tactful in convincing him that his mark was something personal to him. Together, Le Petit Corbeau and Le Fils de Pinchot (Way Ago Enagee) put their marks on the paper. Other Dakota who witnessed the grant signing were Le Grand Partisan (Big Soldier), Le Boeuf qui Marche (Walking Bull) and war chiefs L'Orignal Levé (Rising Moose) and Le Demi Douzen (Six), as well as a Sac chief, Le Becassé ("the Goose" but should be Bras Cassé or "Broken Arm"). At the conclusion of the grant signing, the chiefs and their bands parted for their various villages.

The day after the parlay, the broken flag of Pike's seventy-foot keelboat was discovered drifting past the village of Le Petit Corbeau. This raised an alarm in Petit Corbeau's village that spread like raging fire to neighboring camps, announcing the destroyed keelboat and the murder of peaceful Lieutenant Pike. An act of aggression was made directly against Chief Outard Blanche (White Buzzard), assaulting him for the murder of Pike.

Chief White Buzzard was blamed for the death of Pike and his crew, which was deemed evident by the broken flagstaff and colors disposed of in the Mississippi. A warrior loyal to Petit Corbeau and Pike assaulted White Buzzard without the benefit of question, slashing him with a razor-sharp knife. White Buzzard likely dodged an attack aimed for his throat, but not enough to be missed completely. The blade hit him in the mouth, efficiently removing a lip from his face.

White Buzzard, enraged by the brutal attack, immediately proceeded with his armed warriors to Petit Corbeau. The bloody White Buzzard confronted Petit Corbeau, furious at having his face permanently disfigured. He demanded, "Why assault me?" Petit Corbeau was sympathetic to White Buzzard and agreed that they should band together to search for the "dogs" who had done this bad thing to Pike and his men.

Intent on revenge for the killing of his friend Pike, Petit Corbeau led a great number of armed and painted warriors fifteen miles up the river to Pike's island camp. Petit Corbeau arrived early the next morning at Pike's camp and found his friend lying in bed. Shaking Pike, Le Petit Corbeau woke the lieutenant from his sleep, asking if he and his men had all been killed. Had some accident taken place here? Le Petit Corbeau asked what awful thing had happen here, causing the flag to be broken and thrown overboard.

Le Petit Corbeau informed Pike that many warriors were loading and priming their guns for a great battle that would avenge their deaths and that the lost flag with its broken staff had been found and delivered to him. The knowledge that the missing flag had been found pleased Pike very much.

Then Le Petit Corbeau stood over Pike, stating that this thing so sacred was not taken from the boat by a violent act. He continued that the anger and rage (regarding the flag) should be hushed before any bloodshed occurred. Pike then explained to Petit Corbeau that punishment had already been administered regarding the missing flag.

The morning after the parlay, Pike had discovered his keelboat's flag missing from its stern. Whether it was stolen by Indians or had simply fallen overboard, Pike didn't know. Yet he was so displeased with the loss of the seventeen-star flag that he whipped the soldier who was responsible for staying awake during the night's watch over the craft. Then Pike made a special request of his friend L'Orignal Levé (Rising Moose) to search for the lost flag by exploring three miles downstream.

Part I

Pike noticed that there wasn't any current in the Mississippi River. This indicated a rise in the river's level, likely caused by heavy rains farther downstream. Pike had erroneously concluded that the missing flag should be found fairly close by. He was fortunate to have Le Petit Corbeau's wisdom and protection from so much bloodshed that would have erroneously occurred.

Pike immediately arranged for special gifts for Le Petit Corbeau—a few yards of blue stroud (wool cloth), a few yards of calico, a handkerchief, a knife and some tobacco. He then begged Le Petit Corbeau to make peace among his people, especially Outard Blanche, White Buzzard. Le Petit Corbeau was successful in this.

Zebulon Pike spent a few days at his camp on the island writing in his journal and making plans to portage the expedition's supplies above the Falls of St. Anthony. Just over one hundred years earlier, the Dakota captive missionary Father Louis Hennepin was the first white man to witness the majesty of the shale falls on the prairie. Father Hennepin christened them with the holy name "St. Anthony."

A small barge was being delivered to Pike's camp for the purpose of carrying supplies on the upper Mississippi above the falls made of broken shale. Although not high by any means, St. Anthony Falls would be the limit of navigation on North America's greatest river, a mile-long portage being the only way around it.

Pike was making good use of the area's traders—Frazer, Cameron, Wood and Ferrebault. Native people of the area had access to many goods of cloth, tin and iron. They no longer wore skins or hides, as these were traded for cloth. Cameron delivered (for Pike) an American flag and gift of tobacco to a Dakota camp at the head of the St. Peters River.

Pike and his men were portaging the falls with their canoes and the small barge when they saw a group of black-painted warriors who had been watching them from a distance. Pike realized that these were a group of extremely well-armed Dakota who would go to war at the slightest enticement. Their black-painted faces signified that they had killed an enemy within thirty days. The warriors had guns, bows, arrows, spears and clubs, and some even carried pistols by the pair. Pike and his men were defenseless; the expedition's guns were still below the falls. Pike then offered and shared drinks with the warriors, attempting unsuccessfully to trade for their weapons.

Above the Falls of St. Anthony, Pike discovered a site of many broken canoes, broken oars and bones of Dakota people. The Ojibwe had attacked and killed at a place that was across from the Crow River. Three Frenchmen,

The Perilous St. Croix River Valley Frontier

Pike was told, were among the killed. Here, Pike captured something that he had never seen before—a prairie mole, as it was termed, likely the famed Minnesota gopher.

The expedition's progress above the falls proved to be strenuous, as the weather grew colder; one man vomited blood, and another urinated blood. There was snow on the ground in the middle of October. Pike now wished that he had left in June and not in the middle of August, commenting that the men were killing themselves to obey his orders. He even described himself as being severely discouraged and suffering.

The area to Pike's north was no longer Dakota land but that of the Ojibwe. The men attempted to hunt bison for the first time but succeeded only in wounding them. Pike determined that their rifle caliber was too light to kill bison. Other hunting failures succeeded only in wasting precious rounds of ammunition. An incident in the middle of December soaked most of Pike's goods and reserve ammunition when they fell through the ice. On January 4, 1806, Pike's tent caught fire, burning his leggings, socks and moccasins, which were hung to dry. The next day was Zebulon Pike's twenty-seventh birthday.

The Pike expedition would survive through the winter by camping with traders at Leech Lake. Pike exchanged U.S. flags for British flags held in possession of traders and Ojibwe chiefs. Yet young Pike would fail to entice and escort the great Ojibwe chiefs to St. Louis for peace talks, as instructed by General Wilkinson. With the exception of two young warriors who joined Pike, Bucks and Beaux, the Ojibwe chiefs would not leave on a journey of a thousand miles crossing their enemies' land. Even if Pike had been assured free passport by the Dakota grant agreement, the Ojibwe chiefs were not going anywhere.

Pike identified and mapped Leech Lake as the source of the mighty Mississippi River. Of course, he was mistaken, an error he would never live down.

Spring arrived while Pike made rapid progress traveling down the Mississippi, occasioning personal reunions along the way. One such call was made by invitation at a few lodges just below the mouth of the St. Peters River. Pike visited and received various gifts, including sugar. Then he reciprocated, sharing a small drink of alcohol with the proprietor, after which the man demanded a kettle full. This request Pike refused, upsetting the Dakota man, who threatened to start a war by summer. Pike communicated that he would reply with troops if the war were to take place.

Of the reunions, none would be better than that with head chief Le Petit Corbeau at his camp, O'-ki-zu Wa-kpa', at the mouth of the St. Croix River. Le Petit Corbeau apologized to Pike for the prior misconduct of his people

Part I

and gifted him with a beaver robe and pipe, including a message to General Wilkinson that he was determined to preserve the peace. Le Petit Corbeau then informed Pike that the trader Cameron had sold hard liquor to villages on the St. Peters River. Cameron's partner, Rollet, had been doing the same below the mouth of the St. Croix. The illegal activity now placed a negative image on the other traders of the area, and Pike assured Le Petit Corbeau that he would have the guilty traders prosecuted by law.

Overall, Lieutenant Pike was pleased with the accomplishments of the expedition, along with Le Petit Corbeau's final promise to make a road clear for peace. The large island where Pike had camped the autumn before retained his name, Pike Island, for centuries to come.

It was now the middle of April and time for the expedition to return home. The weather had become pleasing, and the trees were budding. Pike enjoyed simpler pleasures, his men rowing vigorously downstream in a lighter keelboat, having consumed nearly all of the journey's provisions. A welcome wind rose and filled the sail.

Pike was promoted to captain following his return to St. Louis. It was a small consolation for his efforts that held less than the desired results. Peace between the Dakota and Ojibwe was not achieved. Sadly, with merely seven years to live, young Zebulon Pike's troubles were not over.

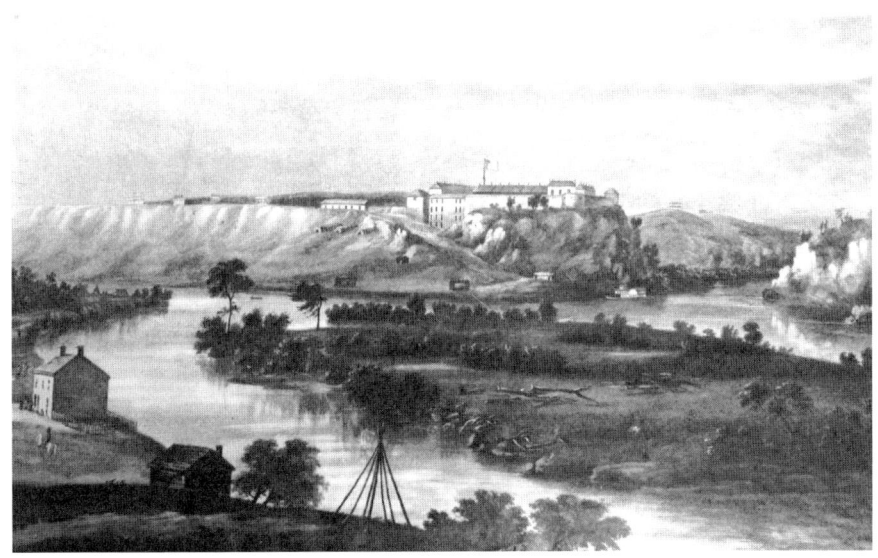

Pike Island sits between the St. Peters and Mississippi Rivers. Traders Faribault and Sibley were located at Mendota (on the left). Fort Snelling was constructed on the bluff, after Pike's death, just as he had envisioned. *Photo courtesy Afton Historical Museum.*

The Perilous St. Croix River Valley Frontier

William and Allan Morrison would claim discovery of the source of the Mississippi and would have shared it with Pike if only Pike had waited at Leech Lake for their arrival. Three decades later (disputed by the Morrisons), Henry Schoolcraft captured America's fascination, having named Lake Itasca as the true source of the mighty Mississippi.

Promoted to general, Zebulon Pike would be killed following the British invasion of America during the War of 1812. General Pike was commanding the American assault on Fort York when the British fled, setting their fort aflame. Tragically, Pike became a victim when he was struck in the back by a stone from the explosion of the fort's powder magazine. Mortally wounded, the general was presented with Fort York's captured colors. Zebulon Pike died a victorious American hero with his head pillowed on the "exchanged" British flag.

PART II

A Land Dispute Settled by Death: The Battle of Zion Hill

Peace between the Dakota and Ojibwe was elusive. The Dakota had unwillingly given up much of their land to the encroaching population of Ojibwe. Both peoples occupied the St. Croix River Valley, and neither was willing to share it. The St. Croix River had become the division between the two tribes, with the lower portion of the river, from the Falls of St. Croix fifty-two miles to the mouth of the river, being hotly contested.

Battles and raids had become so regular among the Dakota and Ojibwe that both feared for the survival of their populations—men, women and children all being victims of great slaughter. As their lodges filled with war trophies and scalps, their family members were being reduced in number. Chiefs on both sides finally realized that the depletion of their numbers could not be sustained. A solution to the ongoing warfare had to be found.

Two of the opposing chiefs met to search for a resolution to the bloody conflict in hopes of achieving peace. The two leaders mutually agreed to settle the war between themselves to minimize any further bloodshed. They agreed that one last battle would decide the future of both tribes, the victor of which would claim the St. Croix River and the valley for their people.

The two chiefs agreed, for the purpose of preserving their people, that they would be the only combatants of the decisive battle. They would fight each other to the death, until one victorious chief was left alive. The victorious chief would hold permanent claim to the valley, and his people would remain there in peace. The people of the deceased chief would peacefully move off the disputed land forever.

A mutually agreed upon battle site was selected on a western hilltop above the St. Croix River at the head of Lake St. Croix, later named Zion Hill. Groups of people from both tribes gathered to witness the warrior spectacle between the two great chiefs. The two were equally armed with tomahawks and knives. War hammers of sharpened stone were extremely effective but had been recently retired in favor of metal-edged tomahawks received from traders. A swift blow delivered by either weapon would invert the skull, instantly taking a life. Knives of the native hunter were sharpened to a razor's edge, one that was required to survive on the raw land. Cuts made with one of these were certain to be clean and deep. The two great chiefs began to fight.

An hour of sparring passed without any conclusion to the battle. Impatient warriors began to wonder if the two chiefs would settle the case. It seemed as if the enemy warriors collected at the scene would sprint into one another and join in on the fray, but they halted just when the chiefs each swung and landed serious blows. Another hour of lunging and slicing had the chiefs covered with gashes and dripping in blood.

It would be the Dakota chief who struck with a tomahawk blow of such brutal force that it nearly halted the Ojibwe for good. The Ojibwe chief had just lost an eye, an ear and the cheek in between. The severely wounded Ojibwe lunged and slashed with great effect, lancing the Dakota deeply across the abdomen. How much longer would the two chiefs last as they weakened and staggered, losing even more blood?

The Ojibwe was quite stunned in the final moments of the fight, and the Dakota was holding his intestines in with one hand as he hurled his tomahawk in a wild and final effort. The tomahawk's effect on the Ojibwe was mortal, and the two bloody chiefs stumbled into each other with a death grip that failed to hold. The two warriors dropped to the ground, unable to deliver another blow. Both chiefs were dying. The question was: which one would be the first?

The Ojibwe chief knew that he had but little time to live, so his people carried him a short distance down the hillside to a beautiful ravine to rest. An hour passed by, and the chief called his people close, having had a vision that was important to share. The dying chief gave this important message to his people: the white man would be coming in great numbers, and they would not be able to remain on the land. The white man would make buildings for

Part II

lodges. One building would be used to settle his quarrels. Another building would be for teaching children to be good and not to fight. The Great Spirit would also build His lodge on the hill for the white people.

The Ojibwe chief died that night and was quietly buried in the peaceful ravine the next day. The Ojibwe people had lost the decisive battle for the St. Croix Valley and returned to their maple sugar camps forty miles distant up the Apple River. A few years later, the ravine would be named Battle Hollow.

The victorious Dakota chief lived only one day longer than the Ojibwe chief. The Dakota's body was carried to a hilltop above Lilly Lake, west of the battle site.

The battle between the two great chiefs would be remembered as the Battle of Zion Hill. It was recalled and documented by Thomas Connor, a trader who had been living in the area since his youth. Connor married a Dakota woman and attained a license to trade with the native people, which gave him permission to live on the native-owned land.

As a rule, immigrants and settlers were not allowed onto native land unless they had permission to be there. Marrying into the people would gain a foreign man permission to reside on native land. Missionaries with government permission to minister to Indian people would be allowed by

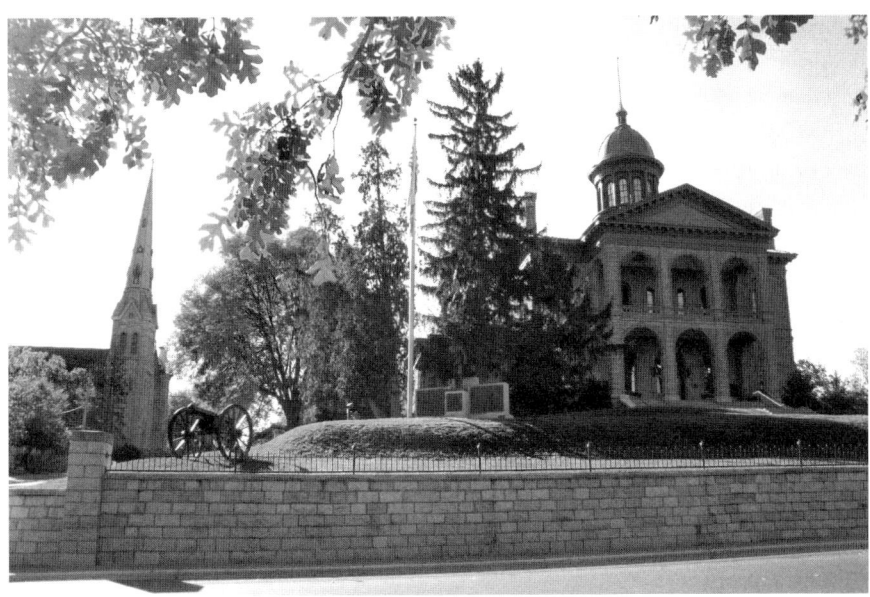

St. Michael's Catholic Church and Washington County's second courthouse constructed on Zion Hill, site of the decisive battle between two great chiefs.

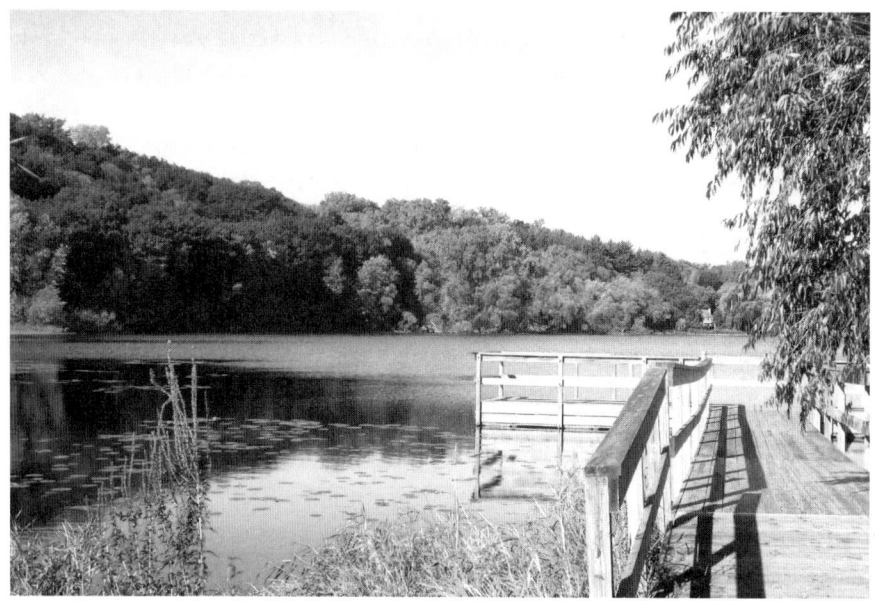

Lilly Lake, Stillwater, Minnesota. Burial mounds were located on the hills above the lake. A grave on the hill was once marked for a chief killed in battle.

the respective tribes onto their land. As for Thomas Connor, his government license to trade with native people added credential to his living at the mouth of Goose Creek on the St. Croix River, above the Falls of St. Croix. If not for trader Connor, this history might have never been preserved.

The Battle of Zion Hill took place about 1830, half a century before the hill was given the heavenly name Zion. In a few decades, the white man would arrive, as predicted by the Ojibwe chief. Two courthouses would be built there, as well as several churches of Stillwater, Minnesota. Lastly, school buildings came to the hill, as envisioned by the dying chief.

THE LAST BUFFALO EAST OF THE MISSISSIPPI, 1832

American bison freely roamed the St. Croix River Valley 250 years ago. American bison are larger and woollier than their eastern hemisphere relative, the yak, and well suited to the extreme weather conditions of the North American continent of the western hemisphere. For centuries, bison were a major resource of the woodland, prairie and plains people. Hunting bison for

Part II

its lean meat provided the people with crucial protein for strength and energy that was necessary for long-term survival on the unforgiving land. Important tools were made from its bones, and shelter and warm bedding were made from its hide. For many native people, a layer or two of hide was their only protection from every weather extreme known to exist on this continent.

When a bison herd was spotted, it was important to the native people to harvest as many animals as possible because no one was certain when such an ideal opportunity would occur again. Tall, dry stalks of prairie grass provided a bold hunter the advantage of concealment when stalking the great animal. Patient hunters would lie silently for long periods of time waiting for the animal to walk over them. An arrow or spear thrust precisely between the animal's third and forth rib would pierce its heart, bringing the beast down. One wrong move on the hunter's part likely meant a painful death from a horn thrust into the abdomen.

Another hunting tactic was to burn off the prairie grass, allowing for fresh green grass to sprout, creating an enticement for the bison to graze. Localizing a prairie burn simplified the search for a herd once the animals found the young, tender grasses on which they would voraciously feed. Lighting a narrow strip of fire on a breezy day allowed hunters to select a specific time and place to organize a great hunt.

Early traders who bought and sold with native people witnessed many of their hunting activities and tactics. In 1805, there was a trader, Robert Dickson, who spent much time living at Chief Wabasha's village on the west bank of the Mississippi. He recorded eleven camps, each with a population

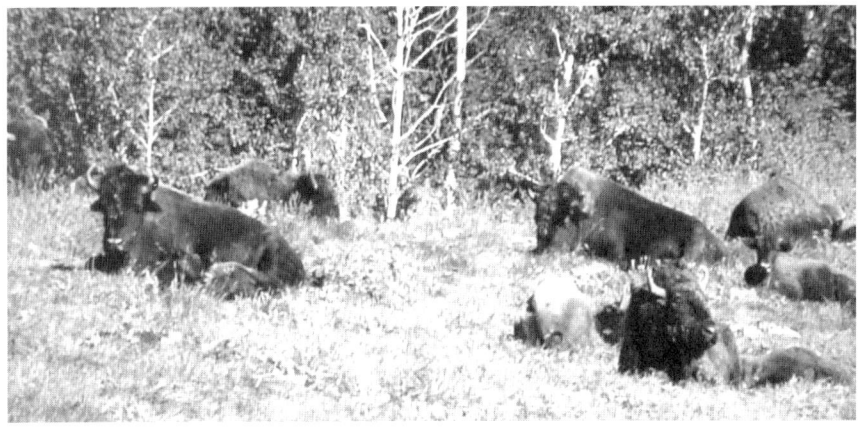

Bison grazing on green grass made them lazy, which simplified the hunt for the powerful animals.

The Perilous St. Croix River Valley Frontier

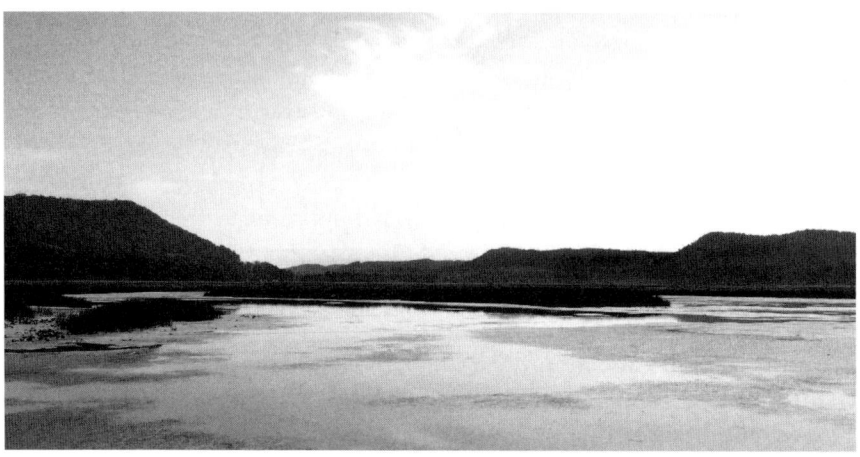

The Buffalo River, a bison hunting ground located in a vast area named Trempealeau, east across from Chief Wabasha's village on the Mississippi.

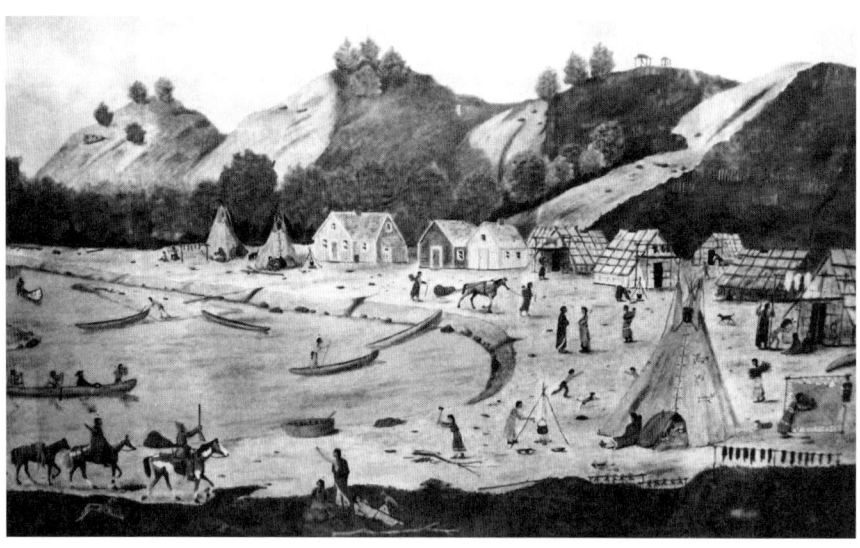

A 1964 painting by F.E. Lawshe depicts a blending of eras on the frontier. The Dakota people were river dwellers who mingled with missionaries and traders. A combination of bark and hide lodges are shown mixed with wood-frame structures.

of one hundred people. Hunters from each of the camps were able to hunt one thousand deer during the year, equaling fewer than ten deer per person annually. The resulting numbers of harvested deer left villagers hungry at times, unless other food sources were located.

Part II

A great bison hunt took place on the Buffalo River during the summer of 1805. The Buffalo River was named for the large population of bison that lived in proximity to its valley and surrounding prairies. Over 1,600 bison were killed and butchered on the site. The butchered meat was then transported as rapidly as possible across the Mississippi River to Wabasha's village for drying. Unfortunately, one-quarter of the bison meat spoiled in the heat before it made it to the canoes. Turkey buzzards gorged themselves on the remains.

Annual hunting was taking its toll on the herds of the St. Croix Valley, and by 1830, they were gone. The vast area south of Lake Pepin, below the mouth of the Buffalo River, was named by the French *Trempealeau*, which means "soaked with water." Bison thrived on the lush wetlands and prairies of this portion of the Mississippi River Valley. Yet their numbers dwindled. Trempealeau is where the last American bison was seen east of the Mississippi River in 1832. It was shot.

Massacre at Battle Hollow: Treaties and Warfare on the New Frontier

In 1836, woodsmen arrived in the St. Croix River Valley and began logging the pines at the Falls of St. Croix. The territory of Wisconsin had been created that year and extended all the way west to the east bank of the Mississippi River. Apparently, these bold men thought they had a right to their chosen activity in the new territory. Galena, Illinois, and the growing city of St. Louis, Missouri, were driving the demand for lumber, and rafting logs down the St. Croix to the Mississippi seemed a profitable solution to the problem.

These particular loggers had made personal agreements with the Ojibwe to operate on land that was still in dispute with the Dakota. The Ojibwe people were somewhat perplexed, though, by the white man's request for trees. This seemed unusual to the native people, but after consideration, the Ojibwe, with the exchange of a few gifts, gave their permission to the loggers to take their trees.

When U.S. Indian agent Lawrence Taliaferro discovered that a logging venture was taking place on Indian-owned land, he was quite upset. Taliaferro, who was in good standing with the tribes, came up the St. Croix River to halt the operation. The law was that you had to own the land from which you were taking trees. Worse yet, the logging site was actually on land that was disputably Dakota. This episode instigated a meeting in 1837 between government treaty agents, the Ojibwe and the Dakota.

Owning land was a European concept that was not part of the native people's culture. Landownership was something mutual among tribes, with the understanding that all people of the tribe owned the land. The idea that money could be exchanged for land was new and difficult to comprehend.

Permission to occupy the land was a concept common to native people; one could have permission to be on it or not. Anyone found on tribal land without permission was committing a serious offense that brought on dire consequences. Once the tribes understood that they were making an exchange for something of value, like a trade, the treaties were agreed to.

In July 1837, the Ojibwe and Dakota chiefs were called to Mendota on the St. Peters River to make separate treaty agreements. The Ojibwe were to sell a portion of their southwestern lands with the understanding that they were retaining the right to remain on them for time to come. The Dakota agreed to a treaty for a large sum of money, surrendering their eastern lands, from which they would vacate, with the intention of moving their villages west of the Mississippi.

The westward migration of the Dakota people had been gradual due to pressure from their blood enemy, the Ojibwe, but now it was coming from American expansion. Other circumstances applied, as bison herds were now absent from the St. Croix Valley. The severe winter and disastrous spring flooding of 1826 resulted in the destruction of a village on the east bank of the Mississippi above Red Rock. Many Dakota people died under great depths of snow and drowned in a record season of floods. Some of the destroyed lodge sites were not rebuilt but moved west across the Mississippi to a camp named Kaposia. All of the bison were west of the Mississippi now, and it seemed to the Dakota that there was more land to live on there as well.

U.S. government functions were very slow and tedious in those times. After much congressional discussion, the Ojibwe and Dakota treaties were ratified in 1838. News spread rapidly among Americans that new land would open for settlement in the St. Croix Valley. One of the first pioneers, James Norris, arrived to the lower valley before treaty ratification was announced.

James Norris staked his claim on an elevation of prairie that was located between the Dakota village of O'-ki-zu Wa-kpa' at the mouth of the St. Croix and the village at Red Rock on the east shore of the Mississippi. Norris was greeted by the Dakota, but it was not a friendly meeting. The Dakota communicated to him that he did not have permission to be there; he was trespassing on their land and dispersing their deer. Norris replied that

Part II

treaty ratification would happen, and the deal would be done. The Dakota explained that this "ratification" document had not been delivered and was not in their hands; therefore, he did not have permission to be on the land. Norris emphasized that the paper would be coming as the government had promised. Although displeased, the Dakota let Norris live.

The year 1839 was when the ratified treaty became the law of the land from the St. Croix River Valley to the eastern shore of the Mississippi River. The land was officially open to pioneering and settlement. The lumber industry was first to begin in earnest on the lower St. Croix River, constructing a sawmill at a site named Marine Mills. Towering white pine trees were being cut far to the north on a tributary of the St. Croix called the Snake River.

The fortification that Zebulon Pike had foreseen in 1805 was eventually built at the mouth of the St. Peters River and the Mississippi. Initially, the stone structure was named Fort St. Anthony in 1819 and then renamed Fort Snelling for Colonel Josiah Snelling, who managed the greatest portion of its construction. There were nine square miles of designated government reserve land on which the post was situated. The fort's reserve land was deemed neutral land on which native warfare was prohibited or the subject parties would face an engagement with heavily armed soldiers from the fort.

At the opening of settlement of the frontier in 1839, Fort Snelling's commanding officer, Major Plympton, organized peace talks between the Ojibwe and Dakota. Many times, Major Plympton had acted as a judge determining innocence or guilt in criminal complaints within the tribes. If guilty were Plympton's decision, then he would release the convict to his respective chief for sentencing. Tribal law would be carried out in this way.

Plympton called tribal peace negotiations in late June 1839. The Ojibwe and Dakota participated in this peaceful event, where both tribes mingled freely and without incident. Several hundred northeastern Ojibwe had come down from the upper St. Croix River, landing their canoes at a place of still water at the head of Lake St. Croix. From this place, the St. Croix Ojibwe embarked on their well-traveled trail twenty-five miles southwest, across the prairie to the Mississippi River crossing, and camped on the Fort Snelling Reserve. Similarly, the Mille Lacs band of Ojibwe traveled one hundred miles south on the Rum River trail to the Mississippi and camped on the fort's reserve.

Major Plympton was well aware that pioneers would be arriving on the open frontier and that the peace must be kept. The year prior to this, a small group of Ojibwe had ambushed seven peaceful Dakota people far to the west on the Chippewa River of Iowa Territory. The Ojibwe people now ranged across a vast area from the Chippewa River border in the east, in Wisconsin, all the way to the Chippewa River in the west, in Iowa Territory. Major Plympton was intent on halting the bloodshed and securing a permanent peace. He was making good progress toward a peace agreement after a week's talk with the two tribes.

About seven miles north of the fort's neutral reserve was a large lake named Calhoun. The lake was named for the U.S. secretary of war in office during the construction of Fort Snelling. At Lake Calhoun lived a band of Dakota people by the same name who practiced farming taught by missionaries Samuel and Gideon Pond. A Dakota named Meekaw was killed at Calhoun by an Ojibwe warrior who was not part of the peace party at the fort. Meekaw had been walking on a trail through tall prairie grass with a young child who was not seen by the Ojibwe. The child ran seven miles to the fort to report the killing, at which point the angry Dakota ended Plympton's peace negotiation. The Ojibwe broke camp, departing for their respective homes.

The St. Croix Ojibwe made night's camp in the ravine by the still water where their canoes were beached. This was the same ravine where they had buried their chief who was killed at the battle between the two chiefs on Zion Hill about ten years before. A trader, William Aitkin, who was well known to them, was also camped in the ravine. Aitkin sold the upset Ojibwe some liquor, and they went to sleep beside the grave of their great chief.

The next morning, July 3, daybreak was sounded by a barrage of musket fire from all three sides of the hollow. Dakota warriors seeking revenge had silently stalked the Ojibwe all the way from Fort Snelling to the hollow, lined the upper elevation and then fired down into the surprised Ojibwe. The Dakota swept down into the ravine, taking twenty-one scalps and wounding twenty-nine Ojibwe. The Ojibwe fled up the St. Croix River in their canoes. Only a few Dakota had been killed, the illegal sales of alcohol being a contributing factor in the uneven casualty count.

The St. Croix Ojibwe made it to the Falls of St. Croix with their wounded, where an old trader named Frazer took them in and tended to their wounds. It was while they were there that word came from the Rum River Trail, four miles above its mouth in the Mississippi, that a battle had taken place on July 4. The news of this terrible battle only increased the grieving of the St. Croix Ojibwe.

Dakota warriors, in retaliation for the Calhoun killing, also struck a large group of Ojibwe at daybreak. The surprised Ojibwe had taken flight while

Part II

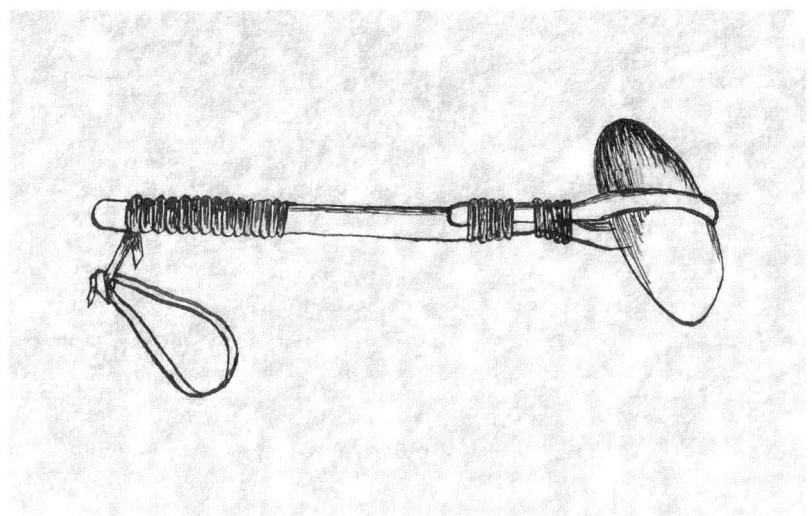

The war club was an essential weapon, as personal confrontation on the battlefield was likely. The force of the club's blow was increased by swinging it from the tether. *Artwork by John Martens.*

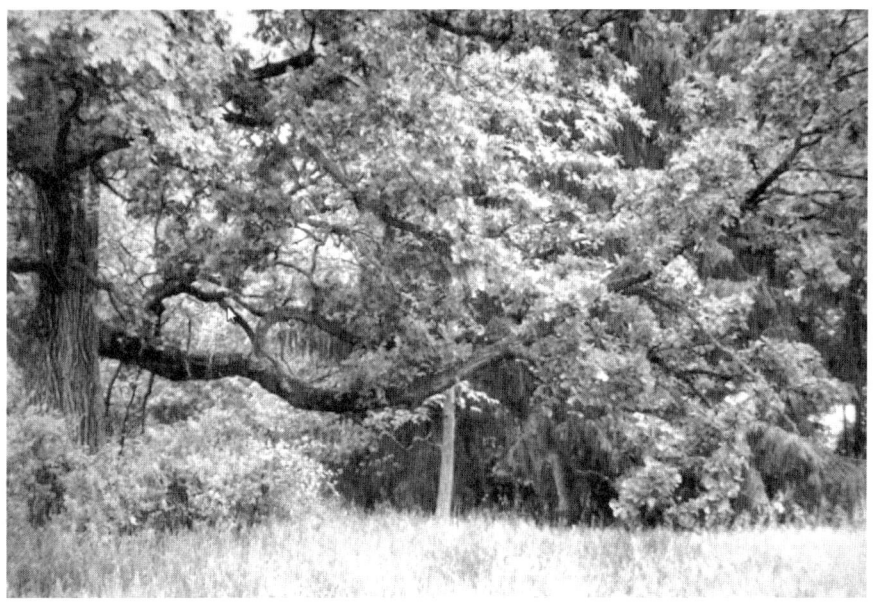

A Rum River Trail native marker tree points the way toward the home camp at Mille Lacs Lake. This marker tree is near the battlefield of the July 4 attack. Marker tree branches were tied and staked to the ground as saplings, being trained to hold their shape as they matured.

the Dakota overtook them one after another. Shots were exchanged with great effect during the battle, but swift Dakota warriors swinging their war clubs overwhelmed the fleeing people.

One incident of the battle that survived (being retold) was that of a forbidden love that took hold during the week of peace talks at the fort. As was common, love at first sight was realized between a young Dakota man and a young Ojibwe girl. They could not hide their affections and were both told to forget that they had ever met. What if peace came true for their people? Then surely their mutual happiness could be possible. Unfortunately, the peace talks ended in disaster, and now the Dakota were swarming over their blood enemy, taking seventy scalps.

What happened on the bloody battlefield that morning was tragic. On that battlefield was the young Dakota man whose heart had been broken when he left his Ojibwe maiden. He had caught up with an enemy from the rear, his war hammer poised for the kill, when the intended victim turned about and saw him. The two lovers recognized each other in an instant. He hesitated to swing his mortal blow, asking himself if he was sworn to kill her or save her life. In that moment, he chose life for her, and in the next moment, another warrior sped from behind, delivering the fatal blow of a war club. She was killed in front of his eyes.

The First Pioneers of the St. Croix Valley: Haskell and Norris Raise Wheat

Joseph Haskell arrived from Maine to the open frontier by way of riverboat, disembarking on the west bank of the Mississippi at Fort Snelling in 1839. Joseph Haskell was given the task of delivering mail, by canoe, to St. Croix Falls. On the return trip, Joseph Haskell left the canoe at Lake St. Croix, taking a native trail as a more direct route to Fort Snelling. This was an opportunity to view the great prairie of tall grasses and intricate flowers to which Haskell took an instant liking. Haskell staked a claim that was over one mile square, located only six miles from James Norris's claim from the year before.

James Norris planted eighty acres of wheat for himself on his claim, which he named Prospect Grove. The best part of the farming venture was the lack of trees on the open prairie. There was no cutting or strenuous stump removal like there was out in wooded lands of the east. Simply put

Part II

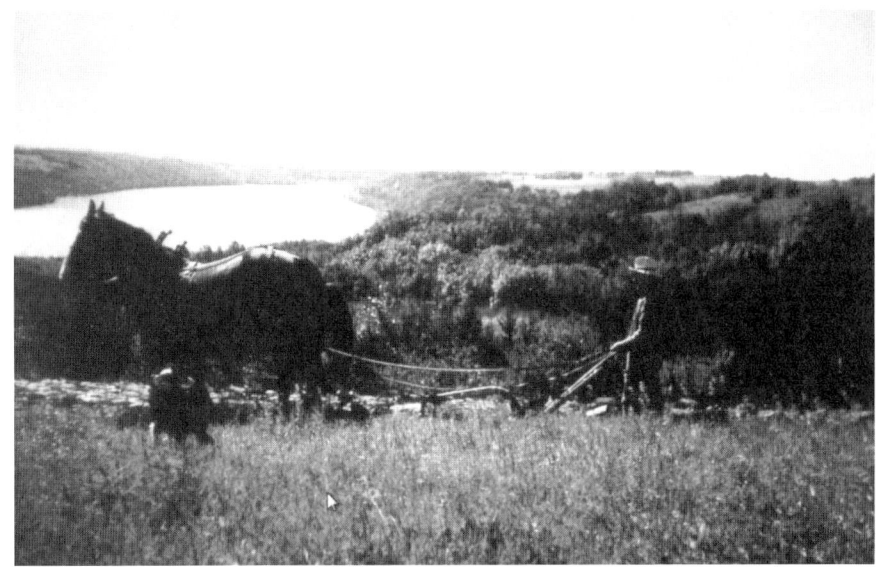

Afton historian Oliver Charley plows sod with a team of horses in 1940. The Afton "terrace" land form is visible in the upper right of the photo. *Photo courtesy Afton Historical Society.*

the newly developed Deering plow to the earth, break the sod and watch it roll over. An Irish oxen driver named Andrew Mackey had claimed a half square mile of land on the west bank of the Lake St. Croix River at Catfish Bar. It took a yoke of oxen to draw the glistening steel of the Deering plow through unbroken prairie sod. Andrew Mackey's oxen were made available at the rate of fifteen dollars an acre. Haskell planted three acres of potatoes and corn.

A clever old-timer named Lemuel Bolles arrived at Catfish, claiming land on a creek above Mackey's claim. Lemuel walked the western shores of Lake St. Croix and found two large, round stones, which he collected. James Norris had plowed and planted his wheat, with Haskell assisting with the harvest, resulting in a need for milling the grain. Lemuel Bolles offered a service, claiming that he could mill the grain into flour with his two round river stones, to which the men agreed. Lemuel charged two dollars for milling three acres' worth of wheat. Norris's eighty acres proved too much to harvest with only minimal labor. Seventy-seven acres of wheat went to rot.

Norris, Mackey, Haskell and Bolles, being the earliest pioneers to the lower St. Croix Valley, had all been to St. Croix Falls and the "pineries,"

The Perilous St. Croix River Valley Frontier

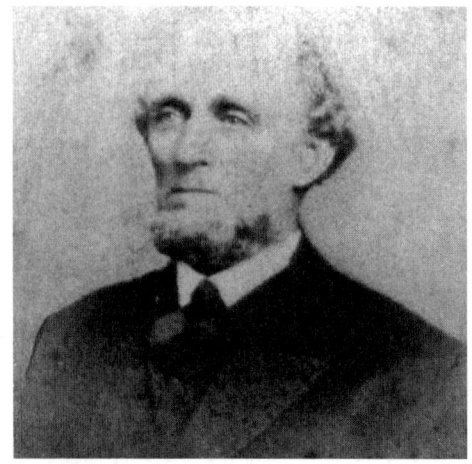

Left: Joseph Haskell came to the frontier to carve out a new life and then traveled back to Maine to escort his sisters to his home once he had reasonable accommodations for them. *Photo courtesy Afton Historical Museum.*

Below: The Afton prairie farmhouse of Minnesota's first commercial farmer, Joseph Haskell. *Photo courtesy Afton Historical Museum.*

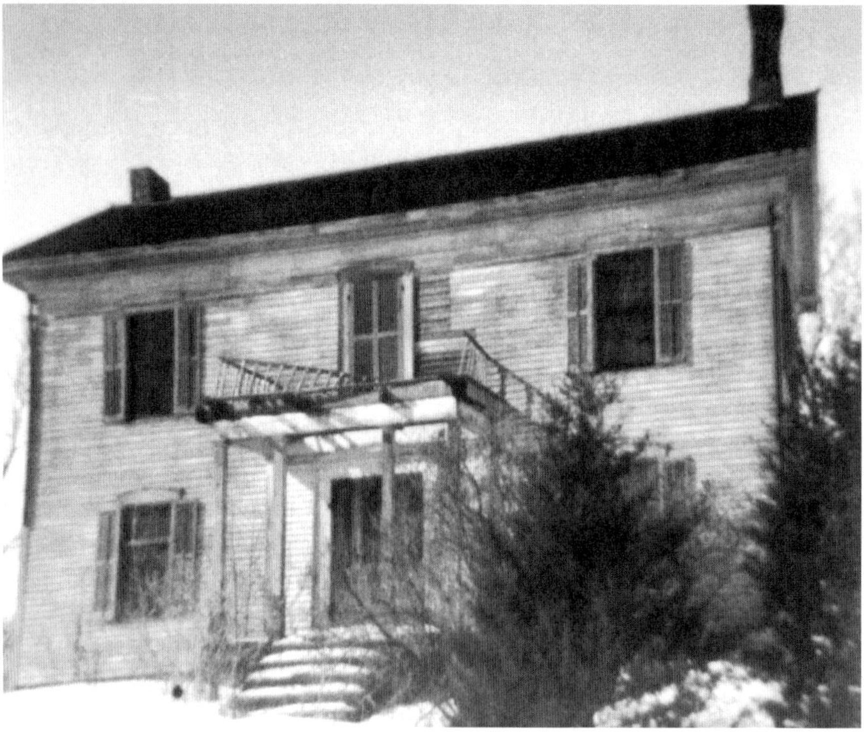

where logging was generating a financial boom. Each of the men had served in some capacity and made good sums of money in a short period of time. There was risk to it, though, and trouble had occurred with the Ojibwe just prior to ratification of the treaty agreement.

Part II

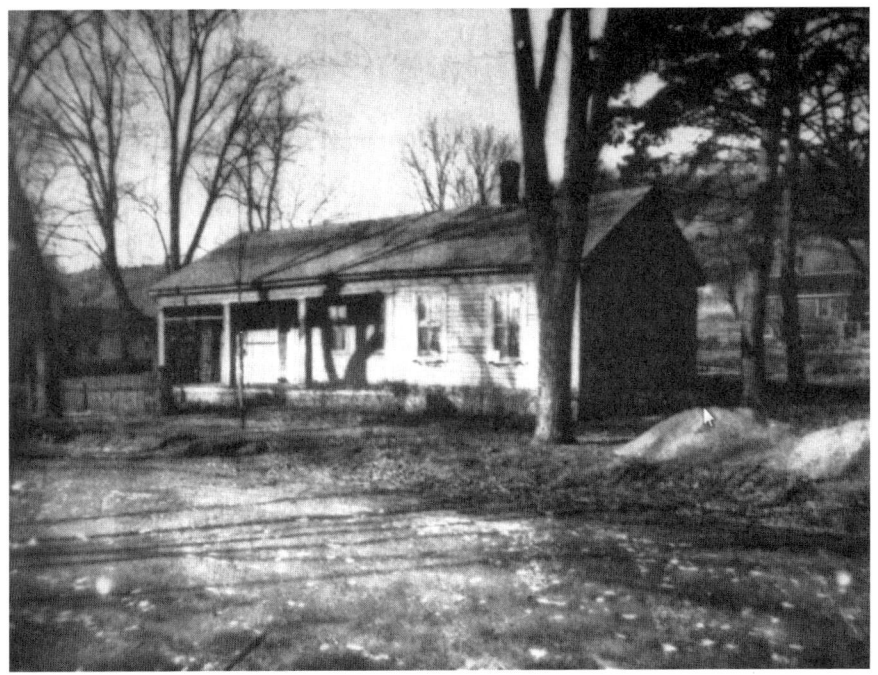

Andrew Mackey was at Chengwatana in 1838, when Dakota chief Pinichon threatened the illegal loggers with two hundred of his warriors. Mackey settled at Catfish in 1841 and lived in a small shack before building this home in 1848. Andrew lived a successful life but never learned to write his own name. *Photo courtesy Afton Historical Museum.*

The Ojibwe knew that ratification of the treaty had not taken place, but the cutting of the great white pines progressed. There was quite a scare in the pine forest, instilling so much fear in the loggers that they fled their camps in canoes down the St. Croix. The fearful men, without regard for the treacherous Falls of St. Croix, shot straight through the water hazard, attempting to place as much distance between them and the fierce Ojibwe as possible.

Winter came in 1839, and Haskell needed shelter, as did Norris. Both men began to dig into a hillside and then built a rough lean-to over the earthen hole where they would spend the winter. Much of the time spent during the long, cold winter was baking bread to survive. The men used their digging shovel to roll the dough and bake it over the open fire.

A few years later, Joseph Haskell raised enough grain to sell 150 miles down the Mississippi from the lower St. Croix River at Prairie Du Chien's market. This successful sale of wheat qualified Joseph Haskell as the first farmer in the St. Croix Valley. Haskell's early pioneer effort would be recorded, as was Norris's, but Joseph Haskell wanted to make clear the story of baking bread on the dirt shovel. Joseph emphasized that the baking shovel was a new shovel.

THE FIRST PIONEER WOMEN IN THE ST. CROIX VALLEY: MARY HONE AND LYDIA CARLI

David Hone arrived at the St. Croix River below the Falls of St. Croix and assisted in establishing the first sawmill in 1839. Operating on water power, it was named Marine Mills after his hometown of Marine, Illinois. The forests of white pine trees farther to the north were destined to be logged and floated down tributaries to the St. Croix River. The logs had to tumble over the Falls of St. Croix and then be collected at Marine Mills for sawing.

David Hone brought his bride of one year, Mary, to the raw frontier. Mary Hone left behind a pleasant home and comfortable living to become the first pioneer woman in the St. Croix Valley. Although there was much activity at the mill, cooking for the crews and chores to do, there were no goods or services, and there wasn't any social life to be found. It was a primitive and lonely place to live.

After a year at Marine Mills, David and Mary Hone moved south to Grey Cloud Island on the Mississippi River, above the mouth of the St. Croix. They farmed on the large island for a few years and then moved a short distance to the mouth of the St. Croix River. A small community began to form there, and David and Mary operated a hotel. Mary Hone began teaching school in 1845. The settlement was merely named the St. Croix Precinct or, more simply, "St. Croix." St. Croix was on the U.S. government reserve land that Zebulon Pike had originally envisioned fortified for the protection of the confluence of the two rivers, granted by Chief La Petit Corbeau. The fort was never built.

Across the river on the east bank is where Philander Prescott began trading and operating a ferry. Prescott had married into the Dakota tribe, raising his mixed-blood family there. Other mixed-blood Dakota people remained at the old O'-ki-zu Wa-kpa' village site, now called Prescott's Landing. The full-blood Dakota villagers moved to the Kaposia Village site up the Mississippi River.

Lydia Carli was the second pioneer woman to arrive in the St. Croix Valley, stepping off a Texas riverboat onto Grey Cloud Island with her

Part II

three children in 1841. Lydia Carli's husband, Paul, was several weeks late to arrive due to a serious illness from which he recovered. The family had followed the invitation to the frontier from Lydia's half brother, Joseph R. Brown, who lived on Grey Cloud. Joseph R. Brown had been a young soldier at Fort Snelling who never left the territory following his mustering out of service. Since that time, Brown had become involved in as many business and political ventures as one could imagine.

Joseph R. Brown had a tamarack log house under construction at the head of Lake St. Croix. The Carli family, along with Brown's family, moved into the unfinished log home. It was named the Tamarack House for the thin pole-like pine logs that formed the walls of the crude, windowless home lit only by candles and constant firelight. It was so primitive that it didn't even have a door but something like a heavy drape, akin to a bison hide. Many visitors graced its entry, as it was the only place to stop for miles around.

The tamarack walls of the house required mud chinking to fill the gaps between the logs. Lydia Carli and family worked to complete the project using mud to fill the gaps. If it rained hard or stormed, the mud chinking washed out and had to be redone. Winters were so cold in the Tamarack House, Lydia said, that the chinking cracked and dropped out of the gaps. Heavy frost built up in the gaps, filling the space where the mud had been. The tamarack pine walls became like sheets of ice as the wood fire kept burning though the long winters.

The tamarack log house was an unusual rarity in an area that was nearly void of conifers and pines. Only a few tamarack trees were found in the area, and none existed south of the Tamarack House. Hardwood trees of oak were common in savannah groves scattered about the prairies.

Next to the Tamarack House, Joseph R. Brown built a city hall for the town he named Dacotah. Brown also made use of the raw, sashless, unfinished two-story structure for the first courthouse of St. Croix County, Wisconsin Territory, serving as a judge (and sometimes jury) in frontier disputes. Although Joseph R. Brown was a Wisconsin territorial legislator and justice of the peace who passed judgment in his court, the town of Dacotah failed to materialize. Joseph R. Brown left Dacotah for parts farther west, expanding his sights on grander adventures.

Both the Dakota and Ojibwe often visited at the Tamarack House merely out of curiosity or for the want of food. Lydia Carli met many of the native travelers who passed by. They always made certain to enter to see what the interior was like. Lydia made many meals for the tribes' people. At certain times, the numbers of native visitors made her feel uncomfortable, but she said that she determined to set those feelings aside because she might need their friendship one day.

Lydia's children slept where it was warm, on crude board planks in the rafters of the house. When Dakota visitors slept on the floor overnight, the children kept a wide eye through the cracks of the planks all night long. The family said that they made many a Dakota friend while at the Tamarack House.

An old Dakota man was a regular visitor of Lydia Carli's at the Tamarack House. The old one was too old to be a warrior and no longer able to hunt. What he could do was help the women of his camp with their chores. Other warriors despised the old one, but the settlers found him to be quite interesting. The old one was a gracious visitor, but when asked if he was hungry, the reply was always an emphatic yes. If there had been any leftover food from Lydia's meal, he would easily have consumed that, too.

The hungry old Dakota also knew John McKusick, a hardworking log rafter who left work at St. Croix Falls, investing in a new venture just below Battle Hollow. John McKusick was a partner in the newly formed Stillwater Lumber Company, which built the first sawmill at the head of Lake St. Croix. The hungry old Dakota visited John McKusick's boardinghouse and was fed by him many times. Both John and Lydia were aware of the old one's amazing digestive ability, so at one dinner, John McKusick prepared enough food for six men and fed the old one.

The old Dakota was able to eat most of the enormous meal but asked if he could stay longer to sleep off his indigestion. After a short time, he awoke, finished the meal and left for the Tamarack House. Arriving there an hour later, he greeted Lydia Carli, stating that he was starved and hadn't eaten for days. Lydia fed him but noticed that he wasn't eating as heartily as at other meals he'd had there. A week later, John McKusick and Lydia met and had a good laugh, realizing the hungry game that was played by the old Dakota.

Life and Death on the New Frontier

Jake Fisher was an eccentric man who worked in the sawmill at St. Croix Falls during 1842. The next year, Jake went downstream to the head of Lake St. Croix and staked a claim of land on the west bank of the river. He

Part II

was able to sell this large claim to John McKusick of the Sillwater Lumber Company and become a partner of McKusick's grand little enterprise.

A small settlement of crude log cabins and slab wood shacks began to cluster around the boardinghouse and sawmill of the Stillwater Lumber

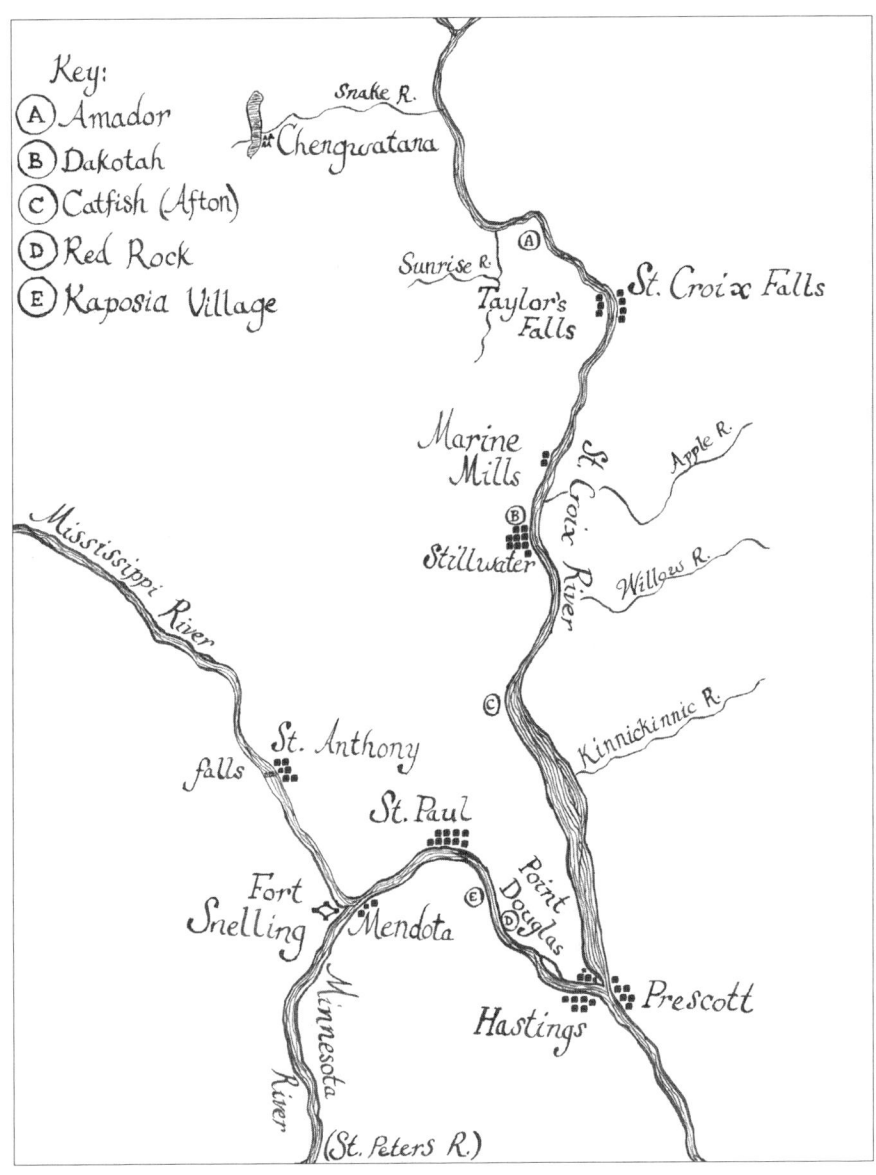

Map of the lower St. Croix River Valley, including the Mississippi River and the historic St. Peters River, which would be renamed the Minnesota River. *Map by John Martens.*

The Perilous St. Croix River Valley Frontier

Company. John McKusick was an instrumental partner in organizing Stillwater as a future site worth developing into a prosperous city on the frontier. Permission was granted by Wisconsin's territorial government to erect a courthouse that established the young town of Stillwater as the new county seat of St. Croix County.

The first frontier deaths to be recorded in the valley occurred when two men working on the river rafting lumber for transport to St. Louis were careless, overexerting themselves in the heat of summer. A man named Mr. Cole was brought to the Tamarack House but died on July 14, 1843. Lydia Carli gave birth to daughter Lisette in the house the next day, July 15. The other heat-stressed man died in the cellar of Brown's Courthouse the next day, July 16; his name remains unknown. Worse, Joseph R. Brown lost a child at the same time. Three burials took place high atop the hill above the Tamarack House.

Joseph R. Brown hired Jake Fisher to build a substantial frame house at a place called St. Mary on Lake St. Croix at the mouth of Lemuel Bolles Creek. A Catholic missionary provided the holy name to the location, having been placed a few miles above there in 1838. Brown asked Paul and Lydia Carli's family to occupy the new farmhouse in 1845. It was a two-story house and the only frame house on the St Croix between the mouth of the river and Marine Mills.

Spring came early in March 1846, and Paul Carli went duck hunting near Bolles Creek, not far from the frame home. Paul was successful in downing some of the foul but had to recover one from the waters of the creek that were flowing toward the open water of the St. Croix. Paul paddled out in a canoe to pick up the duck but capsized the small craft. Paul was unable to swim, wearing his heavy coat in water that was as cold as ice, and drowned. Paul's son was standing on the shore helplessly watching the tragic event. Paul Carli was the first death recorded at the village of Catfish, which is below the mouth of Bolles Creek. Shortly after the tragedy, Lydia, pregnant with Rosaltha, moved with her children eleven miles north, back to the primitive Tamarack House.

Lydia was a grieving widow in mourning for the customary year following her husband's death. When the year was up, she married Dr. Christopher Carli, Paul's brother. The couple lived a long life together and was famed for their dramatic frontier adventures.

PART II

BURIAL GROUND NEEDED: CATFISH BLUFF, WILLOW RIVER, FAHLSTROM'S FAMILY PLOT

The burial ground at Catfish was located high on a bluff overlooking the St. Croix River to the east with a commanding view of prairie sunsets in the west. The first group of settlers staking claims on the new frontier came from unfair circumstances, being evicted from the government reserve land at Fort Snelling. These families would be the first to use the round bluff above Catfish for their burying ground.

For several decades, ox cart drivers and their families freely made their homes on land that was not theirs. Residing on the fort reserve meant that they were not trespassing on native lands. As ox cart drivers, they employed themselves in delivering goods by a crude single-axle cart drawn by a yoke of oxen. These hardy men loaded goods and supplies at the riverboat landings and then traveled northwest for weeks across the vast prairies to settlements on the Red River. The ox carts would return to the fort from the Red River posts and villages loaded with furs and hides. These hardworking drivers regularly traveled over tall grass prairie on journeys of 250 to 400 miles, depending on their destination along the Red River of the north.

By 1840, many of the ox cart drivers had served twenty years or more delivering goods in both directions across the prairie. It might have seemed

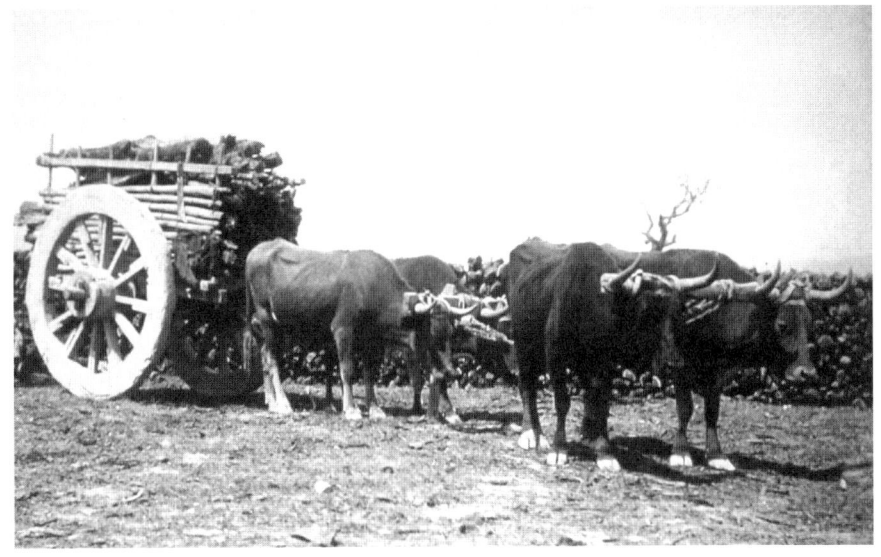

Ox cart teamsters also carried their own firewood for the lengthy journey across the treeless prairie. *Library of Congress, det1994023579/PP.*

The Perilous St. Croix River Valley Frontier

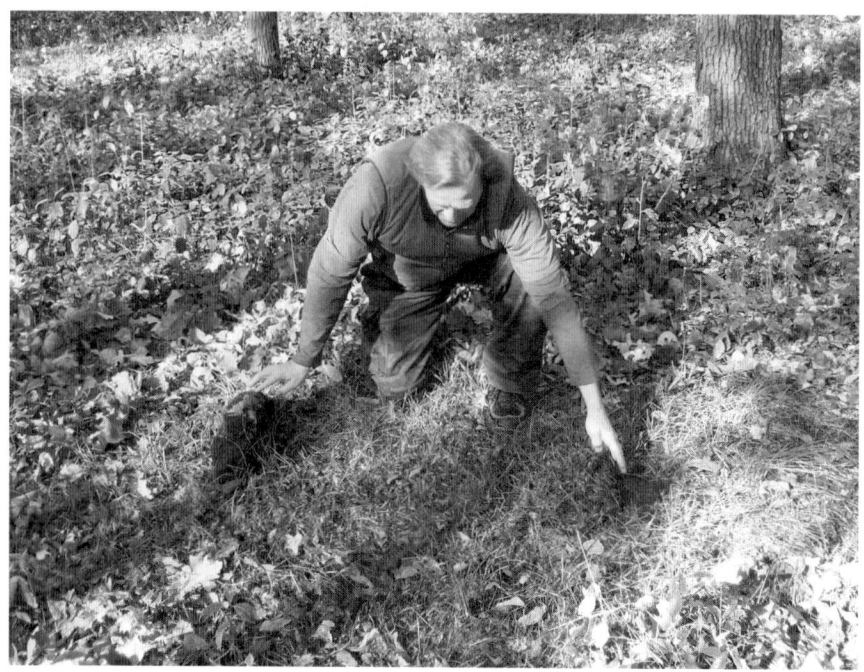

Infant and child burials were marked with lime rock headstones and small footstones on the blufftop burial ground above Catfish on the St. Croix River.

to Major Plympton at the fort that this troop of people was about to retire outside his post on reserve land. Knowing that the frontier had opened to the east of the stone fort the prior year, Plympton took it upon himself to evict the old drivers and their families from the reserve land.

May 6, 1840, was the day Major Plympton issued his ultimatum to the old drivers to vacate their homes and move east off the reserve. Most of the men were of Scottish or French descent and had married native women and were raising children. It was the spring of the season; there was plenty of land to claim and prime time to begin a new life out on the prairie. It seemed reasonable to claim the land, but life instantly became more difficult, as the former ox cart drivers lacked goods, services and shelter. As such, the need for a burial ground grew rapidly, with children suffering the most. Little graves dot the blufftop that overlooks Catfish Bar on the St. Croix.

Among the families evicted by Major Plympton were Brown, Bruce, Leith, Massey, McCoy, Bellonge, Bourcier, Fournier, La Bathe and Mager. These people are a few of the recorded settlers who made a life in the lower St. Croix Valley or near the mouth of the St. Croix River.

Part II

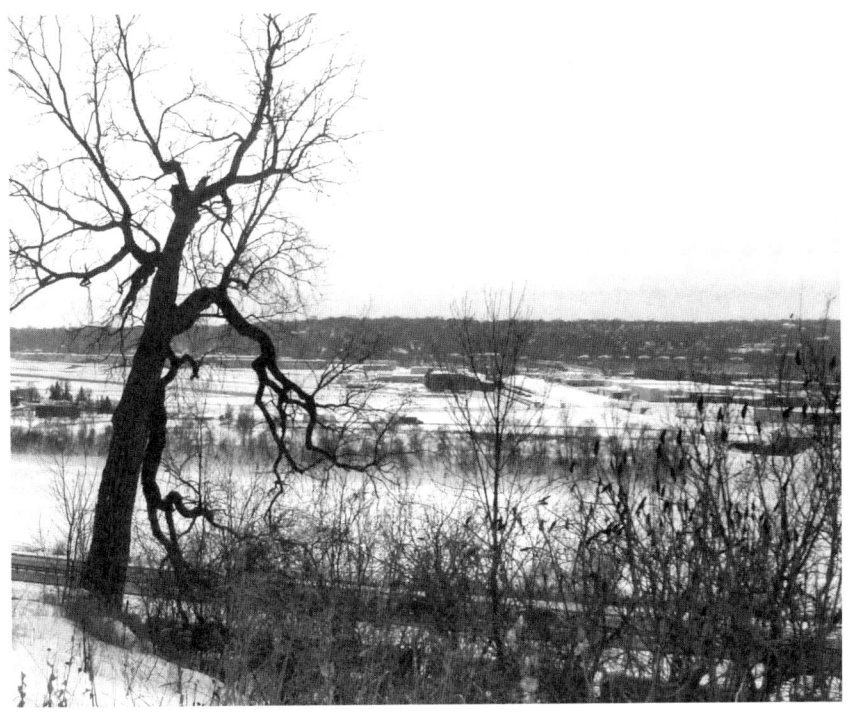

A Dakota marker tree on Mounds Park Bluff in St. Paul points down to the Old Cave settlement site and to the mouth of Carver's historic cave below the bluff.

Louis Massey was a well-respected settler and trader who had lived on the fort's reserve for twenty-two years. Officers of the post felt compassion for Massey's plight and assisted in moving his family and their possessions across the St. Croix, to the mouth of the Willow River. Louis Massey and his family were the first pioneers located on the east bank of Lake St. Croix. Other pioneer-minded people would settle around the Masseys. Their hilltop burial ground would be named for the Willow River.

A Swedish man, Jacob Fahlstrom, was a reluctant pioneer from the fort who argued the order to move, appealing his eviction to the federal government. Fahlstrom's appeal was denied. Jacob moved his mixed-blood family to a ravine near the Old Cave Settlement. The Dakota who had camped in the vicinity of the Old Cave moved some of their lodges across the river to Kaposia, honoring the 1837 Mendota Treaty to clear the east bank for new settlers.

The Old Cave, seven miles below Fort Snelling, was a significant meeting place of the area's native people. During the colonial period, Jonathan Carver,

The Perilous St. Croix River Valley Frontier

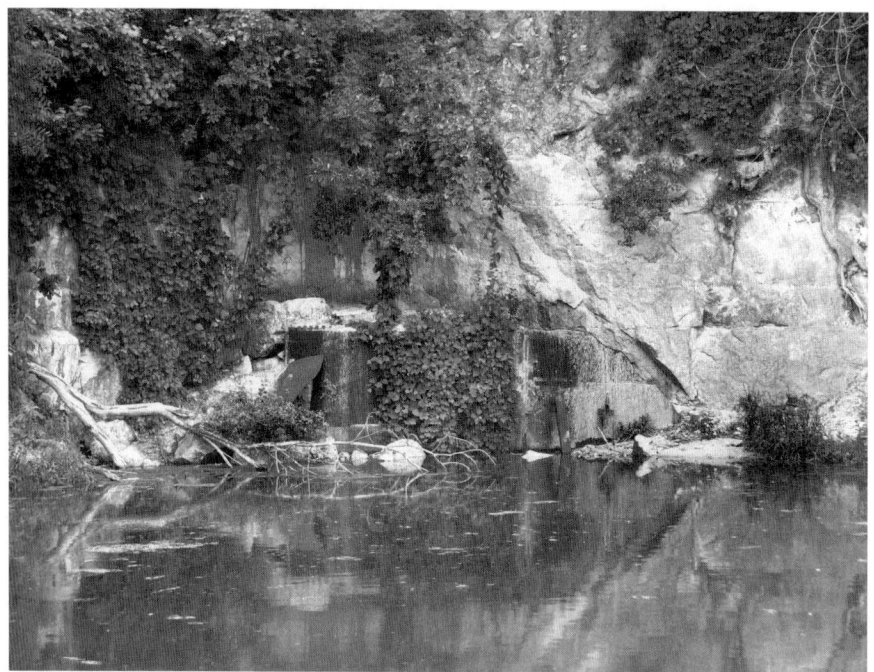

Historic Carver's Cave has since been filled and flooded and had its original entrance dynamited and blocked with an iron barricade.

a former British army captain, led an expedition exploring the Ouisconsin, Mississippi and St. Peters Rivers. During the fall of 1766, Carver met the area's Dakota tribes and was given a tour of the Old Cave, where the Dakota people buried their dead. Carver's expedition was invited to remain for the duration of winter.

Captain Carver became well acquainted with the surrounding area, including St. Anthony Falls and the St. Croix River. Carver and his entourage of explorers also became well acquainted with the Dakota people through the winter of 1766–67. A couple decades later, a band of Dakota people evolved from that winter's stay, calling themselves the Carver band of Dakota, direct descendants of Carver and the men of his expedition. Sometime afterward, the Old Cave would be fondly remembered as Carver's Cave.

Jacob Fahlstrom was serving the fort as a mail carrier prior to the eviction. Jacob delivered mail from Fort Snelling to Fort Crawford at Prairie Du Chien and then to the Indian Agency at La Pointe on Lake Superior. Jacob also served as a trail guide to many traders and explorers. He knew the land above the Falls of St. Anthony quite well. While Jacob was a teenager,

Part II

he was located far to the north at Lord Selkirk's Canadian fur trade colony. Jacob had arrived in North America by sea but came through Hudson Bay and then to the colony by way of the Red River.

As competition increased for furs and hides, a trade war erupted between the Hudson Bay Company and the North West Company at Selkirk. Jacob exited the disputed area when the shooting started, heading south into Ojibwe country. He was found wandering the forest and was taken in by a chief and raised in the Ojibwe culture. Jacob Fahlstrom was the first person of Swedish descent to arrive in the upper Mississippi River region. Jacob was well known for his Ojibwe skills, and to fur traders acquainted with him, he was called the Swede Indian.

Jacob could communicate in English, Ojibwe and Dakota as well as his first language of Swedish. His hair was blond, as was common among Scandinavians; as a result, the Ojibwe and Dakota called him "Yellow Head." The guide named Yellow Head who led famed discoverer Henry Schoolcraft to the source of the Mississippi River was likely Jacob Fahlstrom.

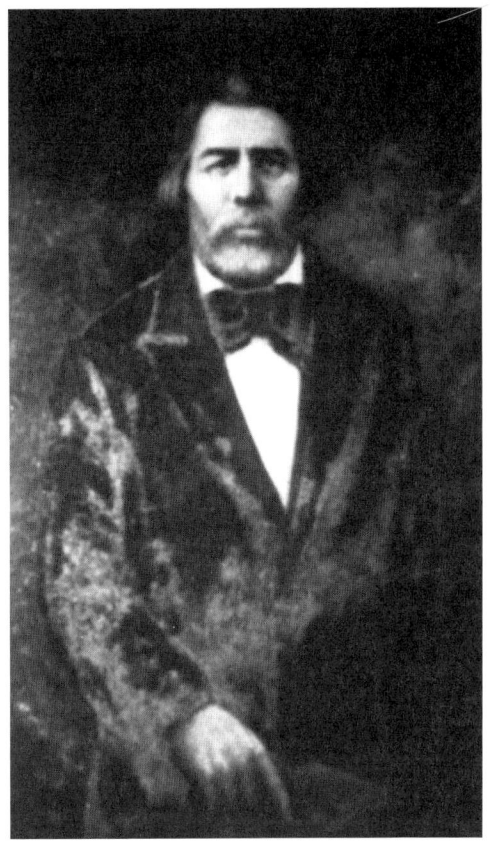

Born in Sweden, Jacob Fahlstrom was a young Canadian settler who was adopted by the Ojibwe. Jacob became a trail guide, a mail carrier, a farmer and a missionary. He is recognized for being the first Swede in what is now called Minnesota. *Photo courtesy Afton Historical Museum.*

Fahlstrom lived in the ravine near the Old Cave for a short time, becoming tired of climbing the steep hills on either side. At forty-five years of age, following a life of trekking great distances, Jacob desired a place less hilly to occupy. Twelve miles farther to the east was rolling prairieland, far more pleasant on which to settle. Jacob Fahlstrom left the ravine, but the place retained a name for its first pioneer: Swede Hollow.

The Perilous St. Croix River Valley Frontier

Jacob built a log cabin next to a pond on a well-traveled native trail that was only four miles from Lake St. Croix. Both Dakota and Ojibwe were welcome at "Father Jacob's" cabin. Jacob had been converted to Methodism just three years prior at the Kaposia Mission site near Red Rock and was passionate about converting anyone who passed through. The Kaposia Mission was ministering to the Dakota people, and Jacob Fahlstrom became the missionary to the Ojibwe.

Jacob Fahlstrom was married to a mixed-blood Ojibwe woman who came from a village far to the north. The difference with Marguarite was that she was part African, being descended from her grandfather Jean Bonga, a slave who served British army captain Daniel Robertson. When Captain Robertson died in 1810, Jean Bonga became a free black who carried on with fur trading, which he had learned during his servitude. As the Bonga family grew, they remained in the north, prospering in the fur trade and marrying into the Ojibwe people.

Both Jacob and Marguarite always welcomed visitors to the cabin, and Father Jacob hosted any missionary wishing to stay with the family. Jacob also attempted to enter local politics in 1842 by running for clerk to the St. Croix County commissioner. Jacob received only one vote in the frontier election; Joseph R. Brown received thirty.

Unfortunately, tragedy struck the native people in the form of a plague that took many lives. Yellow fever was a serious ailment to which the native people had little immunity, and they suffered from it. Smallpox was also destroying native villages from the headwaters of the Mississippi west to the Missouri River. Great numbers of native people were plagued with a horrible death by pox from 1837 to 1842. The year 1842 was when the plague reached its limits at the Fahlstrom place.

Jacob Fahlstrom's cabin was open to the ailing Dakota and became filled with many who were afflicted and dying. The Fahlstrom family nursed as many as they could, but the cabin emptied of patients as the worst cases died from the affliction. A small hill on Jacob's claim became a native cemetery, with too many graves to mark.

It's more than likely that Father Jacob preached salvation to the native people who lived and died. Jacob's efforts contributed to a new clan of native people termed "Christian Indians." These Christian Indians became established as a unique and distinctive group among themselves.

Part II

A Bold Ojibwe Attack: Pine Glen, 1842

Pine Glen was an extensive ravine that branched through the river bluff on the east bank of the Mississippi. It was named for a rare growth of pine trees in an area that was primarily prairie grass and oak trees. The attack there was a surprise that came from the east over the prairie. Targeted were the mixed-blood people who were residing along the banks of the Mississippi in proximity to Red Rock. The full-blood Dakota people vacated their eastern villages and moved west across the Mississippi to comply with the 1837 treaty. The St. Croix Ojibwe chose to pursue their blood enemy's migration beyond the St. Croix Valley.

There was great panic among the people near Pine Glen. Many of the east bank villagers were mixed-blood people who had previously been protected by living on the fort reserve. The confusion was intense as the Dakota villagers—children, women and men—scattered in every direction. Two Dakota women and a boy, working in a garden, were pursued and struck down by the Ojibwe warriors. Mrs. Rattler was shot and instantly killed. Her son was scalped and beheaded.

An old voyager from Fort Snelling, François Gamelle, witnessed the wounding of his Dakota wife by an Ojibwe, whom she could not outrun. The terrified husband rescued his wounded wife, carrying her bleeding body into their family cabin, but the Ojibwe warrior rushed through the cabin's door and scalped the woman while in her husband's arms. Mr. Rattler, or Kha-dayah, was (in Gamelle's cabin) with his second wife, who was sick, but they were not seen by the Ojibwe warrior.

Gamelle placed his dead wife in bed and grabbed his old gun, chasing after the Ojibwe. He fired a shot at the running warrior, striking him in the back of the leg. The warrior painfully limped away with his trophy, the beloved woman's scalp.

The sounds of screaming and gunfire echoed across the river. Dakota warriors, who had received the alarm, took to their canoes to fend off their Ojibwe enemy but were under the influence of liquor, some too drunk to be effective. The women of the Kaposia camp had hidden the warriors' guns, as they typically did during times of heavy drinking. The women knew that shootings would take place, the men killing one another. Once the warriors made it to Pine Glen, they fired on their enemy, the Ojibwe.

The gun battle that took place in the vast ravine lasted over an hour until the attackers left the field on the trail to Battle Hollow, eighteen miles away. The impaired Dakota warriors went on the chase after their enemy, taking

The Perilous St. Croix River Valley Frontier

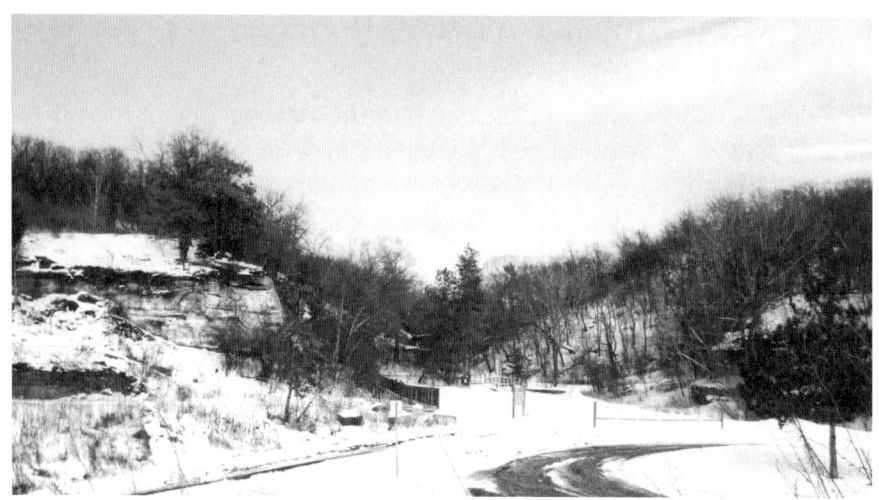

Battle Creek was named for the 1842 Ojibwe attack that was made in proximity to the stream. Originally, the creek flowed from a cave that was explored in 1817 by Major Stephen Long (who was searching for Carver's Cave). Record floods in 1826 washed out the gypsum sand cave that created the park-like ravine.

down as many as five Ojibwe who were in retreat. It was not a good day for the Dakota, either; thirteen of their warriors were killed in the battle.

One of the Dakota boys who participated in the chase had taken an Ojibwe scalp as his trophy. Then he beheaded the Ojibwe and kept that as well. The boy was so proud of the gruesome object that he took it to the trader Henry Sibley, at Mendota, and displayed it for him, too.

The battle that occurred at Pine Glen meant that east bank village sites were no longer safe. These villages did not recover but were dispersed east and west. Some of the mission people moved east toward Lake St. Croix, and others moved to the west bank village of Kaposia, which became a primary encampment of the Dakota people. The Methodist mission of Kaposia was closed.

A Partnership Made to Farm the Land "Unto Death Us Do Part": Educators of the Kaposia Mission

Elizabeth Campbell Randolph and Taylor Fitz Randolph, husband and wife, were the first schoolteachers serving the Dakota mission at Kaposia. The Methodist mission was originally on the west bank of the Mississippi

Part II

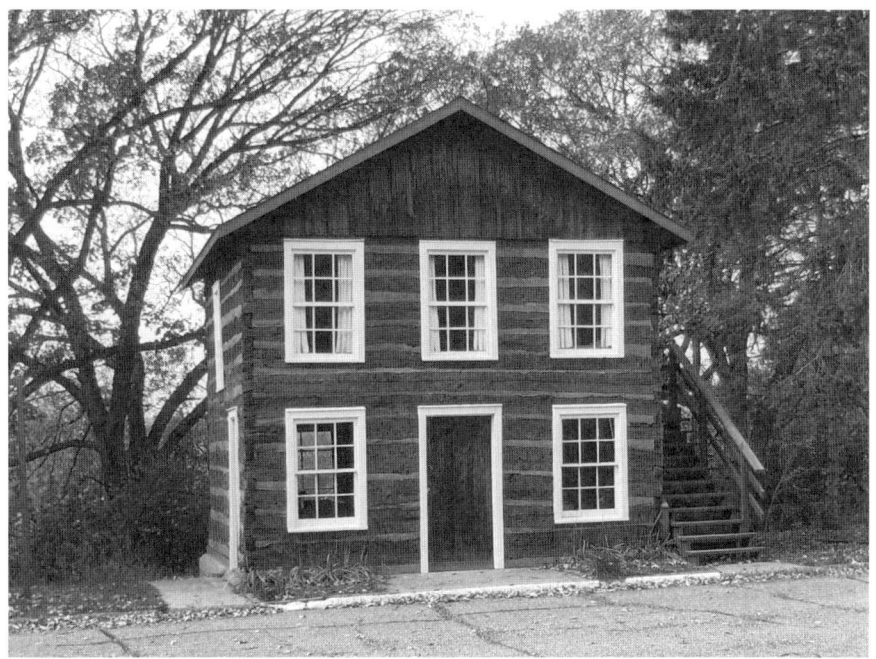

The Kaposia Methodist mission is preserved by the United Methodist Church in Newport, Minnesota, where school was taught on both levels by Elizabeth and Tyler Randolph. *Photo by Leah Junkert.*

but soon moved across the river to Red Rock. The Randolphs began holding two separate classes at the mission in 1837. One class educated full-blood Dakota children; the other class educated mixed-blood and white pioneer children. The married couple taught school for nearly five years at the mission house and then moved away from the mission after the 1842 Battle of Pine Glen. They moved east to farm the prairie near Bissell's Mounds.

Bissell's Mounds are unusual geological land formations of natural limestone remnants of bedrock that failed to erode during the St. Croix Valley's formation. There were four large mounds that were named for Elijah Bissell, the first pioneer to claim land there. Elijah Bissell began farming and raising his sons at the mounds in 1842. Elijah's wife had passed away, so he vacated his claim after marrying his second wife, Mary. The family moved west across the Mississippi to Dakota lands in 1850, but the geological landmark retained Bissell's name.

The Bissell's Mounds prairie that Elizabeth and Taylor Randolph farmed was south of Jacob Fahlstrom's claim but north of the large claim made by Joseph Haskell. The opportunity to prosper on the prairie was obvious to all

The Perilous St. Croix River Valley Frontier

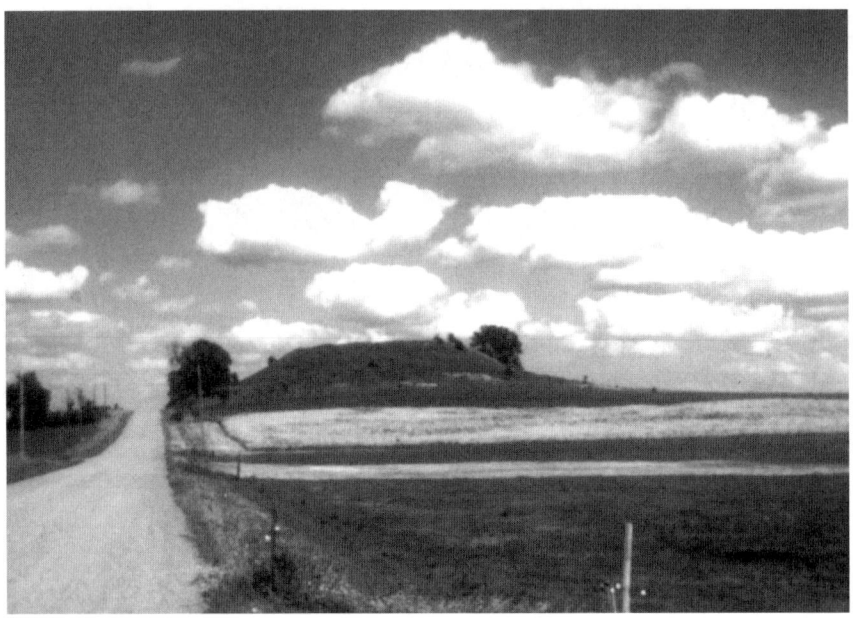

One of Bissell's Mounds on the prairie that is now Afton, Minnesota. *Photo courtesy Afton Historical Museum.*

who came to the St. Croix Valley, but the earliest problem was the lack of available labor to harvest the grain they planted.

During the summer of 1846, Elizabeth Randolph, Taylor Randolph and Jonathan Davis entered into a three-way legal and binding agreement. The three parties decided to assist one another equally on a joint claim. Even though the plotted field was no more than five acres, their mutual goal was to succeed at farming the unforgiving prairie.

In his mid-fifties, Jonathan Davis was an old ox cart driver who had been living on the Fort Snelling reserve but was evicted six years before. Jonathan lost his Dakota wife and was raising their young teenage daughter alone. It made sense for the three partners to help one another, but how would they maintain an equitable division of assets without having written it out legally?

The arrangement was that each of them had a fair chance to own the entire land claim. The deciding factor would be determined by which one of them were to live the longest. The document was signed and sealed by all three people on August 28, 1846.

The fall harvest would proceed immediately, with all three parties assisting equally. Sickle and scythe were put to the wheat, shearing it off with backbreaking effort. Fallen stalks of wheat grass were bundled in shocks that were stacked vertically across the field. The shocks would be collected and localized in a spot suitable for threshing. The grains of wheat were vigorously beaten from the stalks with heavy flails the size of tree limbs. Wheat grain then had to be separated from its useless chaff. A light breeze is required to carry away the loose chaff of the wheat grain casings by tossing it up in the air.

Harvest can be a difficult time but with rewarding results. Unfortunately, the worst happened, and Elizabeth Randolph died before the end of the year. Taylor Randolph was dying, and his death was reported to have taken place. However, he survived. Taylor, childless and alone, gave his portion of the claim to Davis, nullifying the agreement to work the land. Taylor Randolph became a boarder on James Higby's farm next to old Jonathan Davis. After a handful of years, both men disappeared from recorded view.

Delivering Winter Supplies to the St. Croix Valley Alive, If Possible

In December 1845, four teams of horses drawing sleds for freight went down the frozen waterway to Prairie Du Chien to load supplies. Prairie Du Chien on the Mississippi River was the nearest city and supply source for the young establishments of the St. Croix Valley. For a distance exceeding 150 miles, every village between the St. Croix and Prairie Du Chien was of the Dakota people. Some of the trip was made along the river roads, but much of the travel was done on the ice that formed late in autumn. The icy portion of the river route helped to shorten the lengthy journey.

William Dibble, William Folsom, Mr. Tibbetts and Jonathan E. McKusick were driving the teams, halting halfway on the return trip to partake of some whiskey, which was stored on the last sled. William Dibble's team of horses was sledding out in front of the group when the men stopped for a swig from the keg. Dibble left his team unanchored to join in the light revelry, soon after which the horses bolted. The runaway team broke from their harness, one horse running toward shore and the other plunging through a thin spot in the ice.

The jovial men charged up to the hole in the ice to save the thrashing animal using ropes and poles. The struggle to hoist the horse and slide it back onto solid ice was a challenge to the gleeful group, who eventually succeeded in the task. The salvaged horse had lost consciousness, so the men poured the remaining whiskey down its throat in an attempt to revive it. Unfortunately, the horse was dead.

Early Marriages of the St. Croix Frontier

John Kenny of Massachusetts settled at Bissell's Mounds in 1847. John Kenny called on justice of the peace William H. Folsom to join him with a mixed-race woman named Mary Jane. Kenny's neighbor, Robert Kennedy (a Virginian), forbid his friend Folsom to commit the travesty of wedlock between the white man and mulatto woman. Robert Kennedy threatened to never have a single discourse again with William Folsom if he went through with the wedding. Folsom married the Massachusetts couple, commenting that they made an interesting pair. Robert Kennedy moved to St. Paul soon after.

Benjamin Otis married an Ojibwe woman, Ann Little Wolf, at Marine Mills. The Reverend William Boutwell performed the marriage in 1844. Reverend Boutwell himself was married to Hester Crooks, a mixed-blood Ojibwe. It wasn't every man who agreed with these types of unions, with some objecting more strongly than others. Ann Little Wolf gave birth to Henry, who survived, but she did not live long after. Not much was mentioned of the poisoning of Ann Little Wolf, and no one investigated the uncertain circumstances of her death in 1848. Benjamin buried Ann in a native burial mound at Copas, raising Henry and remarrying some years later.

William Dibble married a mixed-blood woman, Eliza McCauslin, at Marine Mills in 1844. These situations were a fairly common occurrence during frontier times. The Dibbles soon began farming at the mouth of the St. Croix, expecting to raise children there. Carver, their first son, lived only a year, and Eliza only a short time longer. William buried Eliza in 1849 in a native mound on the top of the river bluff above their farm.

Part II

A Burial Wish Come True:
Silas Snell on Liberty Hill

The Willow River is an east bank tributary that flows into Lake St. Croix between Stillwater and Catfish Bar. A sawmill operation was running at Stillwater, and riverboats began making deliveries to the small settlements that were developing on the river. The first riverboat to land at the mouth of the Willow River arrived on April 15, 1847. Captain John Page became a father the same spring day when his wife delivered their daughter Abigail. The retired sea captain and his wife had been located at the Willow River for less than a year when they began their family on the frontier. Captain Page had been operating a logging venture on the Willow River. Page's crew was floating the cut timber to Lake St. Croix and then rafting the logs, sending them south on the Mississippi. Trees were fairly plentiful along the banks of the Willow River near the water's edge. Prairies were considered thinly wooded, best suited for sod breaking and farming.

One of the Willow River loggers familiar to Captain Page was Silas Snell. Silas had a special appreciation for the beauty of the St. Croix River. One of the most beautiful locations of the St. Croix was Liberty Hill, an elevation of land at the mouth of the Willow River. Silas Snell commented to Page that Liberty Hill was such a beautiful place that he would like to be buried on the hilltop when that final day came.

Captain John Page agreed with Silas that Liberty Hill was a special place on the St. Croix and said that he wouldn't mind being buried on that spot

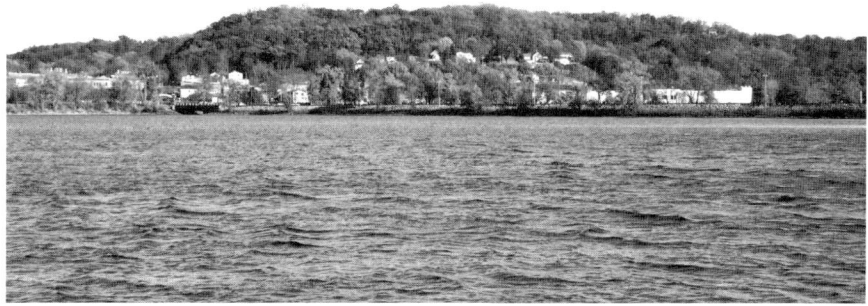

Hudson, Wisconsin's bluff Liberty Hill. Its St. Croix Valley beauty was admired by Silas Snell and Captain John Page.

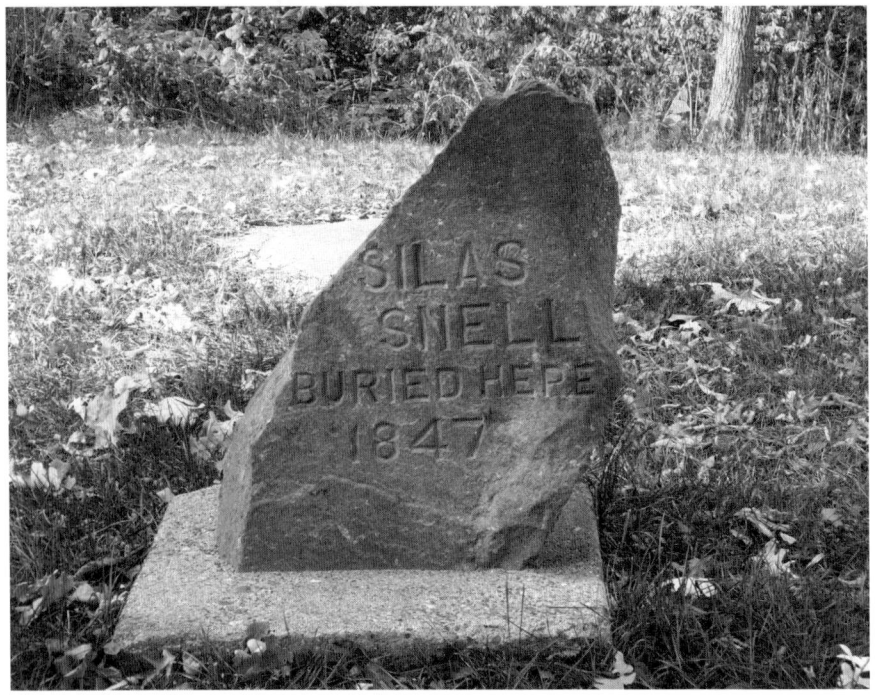

Located in Hudson's Prospect Park on top of Liberty Hill, Silas Snell's grave marker was placed in 1927.

one day as well. Silas Snell promised the captain to bury him on Liberty Hill if he were to die first. The two men came to an agreement that whoever died first would be guaranteed to be buried by the other on Liberty Hill.

Strange as it seems, Silas Snell might have predicted his early demise, passing away soon after the agreement was made. True to his promise, Captain Page and the loggers buried Silas Snell on beautiful Liberty Hill.

Stillwater's First Murder Trial, 1847: The Murder of Henry Rust

Henry Rust was a simple peddler with a small trading house north of the Falls of St. Croix on the Groundhouse River. Much of Henry's trading business had to do with whiskey. Henry Rust was invited by Reverend William Boutwell to come into a logging camp to hear him preach. Henry did not

Part II

attend the sermon and was soon found dead, having been shot. Learning of this tragedy, seventy-five angry loggers collected all the weapons they could find and went directly to Henry's trading house. The men recovered Henry's body and then emptied the house of valuables, dumping out two barrels of whiskey and setting fire to the entire place. The whiskey greatly assisted in setting the liquor establishment ablaze.

Henry Rust was laid to rest at an old mission site with forty of the men in attendance. After the burial, a meeting was held during which it was agreed that whiskey was the cause of many complaints, and it was determined to eliminate it from the country. The force of armed men went out to three other trading houses, destroying whiskey by the barrel in spite of tearful pleas from the traders. The angry purge of liquor was short-lived, and whiskey was soon flowing freely again.

Two arrests were made in the murder of Henry Rust: Nodin and Ne-she-ke-o-ge-ma. Both of the Ojibwe men were charged, having admitted to the crime. Jurors were few and far between, all of them located within a one-hundred-mile radius of Stillwater. The jury's decision was an acquittal, setting the native men free. Whiskey was blamed for the drunken brawl.

Nodin revealed a secret to William Folsom, the sheriff, while being transported to Stillwater for prosecution. He told Folsom of a copper find on the Kanabec River. It's true that copper is extremely rare in the area, nearly beyond the realm of possibility. The story of the copper mine was an intriguing one, and after the criminal case was resolved, Nodin promised to take William Folsom to the find. Nodin's life was unexpectedly cut short after the acquittal, and the Kanabec River copper mine remained undiscovered.

Murder for Hire: Whiskey Rivalries Become Deadly

Competition for whiskey sales developed along the St. Croix River around St. Croix Falls, which led to a conspiracy to put one out of business. The plan was hatched by an old German named Miller, who was located east of the Falls of St. Croix. Miller thought he had rights to sell whiskey where no one else should.

A recently established whiskey seller, Miles Tornell, created a problem for Miller, but Tornell's establishment burned to the ground. Two bodies were found in the rubble, strangely discovered buried in a coal pit. Tornell's was one of them. Questions were asked about the tragedy, and an Ojibwe honestly replied that he had killed the men. The Ojibwe explained that he had been hired by Miller to kill Tornell. The second man, named McLaughlin, was simply in the wrong place at the wrong time.

A speedy trial had been given to the Ojibwe, which ended without a verdict. An overnight discussion of the matter determined that the Ojibwe should be hanged. The condemned was taken at daybreak to a tree, where he was hanged by a rope. The Ojibwe were given the body for a customary burial.

Letting Miller, the true criminal in the matter, get away nearly happened, but he was tied to the hanging tree and whipped. Fifteen strokes with a beech tree branch was hardly corporal punishment for two murders. Miller was then placed on a steamboat and banished, being told never to return.

Pat Collins was a generally spiteful man, having whipped Miller with a passion. Collins's personal hate for Miller contributed to the beating. Some years later, Collins was hanged in California for highway robbery. The assistant hangman, Charles Rowley, farmed until the Civil War but was killed in battle. Rowley's Thirteenth Wisconsin Infantry regiment fought in only one battle during the Civil War, with only five killed. Charles was one of the dead.

White Man's Justice: A Fearsome Thing

An incident of a drunken fight occurred not long after the debacle of the whiskey murders. Two Ojibwe confessed to a fight that killed a whiskey tender. When asked if they knew what had happened, the two Ojibwe men admitted that they were drunk at the time of the murder. Before charges were brought on the men, they committed suicide by musket, having heard of "white man's justice." The resentful pair of Ojibwe so disliked the idea of being hanged from a rope that they preferred to shoot themselves.

PART III

EARLY ELECTIONS IN STILLWATER, ST. CROIX COUNTY, WISCONSIN TERRITORY

Many county positions were open for election in 1847. Three county commissioners, six justices of the peace, one sheriff, a coroner, a treasurer and "Negro suffrage" were on the ballets. One of the earliest black pioneers in the St. Croix Valley was London Peters. London Peters was born in Ohio about 1810, yet his exact birth year was, customarily, not recorded or celebrated. London was never a slave, although it's uncertain if he had been an indentured servant. What is certain is that London Peters was a free black man running for county commissioner of St. Croix County.

Negro suffrage was placed on the ballet to determine if "colored people" (as they were called at the time) had the right to vote in the territorial county. London Peters was a black man with a large claim of land on the north end of Kittson's Point, which was a short distance below Stillwater on the St. Croix. London had a house on the 298-acre claim that he owned free and clear of any encumbrances. As such, the ownership of the frontier acreage, nearly a half square mile of land, qualified London Peters as a free man with the right to vote. Naturally, Negro suffrage had to be placed on the ballot, as blacks were not qualified voters.

There were as many as 490 voters in the election for Stillwater's county commissioner. London Peters was on the ballot to be elected commissioner if he received the majority of votes. He received only 1 vote. On the issue of

Negro suffrage, there were 126 "no" votes and only 1 "yes" vote. The next year, London sold his claim for $298 and moved to the point of land at the south end of the county now called Mouth of the St. Croix.

Gateway to the Raw Frontier, Stillwater

The year 1847 was when land surveyors from Dubuque, Iowa, came to Mouth of the St. Croix to create section lines and township borders. The hardy men struck out from the west bank of Lake St. Croix, above the mouth of the river, near the forty-fifth parallel. They pushed through tall prairie grass, measuring with their iron links and chains using oak trees and boulders (when they could be found) and designating reference points and markers.

A few square miles of virgin prairie still exist in central Washington County of Minnesota. The grazing of cattle prevented the growth of invasive plants and trees.

The survey crew began each day's work on the prairie soaked by morning dew, which was followed by a good caking of mud. Terrible battles occurred between the valiant crew and bloodthirsty mosquitoes, which attacked from the numerous ponds and lakes on the prairie.

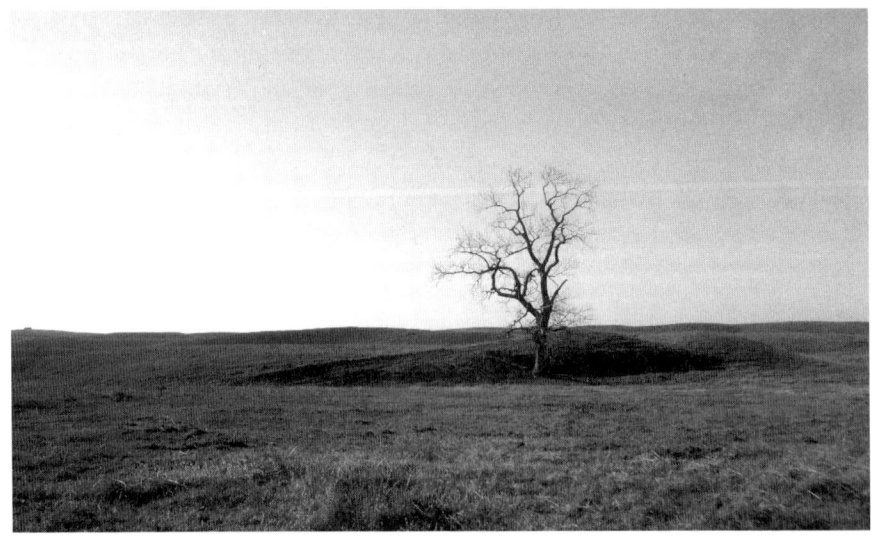

A few square miles of virgin prairie still exist in central Washington County of Minnesota. The grazing of cattle prevented the growth of invasive plants and trees.

Part III

The surveyors measured, mapped and marked township lines and section corners with wooden stakes or rocks and trees, creating legal descriptions for blocks of land that would be sold to pioneers. Frontier acreage could be purchased from the U.S. government at the land office for $1.25 an acre, in Taylors Falls, on August 14, 1848. The days of staking claims on the frontier were ending.

Illinois senator Stephen A. Douglas visited the Mississippi River Valley in 1848. Douglas, as chairman of the Committee on Territories, toured special river sites that included Mouth of the St. Croix, Fort Snelling and Pilot Knob. Douglas recommended developing St. Paul as a future territorial capital after ruling out St. Peter, St. Anthony, Mendota, Lakeland and Stillwater.

Stillwater had become the gateway city to the frontier. The small settlement that was planted by John McKusick (and lumber partners) was rapidly developing around the sawmill their lumber company had built at the head of Lake St. Croix. Solid frame structures were being constructed, and a real city was taking shape. The early shacks that were constructed of slab wood and random boards were taken down, salvaged and reused with none of the material going to waste.

Shortly after Senator Douglas departed the St. Croix Valley for Washington, his name was placed on a point of land, out of great respect, that had once been chosen by Zebulon Pike for a military fortification. After Pike's ratification of the land granted by the great chief La Petit Corbeau, it was under the title of the U.S. government reserve. Later, the name St. Croix, or St. Croix Precinct, was attached to the vast area. Then the Mouth of St. Croix post office was moved west across the St. Croix, from the east bank, providing a more specific locale. The east bank is where Prescott's Landing was located, named for the ferry operation there. Ultimately, the name Point Douglas stuck as a frontier village grew with a store, hotel, school, church, sawmill and boardinghouse.

Whose Baby Is Whose?: Early Socializing in Stillwater

Women were quite the minority in Stillwater's early sawmill days. The hardworking laborers, sawyers and men of industry searched for wives for pleasant company. A society was developing as the ladies met for tea in small numbers. Special occasions did occur when large parties, or balls, were thrown, the grand affairs being well attended. Families were growing during these early times, and there were many newborn infants who came with their parents to the balls.

These events were a rare occasion for the women of the frontier to socialize and engage in real conversation. They were not to be missed. One of the young women brought an eleven-day-old baby with her, but there was another baby there that was younger than hers. A nursery was set up in Anson Northrop's new hotel, where the babes were bundled and put to sleep. This arrangement worked quite well, as the babies slept until first daylight, when the hardy partiers could see to find their ways home.

On a particular occurrence, the upper-level nursery at the party hall had eleven babies all sleeping together. Oddly, though, a mischievous visitor to the nursery unwrapped the bundled babies and switched their wraps; he also rearranged the infants' sleeping positions. All of the infants were mismatched and mixed up. Their mothers arrived at 5:00 a.m., the party having concluded, gathered their little ones from the nursery and headed for home.

The story of the secret swap was told, but it remained a quiet one. No one has ever heard if the women discovered the mistaken identities of their babies or if the ill-behaved error was ever corrected. Yet some folks told of frantic mothers running to and fro through Stillwater at six o'clock in the morning, searching for their rightful children.

Border Country and Statehood

On May 29, 1848, the state of Wisconsin was created from the established territory of 1836, except that the St. Croix River had become the western border of the new state. Stillwater had been the territorial county seat of St. Croix County, but now that county terminated on the east bank of the river, and Stillwater was on the west.

This meant that Stillwater was at the head of western expansion on the frontier. It was just Stillwater. There was no other name for the west unless one called it a no-man's land, and many did. For ten months following Wisconsin's statehood, Stillwater was, generally speaking, the capital of the nameless frontier.

The St. Croix River also served as another border and no-man's land between the Dakota and Ojibwe, who continued to be hostile toward each other. Neither tribe could enter the river valley without consequence or confrontation.

Part III

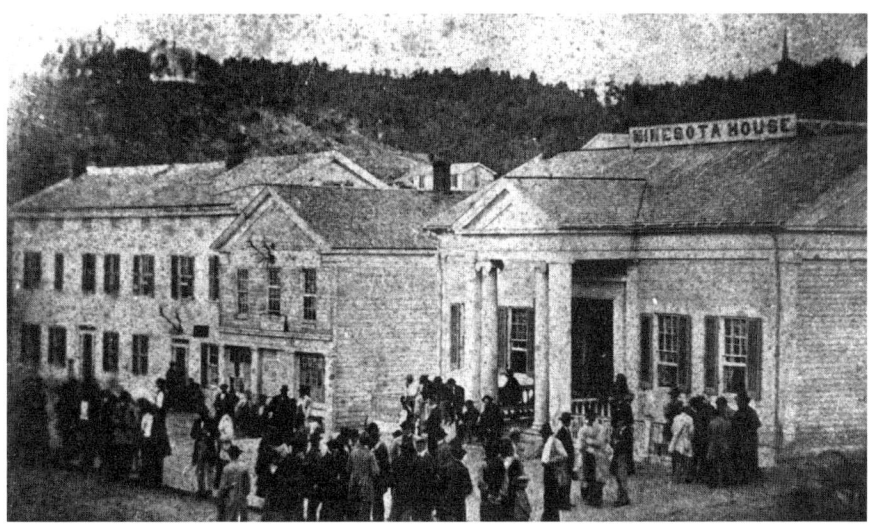

Stillwater's Minesota House, located on Main Street, is where the territory of Minnesota was first proposed. *Photo courtesy Washington County Historical Society.*

As pioneers arrived in the valley with each riverboat, they witnessed the coming and going of native people. Even though the binding treaty agreements were honored and the tribes lived on their prescribed lands, they regularly conducted business in the area. Native people never struggled with a twenty- to twenty-five-mile walk to a chosen destination, sometimes staying the night or returning to their point of origin the same day. The Dakota people entering Stillwater came from their western camp at Kaposia. The Ojibwe people came from small, eastern lodges on the Apple River or from St. Croix Falls to the north.

On August 26, 1848, a small convention was held. Joseph R. Brown, John McKusick, Jonathon E. McKusick, James Norris and Joseph Haskell were among sixty-one motivated men in an upper room belonging to John McKusick. The unnamed frontier required organizing, so territorial resolutions were passed, written and delivered to the state of Wisconsin's House of Representatives, as if Stillwater were still part of Wisconsin Territory. The raw frontier was named "Minesota," (spelled with one *n*), with the territorial government being formed at Stillwater. Washington County was the first county created, named for America's first president. A resolution was soon passed incorporating a second *n* in the name Minnesota Territory. Progress was being made.

The Perilous St. Croix River Valley Frontier

Black Pioneer Dick: Joel Foster's Indentured Servant

Wisconsin statehood brought change to the St. Croix Valley. In 1848, the United States had won an overwhelming victory in the war with Mexico, the Mexican army suffering great losses in battle against the Americans. Massey and Bouche's settlement of Willow River was renamed Buena Vista in 1848 for a resounding U.S. victory at a battle of the same name. In most of the battles fought in the Mexican War, the results were disastrous for the Mexicans, as if the lives of David Crockett, Jim Bowie and the heroes lost at the Alamo were being avenged seventy-seven times.

Late in 1848, Captain Joel Foster, with pioneering in mind, came to a tributary on the east bank of the St. Croix named Kinnickinnic. The unusual name of the tributary is an Ojibwe word meaning "blended smoking tobacco." Joel Foster had received his captain's commission, serving as quartermaster during the Mexican War. Now that the war was over, America was on the move, having victoriously gained much more western territory from Mexico.

Joel Foster had served in an Illinois infantry regiment, but his black servant, Dick, was from Indiana. Slavery did exist but not in the usual way in the Northern states, which were considered free states. Slave owners could and did bring their human property to the North, as they were guaranteed this right by the Fifth Amendment of the United States Constitution. In the case of Dick, a black indentured servant, his time could be "made good," and then he would be released from service.

Indentured servitude had its conditions, and in this situation, Joel Foster was required by law to have a court order to remove Dick from Indiana. Foster went before an Indiana judge with his request to take young Dick to the new state of Wisconsin. Not seeing any difficulty with the request, the judge approved the legal transportation of the black indentured servant.

The two men arrived at the Falls of the Kinnickinnic late in the autumn of 1848. There was an overhanging ledge of rock next to the falls where many native people had camped, and Joel and Dick made use of it for themselves. Together they worked hard cutting trees to construct a log home above the rock ledge at the falls. Winter came too soon that fall; the unfinished cabin was still without a roof for shelter. Desperate for protection from bitterly cold weather, they dug a hole in the ground inside the four walls of the log structure. The hole, or cave cabin, is where the two men spent the cold winter, continuing work on the roof and mud chinking the logs when weather permitted.

Part III

Joel and Dick were the first two pioneers in that part of the country. Without goods and services, they had to hunt for most of their food. Dick was quite the marksman and would challenge anyone to a target shoot—and win. A few other pioneers became acquainted with the pair and joined in hunting wild game. Dick trekked across the rolling terrain and was quite jovial about the others' inability to keep pace with him.

As summer arrived, Dick reached his estimated twenty-first year of life. Dick's indentured service contract was up, having "made good" his time with Joel Foster. Dick was his own man now, and he desired very much to be married. Dick told Joel that he wanted a black woman for a wife and that he would be certain to find one in St. Louis, Missouri.

Dick left on his matrimonial journey and had been gone a matter of weeks when he communicated to Joel Foster that he had found his mate. Dick was in love, and his black gal was free to come north and make a life with him. Unfortunately, his bride's family objected to taking their daughter away to the frozen northland. It was just too cold for their girl to live up north. Dick stayed with his bride, living as a free man in St. Louis, not returning to pioneer the frontier.

Scalp Dance in Downtown Stillwater: Terror on Broadway

In the spring of 1850, thirteen painted warriors from Kaposia entered the frontier city of Stillwater. This band had been advised by Chief Red Wing to organize a war party, but these warriors were led by a questionable war chief who had been in Fort Snelling's jail for scalping his wife. The war-painted Dakota were curious about what they might find in Stillwater as they explored various stores of goods and wares. The warriors were not there very long when they noticed their blood enemy, the Ojibwe, on the north end of town entering a store.

The Dakota were cautious not to reveal themselves, returning to their war chief, who was still at the south end of the street. The alarmed warriors notified their chief and suggested they attack and destroy the enemy right there in the town. The war chief put a halt to that thought, stating, "Not here." The perturbed warriors replied that the element of surprise would be lost if they failed to act. Furthermore, it appeared that these were the same Ojibwe who had raided their camp and were responsible for scalping the war chief's wife. The chief repeated, "Do nothing."

The Perilous St. Croix River Valley Frontier

The warriors questioned their chief, "Have you become weak?" The wise chief advised them to simply watch and see where the Ojibwe went. They responded that he was weak, but the chief explained that these Ojibwe would lead them to more, and then they would attack. The warriors understood that the plan was to stalk the Ojibwe without revealing their presence and then launch the attack to avenge their people.

The Ojibwe eventually left Stillwater, heading north on the river and then northeast up the Apple River a handful of miles to a bark lodge on the embankment. The Dakota followed tracks in the snow, which included evidence that the Ojibwe were dragging a keg of whiskey. The war party discovered fifteen Ojibwe drinking at the lodge, supporting the chief's tactical wisdom. When morning came, the Dakota let out their vicious war cries, startling their enemy, and then fired their muskets with full effect. Swinging war clubs with brutal accuracy, the painted war party fiercely chased down any Ojibwe who ran.

All of the Ojibwe were killed and scalped except for one boy, who was spared when the war chief halted the killing. "One must remain alive to tell the tale of the battle that occurred that day," stated the chief. The next day, the war party returned on the trail to Stillwater (populated by six hundred people) with their young captive. On Broadway Street of downtown Stillwater, thirteen painted warriors displayed their blood-soaked scalps, some of which belonged to relatives of the captive nine-year-old boy. On the street, the warriors surrounded the boy, parading the scalps in a victory dance that increased with intensity. As the warriors danced round and round, they sang and slapped the boy in the face with their bloody trophies.

After the scalp dance, the Dakota victors returned to Kaposia Village, where the chief adopted the captive Ojibwe boy. News of the event reached Minnesota's territorial governor, Alexander Ramsey, who called for the captive boy to be delivered to him in St. Paul. Alexander Ramsey intended to clothe the boy, feed him, educate him and raise him in the white way, in effect replacing a young son that the Ramseys had recently lost. The scared boy cried bitterly, preferring to be held captive by his blood enemy. He attempted several escapes from the residence. Alexander Ramsey had the doors of his house locked, preventing the boy's escape.

Territorial governor Ramsey had arrested the thirteen Dakota warriors who were responsible for the Apple River killings, placing them in Fort Snelling's jail. Soon after this, the great Ojibwe chief Hole-in-the-Day came from his Gull Lake home to the Mississippi River near St. Paul and killed a Dakota in retaliation for the Apple River attack. Ramsey realized the futility

Part III

of arresting the chief of the sovereign nation and released the thirteen Dakota from jail.

During a late-night dinner party at Ramsey's home, the Ojibwe boy was allowed to be in the kitchen with the servant and cook. The servant, who felt quite badly for the poor lad, intentionally left the back door unlocked. About midnight, the boy discovered the open door and fled into the dark. He was never seen again.

Rats Attacked by Tom the Cat: Terror in Stillwater

Stillwater's first cat of notable record was one by the name of Tom. Tom was often kept penned up in a small cage that was fairly tight quarters for the feline. Tom suffered from lethargy in the crate—so much so that he appeared to have given up his spirit and died. Reported dead, Jonathon E. McKusick came to inspect the remains of the once proud cat. Jonathan E. McKusick was able to detect a faint sign of life left in its veins and proceeded with a bloodletting cure for the cat. By a medical miracle, the cat regained consciousness after being cut by McKusick's sharp knife. Tom the cat lived for many more years, reducing Stillwater's rat infestation by using feline stealth, terror, claws and fangs.

Rain, Lightning and Thunderbird: Terror from the Sky

Stillwater was planted in a bowl-like semicircular hollow with five ravines all directed into it. The spring of 1852 was an unusually wet one. Then rain fell continuous for two days in May, culminating on a third day, the fourteenth, with a great deluge of inconceivable power. The saturated soil along a ravine that led from McKusick's sawmill up to McKusick Lake let loose, creating a landslide through Stillwater to the mill on the river's shore.

Lake McKusick's level had risen high enough to wash out the sawmill's spillway dam. The dam burst created a second landslide down the ravine worse than the first. So much mud had slid down in the two landslides that Stillwater's waterfront was twenty feet higher than before. Many shacks and shanties were completely buried with earth. The McKusick sawmill was surrounded and filled with mud. The steam engine and water wheel inside the mill were dug out, and the machinery was repaired to working condition. In a strange way, the sawmill worked even better with the new soil surrounding the outer walls of the structure.

It was said that the disaster permanently improved the waterfront at Stillwater by increasing its height and leveling it out. It was also said that if anyone were to have been inside the shanties or shacks, they are still there, never having been recovered.

A powerful thunderstorm passed over the St. Croix River at the mouth of the Willow River about the same time Stillwater suffered from its landslide. There was a tent pitched just south of the Willow River with sixteen men inside while the rains fell, but at about 9:00 p.m., a great bolt of lightning struck the tent.

Two of the men in the tent, Carson and Witham, were killed instantly, the electricity entering their heads, passing through their bodies and exiting their feet. Two more men suffered from the effects of the electric shock and were presumed dead. Both Oaks and Rand were stunned and unable to move. Mr. Oaks was struck with electricity in the arm; it traveled through his body, leaving small burn marks all over his skin. Permanent scars welted up on his skin showing the path that the voltage took through him. Mr. Oaks was nearly a year in recovery.

Mr. Rand was physically frozen, seemingly unconscious for a day, yet he was completely aware the entire time. Rand was severely burned and blistered on one side of his body. He recovered from his burns, and his prior vision impairment was mysteriously cured.

The Dakota people at Kaposia spoke of the greatest bird seen in the sky. The Dakota, like other native people, had always admired the bald eagle for its ability to fly higher than any other bird in the air. Eagles were known to fly at cloud-level elevations that were nearest to where the Great Spirit resided. There was one other rare bird of the sky that eclipsed the size of a bald eagle, and that one was named the Thunderbird.

The Kaposia people told of a time when one of the fearsome birds was killed and examined. The Dakota had spread out the Thunderbird's wings, which were double the span of a mature bald eagle, likely fifteen feet in width. Another feature of the bird's wings was the strange zigzag shape that could have been compared to bolts of lightning. Even stranger was the head of the bird, which was comparable in size to that of a man and also resembled a man's face, except for a very large beak.

PART III

RISKY OPPORTUNITY IN THE "PINERIES"

Loggers found work in the "pineries," sixty miles north of Stillwater. The pineries, as they were called, were where the great stands of white pine grew. White pines are tall and straight, exceeding one hundred feet in height and sometimes towering three hundred feet tall. The area was called Chengwatana, and the Snake River, a St. Croix tributary, was of central importance.

White pines were cut during the winter when the ground was frozen so the logs could be dragged or sledded to the Snake River. Logging in the spring or summer was simply impossible, as the logs, mules and sleds sunk into the muddy ground. The pinesap was in the roots of the tree, making it far better for lumber to be cut in the winter. When the Snake River thawed in the spring, the immense logs were floated downstream to the St. Croix. On the journey down the St. Croix, the logs had to tumble over the falls. Many

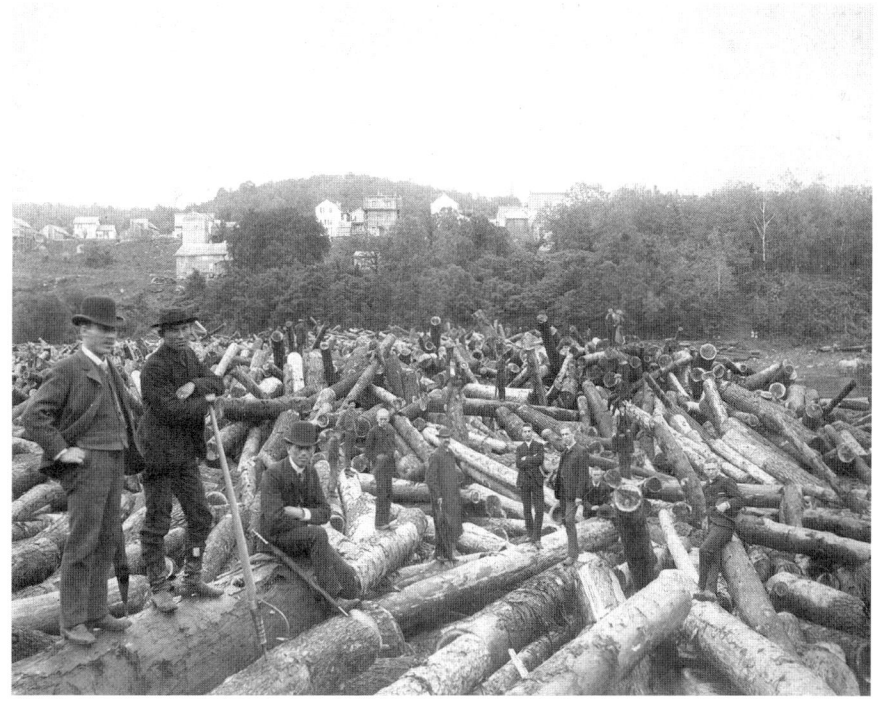

Log jams occurred at the Falls of St. Croix during periods of drought, when the water was at its lowest. Horses on the right can be seen wading in ankle-deep water. *Photo courtesy Washington County Historical Society.*

times, the logs jammed at the foot of the St. Croix's falls, requiring much effort and expensive dynamite to dislodge them.

At Marine Mills, the logs that had been stamped (or branded) for sawing had to be separated out from the others that were destined for other sawmills at Stillwater. Again at Stillwater, the logs had to be identified, separated out on the water and distributed to their various destinations. The separation process was done on the water at a place called the Boom Site just above Stillwater.

Most of the logs were joined together in great rafts that could be measured by the acre in size. These log rafts were destined for great cities down the Mississippi, primarily St. Louis, Missouri. Other logs went through Stillwater's sawmills, being cut into dimensional lumber for constructing buildings. This dimensional lumber went back into the river bound into large lumber rafts destined for new cities being built out on the frontier, primarily St. Paul.

During the early days of rafting logs downstream, a crew had to set up tent camps to live in while on the raft. Rafts also utilized sails and poles to direct them on somewhat treacherous journeys hundreds of miles to their destinations in all sorts of weather. Much money could be made on a successful rafting venture, or everything could be lost if something went wrong with the raft along the hazardous journey.

Big Joe Perraux, or "Perro," as he was popularly known, was a mixed-blood Frenchman from Illinois who earned fame as a St. Croix River pilot of steamboats and rafts. One of Big Joe's deliveries terminated at St. Louis, where he spent some leisure time on the streets of the city. There, Big Joe witnessed a peanut vendor cheat a young black boy of ten cents in change. The crying boy begged for his dime, but to no avail. Big Joe approached the crooked vendor and demanded that the correct change be given to the boy. When the man refused, Big Joe delivered a blast from his clenched fist, knocking over the vendor and the whole peanut stand.

Census takers made their rounds in 1848 for a prospective territory that, in time, would be named Minnesota. Then, in 1849, the first Minnesota territorial census was taken. In 1850, the U.S. census takers passed through again. One of the Stillwater area's early census takers was Dr. Francis Noyes, who had a bad habit of misidentifying mixed-race people. Little did the mixed-blood Indian people (as recorded by Dr. Noyes) know that they had been labeled as mixed-race black with the notation "mulatto." Joe Perro and many other mixed-blood natives like him were misidentified. Big Joe's father was French, and his mother was Native American.

Part III

Big Joe Perro was a successful steamboat river pilot, but the career was not without risk. A great storm gained ferocity over Lake Pepin on the Mississippi on May 21, 1859. Captain Perro's luck ran short that day when enormous waves created by the storm broke up the log raft he was delivering to St. Louis. Several acres of white pine logs, valued at nine dollars per log, were scattered over twenty square miles of water and were virtually impossible to recover.

Risky Opportunity on the Frontier

Farming the virgin prairie of the frontier seemed like a much easier way to prosper in agriculture, and truthfully it was. Gone were the exhausting days of stump pulling to create more acreage; simply put the advanced sod-breaking Deering plow to the land in the spring and seed your crop. Construct your log home from oak trees taken from a savannah grove while your plantings grow and then harvest your crops in the autumn. There never was such an opportunity for success as this.

William H. Guernsey was an early farming pioneer to the lower St. Croix Valley, settling near farmer Haskell and oxen driver Mackey. Guernsey first spent the season of 1847–48 harvesting logs in the pineries, earning quite a bit of money at hard labor. William returned to his Illinois home, collected his family and returned to the frontier, staking a claim in Township 28 at Catfish. Once there, William successfully tilled and expanded his farm. Like William Guernsey, many of the early pioneers made good sums of money laboring in the logging industry and then settling on the frontier. Logging the pineries was such hard, demanding work that few men served there for more than one season.

Englishman David Berry was a pioneer who came to America three times before settling on the frontier. Berry was five years old when his mother brought him to America for a visit. In 1837, he returned to America to enlist in the U.S. Army at the age of twenty-three. He served in Florida during the Second Seminole War, being promoted to sergeant. After five years of Indian war service, Berry returned to England, where he married Elizabeth Holt and continued in the family's merchant and grain business.

David Berry brought the family to the frontier of the lower St. Croix Valley, settling at Catfish, now named Milton Mills for the first commercial flour mill in Minnesota Territory, built by Lemuel Bolles. Berry invested in a large amount of land, approximately 640 acres. Sadly, two of David and Elizabeth's young sons died shortly after their arrival to the frontier, in 1854.

The hot summer day of August 23 was the last one on earth for one-year-old Charlie Berry. A week and a half later, Henry, age seven, passed away, too. Cholera was earning a reputation as a summer killer of the young. The boys were buried together on the blufftop in the established burial ground that was begun over a dozen years earlier. David Berry would initiate improvements to the burial ground, resulting in a dedicated cemetery on the hill named Mount Hope in 1855. Soon, William Guernsey's children began to occupy the improved cemetery next to the Berry's plot.

David and Elizabeth continued with farming and raising their family. He sold off small sections from his original farm, always turning a profit when he did. He also lent money to other frontier folks hopeful of finding success on the prairie. There were no banks or mortgages in that time, and borrowers searched for affluent pioneers for their financing; 2½ percent interest was a common rate charged to carry a loan. Berry assisted many pioneers in making their financial starts on the frontier.

David Berry spent the rest of his life on the farm. One notable incident was recorded when a bear came to eat from his garden outside the back door of his home. This bear was stealing precious food, so David rushed out his back door, angrily chasing the hungry bear far from his garden.

Taken from the High Chair: Struggles on the Frontier

The earliest pioneers had many visits from native men and women who were curious about log house living and the mysterious implements with which these settlers came. When local natives arrived to a frontier home, they would open the front door, enter unannounced and begin their exploration of the household, which was filled with objects quite foreign to them. These inspections shook the nerves of many pioneers, but those who understood the native method fared well.

To the native forager, of special interest was the kitchen, where a bounty a food and supplies would be found. Finding bread by the loaf was like manna from heaven. Flour by the sack was of particular interest, and good use could be made of it. The taste of sugar is especially instinctive among all people, and this the natives collected as if foraging for berries in a glen.

Part III

Butter presented a mystery with its unusual dairy taste in a strange mellow paste. Butter was collected by the box but later rejected as the native foragers discovered the severe indigestion it produced when eating it straight.

An incident occurred in 1838 at the Ojibwe treaty ratification after the steamboat *Palmyra* arrived on the St. Croix with food supplies that had been terms of the agreement. Two barrels of pork worth $200 and a barrel of butter valued at $150 had disappeared from the food stores without payment. At the same time, many of the Ojibwe were discovered to be ill, nearly unconscious, writhing in pain from indigestion. The sick natives were accused of stealing the food when two empty barrels of pork and a barrel two-thirds full of butter were found floating down the St. Croix. When ordered to pay for the eaten food, the Ojibwe said they would pay for the pork but would not be paying for the butter.

Native foraging, whether on the prairie, in the forest or in a pioneer kitchen, was all the same—food was there for the taking and sharing. One difference was, in the case of a gracious pioneer host, a hunted deer might be found a week or so later at his front door, having been placed there by a grateful forager. These "trades"—food for venison—were fairly common.

Unusual happenings were not foreign on the frontier, though. One episode took place on the prairie not far from Haskell and Norris, at the claim of Mr. Gorham Davies. Something happened when Mrs. Davies left her infant daughter in the kitchen to attend to chores at the rear of the home. The mother went to the well for some water, thinking the child would be safe in the highchair for a few moments unattended. After filling a bucket of water, she turned toward the house and saw a buckskin-clad man running away from her home toward the St. Croix River. "There goes an Ojibwe," were her thoughts, "but what was he carrying in his arms as he fled?"

Instantly, a bolt of fear sped through her veins as she dashed from the well into the kitchen, where she found her daughter's highchair empty. In a panic, the woman searched the small house and then the front yard, but her daughter was not to be found. The Ojibwe who had taken the girl was out of sight.

The Ojibwe man who took the girl might have suffered a personal loss, the loss of a child. He likely was planning to raise the captive girl as one of his own family. The young pioneer girl might not have recalled her culture, never knowing from where she had come. She could have had a long life and a large family, but no one knows that for certain. Small consolation to the stricken family was the understanding that native culture functioned in this way. Pioneers who took time to understand the native culture fared much better than those who feared the native population. The Davieses moved away from the native trail and started over.

Struggle for Life on the Frontier: Sophia and James Norris Begin a Family

James Norris and his new wife, Sophia Haskell (sister of Joseph Haskell), did not have children on their large farm at Prospect Grove. Desiring to raise a family, they were able to adopt an orphaned Dakota girl. The girl was quite young and enjoyed being with her new family; she also enjoyed time spent outside of the house. Of concern were the upset Ojibwe, who discovered the arrangement that the Norrises had made with the Dakota. The young girl was told to stay in the house, keeping the doors and windows locked. The Ojibwe secretly stalked the Norris home until the little one inadvertently made it outdoors. Then her blood enemy swept in for the kill, taking the young Dakota girl's life. After the sad and tragic episode, the Norrises took in male borders to work the farm.

Drowned on the Fourth of July: Martin Atkinson

President-elect Martin Van Buren had just won the November election and was to be sworn in on inauguration day. Martin Van Buren Atkinson was born in Maine on December 18, 1836. Martin's parents, John and Hannah, must have had patriotic pride, proudly christening their son with the new president-elect's name.

Martin's parents brought their two sons to Cottage Grove on the new frontier, where he celebrated his tenth birthday. Claiming land on the frontier, where there was every hope of success and a full life, was the true meaning of liberty and freedom to John Atkinson.

In 1854, Martin Atkinson, now a sixteen-year-old, was celebrating the nation's independence from King George of England on the Fourth of July. The warm day was celebrated by bathing in the Mississippi River.

Part III

People of the era were not swimming or trained to swim but enjoyed the simple pleasure of bathing. Something went very badly for Martin that day. Slipping off a ledge into a deeper portion of the water is how people were commonly lost. Tragically, Martin Van Buren Atkinson, namesake of an admired American Patriot, drowned on the Fourth of July.

Diphtheria Attack: The Stouffer Children

John and Hannah Stouffer were born and married in Pennsylvania, moving a short distance to northern Virginia to begin a new farm and continue to raise a family there. New opportunity in the Minnesota Territory enticed the Stouffers to travel over one thousand miles to settle in the lower St. Croix Valley. The Stouffers selected land near Joseph Haskell, beginning fresh on the prairie. John and Hannah brought their small children, Sarah, George and John, on the long trip; Amanda was born in 1852, quite soon after their arrival to the frontier.

The Stouffers, both in their mid-thirties, worked hard on their primitive farm, raising little children. Daughter Susan was born there in 1854. Tragically, illness and death entered the Stouffer farmhouse late in the spring of 1855. Diphtheria infections—what they termed "putrid sore throat"—were suffered by the children. The Stouffer children endured severe throat infections combined with high fevers, but Georgie, almost eight years old, died. Georgie was buried the next day, Sunday, June 17, in the back row of the old burial ground located high on the bluff with a tremendous view of the St. Croix River and valleys that surrounded it.

The Stouffers were not wealthy by any means; placing Georgie in the back row of the burial ground meant that they didn't have the money to purchase a typical plot. The burial ground was in the process of being organized into a designated cemetery. A primitive headstone and footstone were placed over Georgie, but these stones were just that—raw rocks of broken fieldstone that were found fifty feet away near the west edge of the limestone bluff. It was a sad burial.

One week after Georgie died, little Amanda, just three years old, lost her battle with the putrid sore throat. The fever caused by the infected throat was just too high for the little one to endure. She was buried next to Georgie the day after she died, also on a Sunday. Reverend Simon Putnam spoke at Amanda's interment at the burial ground. Putnam was the new preacher in the village developing at the foot of the bluff. Although Reverend Putnam was not a well man, he spoke in place of the Episcopal minister, who did not show up.

The suffering was not over for John and Hannah; six days after Amanda's passing, five-year-old Johnny died. It was a heartbreaking Saturday burial next to Georgie and Amanda. Another trip had been made up the steep, primitive hearse road, the third one in merely two weeks' time. More fieldstone rocks were found at the edge of the bluff to place as headstones and footstones on the little graves. There was much grief to be found on the hill that was to be named Mount Hope.

The pioneer burial ground received its official dedication and naming of Mount Hope. The Stouffer family still had Sarah and Susan, who survived the plague. Andrew was later born, named after John Stouffer's brother Andrew, who came from Pennsylvania to live on the farm. Life continued even if it seemed that all was lost. Reverend Simon Putnam was a passionate man who could be heard to repeat something Jesus said: "Suffer the little children, to come unto me."

Deer Harvested by the Thousands: Grand Hunt on the "Sunrise Prairie"

Early pioneers on the upper St. Croix River witnessed the spectacle of a Dakota hunt. Deer herds by the thousands were seen regularly on the frontier prairies. The Sunrise River is a tributary of the St. Croix that sources out on the western prairie. It was on this prairie that Dakota hunters harvested 1,200 deer per week during their summer hunt of a few weeks in 1855. The deer were taken as rapidly as possible, as it was unknown to the hunters when another opportunity like this would take place. The hunt was made on their old hunting grounds, which were now claimed by the Ojibwe.

Unfortunately, a percentage of the venison—at least two hundred deer each week—was wasted, going to rot in the sun. The depopulation of the deer herds left little to none for the Ojibwe or the pioneers to hunt.

Part III

Afton Water: Electa Getchell

The year 1855 was a great arrival time for the settlement of Catfish, now named Milton Mills. To one New England lady who stepped off of the steamboat, Milton Mills seemed an ugly name for such a pretty place. Electa Getchell saw the immense beauty of the blue St. Croix bordered by limestone bluffs, with the breeze flowing across prairie grasses and over rolling hills that were divided by trickling streams.

Electa Getchell instantly thought of the popular poem "Afton Water," written many decades before by Scotsman Robert Burns:

Flow gently, sweet Afton, among thy green braes,
Flow gently, I'll sing thee a song in thy praise,
My Mary's asleep by thy murmuring stream,
Flow gently, sweet Afton disturb not her dream.

Afton should be the name of this beautiful place, she thought. Electa Getchell had her way, as her husband, Charles Getchell, was one of the organizers of the new village. Charles Getchell came from Maine to the settlement with his brothers, James and William. William Getchell chose to farm the prairie, James Getchell would build a sawmill on the river and Charles Getchell set up a store to sell goods and lumber.

Other 1855 arrivals to the small settlement were the Thomas family from Indiana. Together, the Thomas boys, Minor T., William and Meredith, and their father Hewitt helped Charles Getchell, along with Joseph Haskell and Ralzaman Haskell, purchase the original land claim of oxen driver Andrew Mackey. It was on this claim that the group of civic-minded men would survey and plat a real community, naming it Afton.

Charles and Electa were raising their young son in the small community of Afton. Electa was expecting the birth of another child. Happily, daughter Ada was born in mid-January 1857. Electa had survived the frontier delivery of baby Ada, but tragedy soon set in. Infection spread and Electa developed septicemia, for which there was little to do but wait for death. Electa weakened, clinging to life for two months, and then passed away. Charles buried his charming wife in the dedicated cemetery, Mount Hope. Electa was twenty-seven.

Widower Charles Getchell had six-year-old Gustavus and infant Ada to raise. He took in a housekeeper, Ellen Eagan, to do the housework while he ran the store. Ellen also was aiding Charles's aged mother,

Emma, and hosting boarders, McClusky, Norcross and Hartland. The men were employed as sawmill and store labor. The sixteen-year-old Irish Ellen (considered an emancipated adult) was a busy young housekeeper. Although Charles Getchell stayed busy with the store and family, he never forgot Electa.

Fear the "Zephyrs" of Spring: The Radinzel Family's Funeral

Pioneers feared each spring thaw, especially when west winds blew. The fall harvest would run low, and mold had to be scraped from the pork and potatoes that came from the cellar. Malnourishment and damp winds likely brought death to the youngest and oldest of the families. That someone would die was their springtime fear.

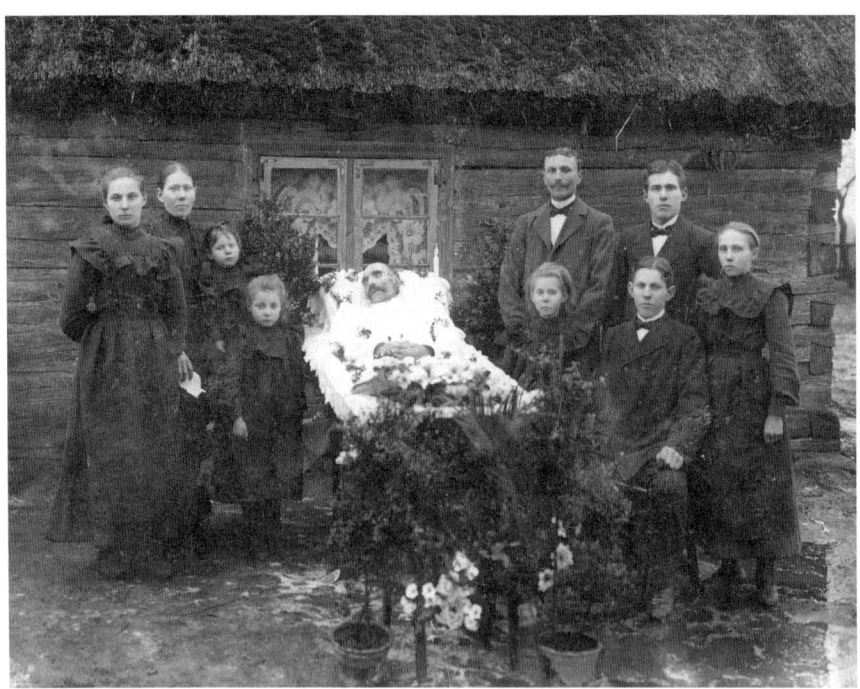

The Radinzel family stands amid water, mud and ice for the funeral of Julius Radinzel, who had brought them from Germany to Lakeland, Minnesota. *Photo courtesy Washington County Historical Society.*

Part III

Under the Ice: Thomas and Anne McDonald

Thomas and Anne McDonald were merely Irish teenagers in the mid-1830s when they settled in Missouri, raising their young children, Hellen, Tom and John. A decade later, a large community of impoverished Irish formed just outside St. Louis, Missouri, as people fled Ireland due to the potato famine that was devastating the isle. These poor, uneducated Irish were not accepted well in America, and little chance for opportunity was offered them. Thomas and Ann McDonald left this dark chapter of Missouri for a brighter future on the frontier at Mouth of the St. Croix.

Son Hugh was born at Mouth of the St. Croix late in 1847; siblings Mary, Edith and Edward would follow during early territorial times in Minnesota. Unfortunately, Edith did not survive her birth in 1853, but her twin, Edward, did. The Thomas McDonald family was not wealthy. Thomas sold two cows and three hogs to raise sixty dollars for the construction of their small house.

When Edith died, they carried her ten miles north to the early pioneer burial ground near Milton Mills. Burial grounds on the prairie were not suitable for Edith McDonald because the family feared a wagon might come along and roll over her beloved grave. Burial on a hill ensured the safety of the loved one, as wagons would not risk a hill climb or a crash down the other side. Wagons drove around hills.

Edith was buried in the rear row among other frontier children, near the western edge of the blufftop. Edith's tiny body was placed in the ground facing east, just like virtually all of the Christian pioneer burials. The Christian families were certain that Christ would make his second coming to earth bright and shining like the rising sun. Facing the burial in any other direction meant they might miss the glorious view when their earthly bodies were resurrected. A pointed fieldstone rock was placed at the head of Edith's small grave and crudely inscribed, "Edith O. McDonald, 1853."

Five years passed, and the frontier became more populated and active. The McDonald farm and children were doing well. Hellen was of marriageable age and moved away to begin her new life. A busy sawmill had been constructed at Point Douglas, and across the Mississippi from the McDonalds' claim was the rapidly growing river town of Hastings. Hastings was lively with heavy river traffic, many goods and services being offered there. A ferry across from Point Douglas to Hastings was operated regularly, even through the winter months when the river froze over. The current was such that half of the river remained open water unless temperatures held below zero.

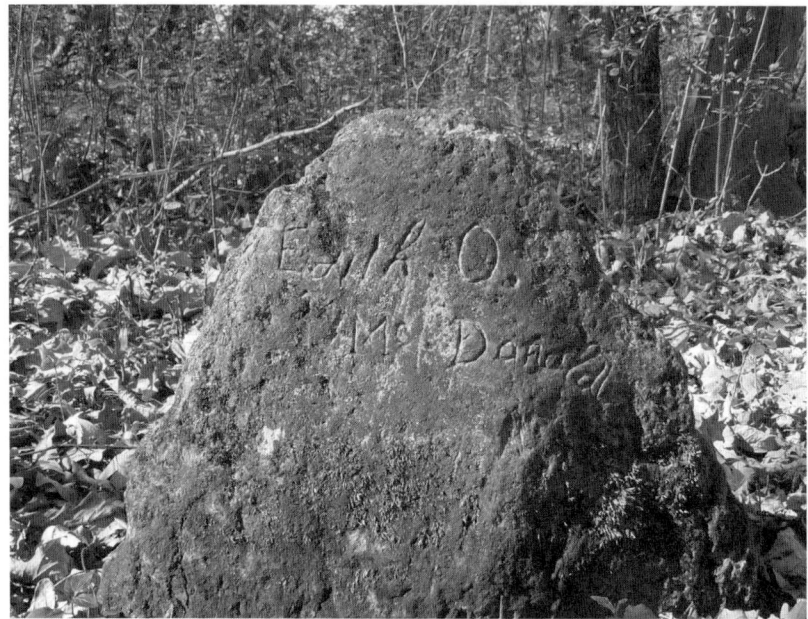

A crudely inscribed primitive burial stone was placed by Edith McDonald's poor Irish family in the pioneer burial ground above Catfish on the St. Croix. Many other infants and children, known and unknown, are buried near Edith.

Thomas and Ann McDonald had business in Hastings, using the ferry as they needed. Even during the winter, there was a need to be in Hastings, and this was the case on January 28, 1858. The ferry, as such, did not run during times of ice, but a skiff or rowboat could be boarded for a fee. If the Mississippi was solid with ice, the skiff would have been sledded across by rope. The McDonalds went to Hastings on the skiff during the morning of the twenty-eighth, conducted their business and returned in the evening. It was a typical midwinter day with both ice and open water.

The skiff was run by rope utilizing three operators, one on each side of the river and one on the skiff whose name was Welch. There were four occupants in the skiff on this trip across, including a tailor from Hastings making the crossing to the Point Douglas side of the river.

Tragically, something went wrong with the skiff as it approached the ledge of ice where the passengers were to disembark. The front of the skiff dipped low into the water and then was pulled farther down by the current. The fragile craft rapidly took on water and then sank, dumping Thomas and Ann McDonald, the tailor and Mr. Welch into the icy cold current of murky river water.

Part III

There was little hope for the heavily clothed passengers, who disappeared, swept under the ledge of ice. The skiff's ferry operator, Mr. Welch, was clinging on the ice ledge but was unable to raise himself. Even with the ferry rope present, Welch was wearing clothes too heavy to remain there for long. The rope man on the riverbank immediately scrambled to rescue Mr. Welch, but the ice ledge caved in, and Welch disappeared into the chilly waters. Now the rope man struggled for his own life in the Mississippi and somehow made it back onto the icy ledge.

The tragedy was labeled "Sad Accident" for the four who went under the ice. A search was carried out below Hastings, but the McDonalds could not be found, nor could the tailor or Mr. Welch. There were five orphaned children at the McDonald home when the terrible news came. There was no hope for the return of their mother and father. An Irish family north of Point Douglas in Denmark Township took in the orphans Thomas, John, Hugh, Mary and Edward. John Sinclair had five children, too, and the McDonalds made it ten. The Sinclairs took care of their own, true to the way of the Irish.

Bodies Found Drifting in the Mississippi

Recovering people lost in the rivers was a prime concern, whatever the reason might be. Not long after the McDonalds' "Sad Accident," a body was located floating in the Mississippi River, but it was found several miles above Hastings. This body could not have traveled upstream, ruling out the possibility that it was one of the McDonalds.

The unknown body was described to be that of a man twenty years of age wearing frontier buckskin trousers and a buckskin coat. He also had twenty dollars in his possession, triggering the assumption that he might have fallen into the river up at St. Paul, likely the result of a drunken stupor. News was put out that if anyone could describe the man, they could have the body and the twenty dollars. If no one claimed the body within a week, it would be buried.

Another body was located above Hastings, described from his features as an Irishman. The dead man's only possessions were his smoking pipe and comb.

A woman's body was also found adrift in the same area about that same time. She had no possessions, and there was no way to identify the woman. Of note was her throat, which was slit from ear to ear.

Coroner's Report!: Body Identified

An identifiable body recovered from the Mississippi River was that of Mr. Welch, the ferry operator who had been aboard the "Sad Accident" skiff. The McDonalds and the Prescott tailor had yet to be found.

Drowned at the River's Ford!

Springtime on the rivers meant that ice dissipated, allowing for normal ferry traffic to resume. In 1858, the river's level dropped instead of experiencing its typical rise with snow melt and rain. This opportunity was taken advantage of by the stage route drivers, who disliked paying the ferry toll for each person on the stage, as well as for their four horses and the coach's two axels. If the river was low, then the stagecoach would attempt to ford the river by driving straight through it at a shallow location. On a mid-March day, there were four passengers on the stage when the coach drivers informed them that they would ford the Mississippi from Point Douglas, just below Hastings.

A talkative Frenchman was one of the passengers on the coach that springtime day, intent on "seeing the West before it was gone," as he put it. The Frenchman also made it known that he was carrying $200 (secreted in his money belt), being well prepared for an extensive journey. Unfortunately, the Frenchman became upset when the passengers were told about fording the Mississippi, exclaiming that they "would surely die inside the rolling coffin!"

The fearful foreigner desired to get out and cross by foot; he convinced another male passenger that it was safer to do this, too. The two men would follow the coach across the river, avoiding any holes that the stage dropped into. The coach made it safely across in short order, but the two men slipped off the ford into deep water, and neither was able to swim. The struggle was awful, with each attempting to cling to the other in hopes of getting out. Somehow the second man was able to climb up and get clear of the deep, but the nameless Frenchman was nowhere to be seen.

Part III

Body Discovered!

A search was conducted for the Frenchman but with an unexpected result—a body wearing women's clothing was discovered. She had been in the water far too long for any sort of reliable identification but was assumed to be Ann McDonald, lost seven weeks prior.

These recoveries were quite unpleasant, and the remains were disposed of as rapidly as possible. Many times, the bodies were buried right on the riverbank where they were found, unless there was an actual cemetery nearby. The Point Douglas Cemetery was a mile north of Ann's discovery location. She was rapidly taken there and interred.

Ann McDonald's Grave

The five orphaned McDonald children now had a special place to grieve the loss of their mother, but they discovered the lack of a gravestone at the grave. Not just any grave marker would satisfy them; it had to be a rock from the river where their mother was found. The kids found a pointed fieldstone on the river's shore that had been well worn by water. Similarly, the pointed

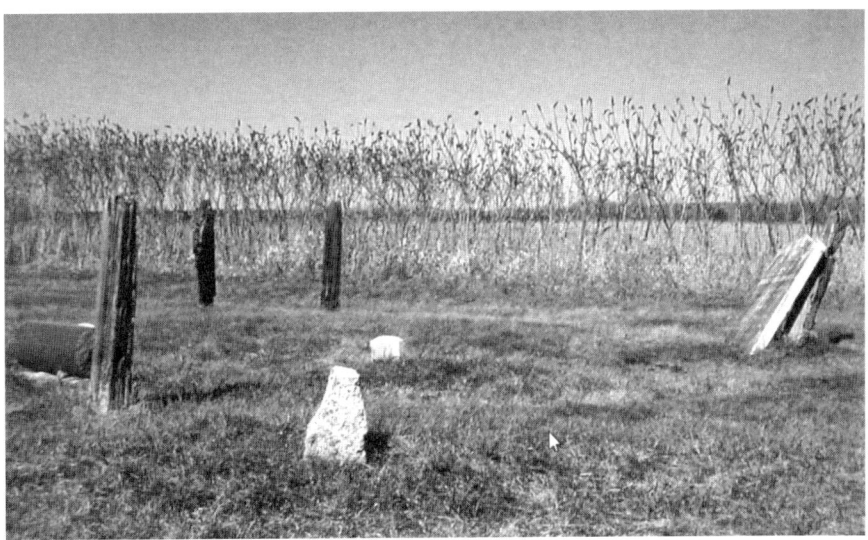

Ann McDonald's gravestone in the foreground. The Point Douglas (pioneer) Cemetery was the closest burial ground to where Ann's body was recovered.

river rock resembled the one they had placed over their sister Edith five years earlier. Their mother's river rock was a bit smaller than Edith's, as they were able to rub only an *A* and *M* faintly into its surface.

The McDonald children never saw their father, Thomas, again. During the hot summer months, the large body of an unidentifiable man was discovered in a Mississippi slough two miles below Hastings. The body had been in the water quite a long time. It might have been that of Mr. McDonald or the tailor, but there was no way to tell. The orphaned McDonald children were raised well by the Sinclairs in Denmark Township. John served in the Minnesota cavalry during the Civil War, and Thomas served in the Second Minnesota Infantry. Edward, Edith's twin, became a teacher at the Langdon School.

Gone Missing: The Prescott Ferry Operator

The spring of 1858 brought news of a missing man, Prescott's ferry operator. Philander Prescott had been trading with the native people at his landing but had moved farther west with his mixed-blood family to continue trade at the new Dakota reservation. The Prescott ferry crossed the mouth of the St. Croix River from Prescott to Point Douglas. The man's wife was upset when he did not return to their cabin located across the Mississippi River.

As each day passed, the ferry operator's wife became more distraught, to the point of being grief-stricken. Prescott citizens spread the word, begging the man to return to his wife or send word of his whereabouts. Eventually, a search was conducted without success. It was assumed by some who knew the man that he had stowed a secret bottle of spirits on the ferry. Most likely, the ferry operator had consumed too much alcohol, causing him to quietly slip into the water at mouth of the St. Croix.

Body Found Floating: Value $200

A steamboat traveling upstream from Red Wing to Hastings discovered a body floating in the Mississippi a few miles below Prescott. The boat's captain piloted the craft toward the body, allowing it to be retrieved from the water. A search of the body was performed for any papers or identification,

Part III

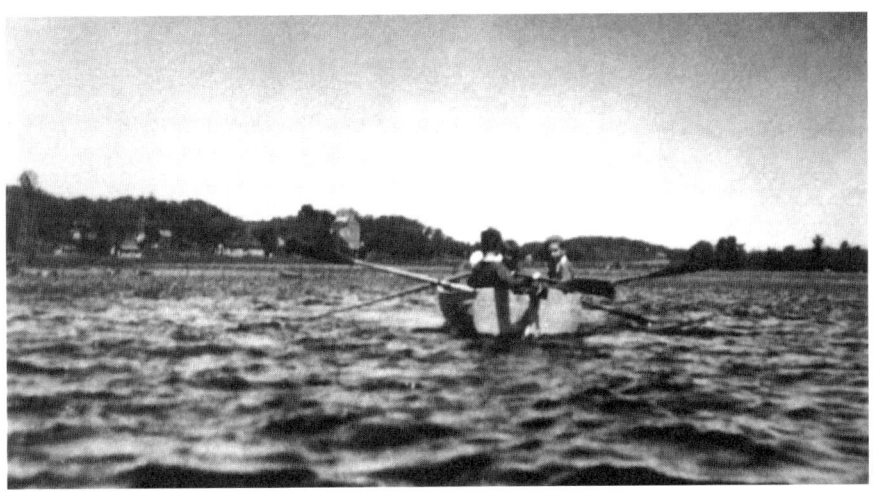

Three boys in a skiff, a common sight on the St. Croix at Afton, Minnesota. *Photo courtesy Afton Historical Museum.*

but none was found. Something of interest was revealed, though: a money belt under the man's clothing containing $200. Without any identification of the man, a speedy burial was the only option left to the captain. The steamboat headed to the east bank of the Mississippi shore, where a grave was quickly dug for the mystery man found floating in the river.

Disappeared: Four Men in a Skiff

Springtime weather also arrives with its unexpected storms. Four men were seen in a skiff, rowing across Lake St. Croix a short distance above the mouth of the river. Rapidly, the weather changed, becoming a squall with blinding rain and a stiff wind. When the short-lived storm cleared, there was an empty skiff on the water. The four men were never seen again.

A Failure to Arrive: Brewer Augustus Benz

In late May of the next year, a German by the name of Benz boarded his skiff north of Stillwater, making a business trip rowing downstream to

Hudson. Mr. Benz was a brewer, and it's likely he had some of his wares with him in the light craft. He never did arrive to his destination, but his skiff was found floating, empty, at about the midpoint of his journey. There had been unpredictable and severe weather recently, but no waves of any particular scale were noted on the day of his disappearance.

Two weeks later, a body was discovered north of Hudson on the Wisconsin bank of the St. Croix; it was that of thirty-one-year-old Augustus Benz. He left a distraught widow, Elizabeth.

Travel on the Turbulent Waters: Harry Wheeler

Harry Wheeler made many trips by rowboat on the St. Croix from his Stillwater home upriver to Osceola, Wisconsin. Harry was criticized for continuing these trips on the turbulent St. Croix now that he was married and had a baby. He was certain to meet his doom and widow his wife.

On a particular return trip from Osceola, Harry Wheeler's intent was to reach Arcola, the midway point to Stillwater, but a storm arose accompanied by furious winds. Harry's frail boat was "tempest tossed" as he struggled to row toward shore, but he broke an oar. Frantic for survival, with only one oar, Harry had visions of a watery grave and food for fishes dancing before his eyes.

Good fortune smiled on Harry Wheeler that day when the storm passed and the sky cleared. He was able to make it to Arcola alive, staying with J.E. Mower for the night. The storm was reported to have been brief, but the intensity of it dropped over an inch and a half of rain. Grass that was thought to have been killed by drought was quickly revived, much to the delight of the cattle and other animals.

Death Rock: Deadly St. Croix Falls

Three men at Taylors Falls boarded a skiff in an effort to cross the river to St. Croix Falls, Wisconsin. This was a direct route between the towns but not an intelligent one, as these were the violent waters of the Falls of St. Croix. Witnesses from the towns on the cliff saw the men in the skiff and thought

Part III

them to be stupefied with whiskey to tempt fate in such a way. The three made it to the center of the churning river but were carried downstream at a rapid pace straight toward a singular large, upright boulder in the water. The skiff was crushed against the "death rock," and the three men were never seen again.

Traveling on Highways of Water: Steamboat Adventures

Steamboats were the chief mode of transportation during frontier times. The first steamboat on the St Croix River, the *Palmyra*, landed at Marine Mills in 1838. Since that time, steamboat activity increased with each year, generating competition between riverboat companies and rivalries between steamboat captains. Frontier-minded people arrived by steamboat seeking fresh opportunities farming on the prairie, logging in the "pineries" or working in the sawmills.

The use of steamboats increased the efficiency of river rafting. Rafts could be pushed or pulled by steamboat, depending on their construction.

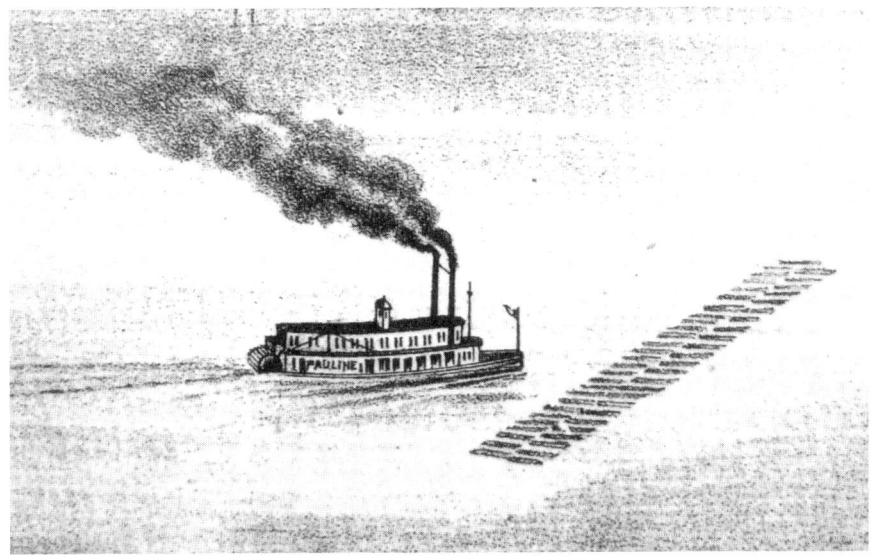

The *Pauline* nudges a segment of rafted logs near Stillwater. Steamboats acted as working craft to assemble segments into immense log rafts for delivery far to the south.

The Perilous St. Croix River Valley Frontier

Steamboats had their risks, too, many times being overloaded or exceeding their mechanical limits by steaming into headwinds. Exerting too much pressure on the boats' boilers caused them to explode, and many did. Fires were started aboard ship from sparks that spewed from smokestacks, ships ran aground on sand bars or hulls were punctured by tree snags, ending many excursions. The average life expectancy of a steamboat was merely five years.

Stillwater was the growing community that attracted the majority of steamboat traffic. Water levels on the St. Croix fluctuated with the seasons or were affected by times of drought or heavy rains. Flooding of downtown Stillwater was common, and Main Street went under water often. One event of note was when a steamboat arrived by sailing onto Main Street, lowering its gangplank down on the boardwalk in front of the Minesota House.

Steamboat captains, as if they were racing the clock, were constantly trying to improve on arrival times to their destinations. Passengers spent their time in merriment, consuming the alcohol that flowed freely on the ship. A tragic incident was witnessed when two members of a tipsy crowd fell over the railing from the top deck of the ship. They plunged below the surface of the water but reappeared after several seconds. A small number of people saw that the men were too drunk to swim or didn't know how; they watched as the two men went under again. From the top deck, one witness threw a wooden deck chair in the water for the men to clasp on to. There was nothing more to do but view the horror of the incident as the steamboat put distance between it and the drowning men. The merriment soon regained its momentum aboard the ship.

Attacking the *Banjo*: Or, We Haven't Any Shingles!

A steamboat named the *Banjo* made several appearances in Stillwater with its theatrics and circus aboard. Entertainment such as this was such a rarity that the *Banjo*'s popularity became notable. The program for this night included a burlesque drama troupe, a minstrel show, trained dogs, bearded Pigmy women and the Great Monkey Circus. The captain collected admission to the onboard theater, and many men from the sawmills were in attendance. A few of the young fellows had not been paid for their work at the mill but were fortunate enough to receive wood

Part III

shingles in lieu of payment. The captain of the vessel was willing to accept these shingles as admission to the entertainment.

There were still many men who had neither money nor shingles and were unable to attend the event. This unfortunate group of penniless men was frustrated and angry for missing out on the program. They plotted their revenge against the *Banjo* in the darkness of night. After the show was over and the lucky show-goers had left for home, the malcontents formed a mob and assaulted the ship with heavy stones found along the shore. The stone barrage was very effective in shaking the timbers and beams of the ship—so much so that the ship's crew went for their guns.

The armed crew fired buckshot into the dark from which the large stones had been violently hurled. The mob on shore beat a hasty retreat, seeking shelter in the tree line beyond the shore. The crewmen rapidly cut the mooring lines, and the steamboat reversed into the murkiness of the river. The showboat *Banjo* steamed away like a ghost in the blackness, never returning to Stillwater again. Nobody knew how much damage was done to the *Banjo*, but the riffraff were heard to say, "No one was hurt on our side."

PART IV

A Ship's Carpenter's Luck Runs Out: Thomas Ramsden

As a young lad of eight, Thomas Ramsden left his English home and went to sea as a cabin boy learning the trade of a ship's carpenter. Wooden sailing vessels were in constant need of maintenance, repair and, in many instances, replacement of parts. A ship's carpenter had to be skilled in making detailed wooden members from raw stock with nothing more than hand tools, saws, planes, hammers and chisels. After sailing several times around the world and completing his term of duties, Thomas Ramsden married his sweetheart, Charity Jose. The couple left England with their young son, Tom Jr., to pioneer the new frontier of the St. Croix Valley, just a few miles west of Stillwater.

The couple had not been on the prairie for long when tragedy struck home. Thomas Ramsden's wife passed away during childbirth. Thomas buried his dear wife on a lonely hill near their farm and returned to England with Tom. While in England, Thomas found another bride, Jane, who was willing to settle on his claim out on the frontier.

Traversing the world was no simple matter in the mid-1800s, but Ramsden, whose career had been on the open seas, was quite accustomed to it. In that time period, entering America at the port of New Orleans was the chief entry point to the St. Croix Valley via the Mississippi River, a route that

Ramsden followed several times. Thomas Ramsden was a common traveler passing through New Orleans as he made trips to England and back.

Ramsden witnessed a tragic scene on one of the trips that took him through the St. Lawrence Seaway to the Great Lakes. A seagoing vessel was sinking within sight of Ramsden's ship, and he just watched helplessly as passengers drowned one by one. The horrible episode affected the seasoned seafarer like nothing he had ever experienced before.

Once again, Thomas planned to raise crops on the farm with his new wife when there was news of disaster in New Orleans. A plague of yellow fever swept over the coastal city in 1852; thousands of people became ill and far too many of them died. The dead from the plague were literally piling up, generating a dire need for caskets.

Thomas Ramsden was familiar with the river route to New Orleans and packed his carpentry tools for another steamboat journey to the city. The city of New Orleans was a wealthy one, and it paid Ramsden extremely well—all in gold—for his time building casket upon casket.

The New Orleans plague eventually ran its course, and Ramsden boarded a Mississippi riverboat for the St. Croix and home. The trip did not progress well; the northern-bound steamboat's boiler exploded, sinking the entire vessel in the Mississippi. It was fortunate that Thomas survived the catastrophe, but that was the sum total of his luck. Ramsden's possessions went to the bottom of the Mississippi—all of his carpentry tools were gone, as was his payment in gold. Having arrived penniless in Stillwater, Thomas Ramsden contracted himself as an indentured servant to lumberman John McKusick.

Not all was lost for Thomas Ramsden, though. He still had his wife, their children, their homestead and, especially, his life, making it a good one on the new frontier.

Arrival on a Plague Ship:
Ambrose Secrest's Pioneer Crisis

When Ambrose Secrest departed Indiana for the frontier, he brought his entire family, including his parents and siblings. The Secrest family traveled by steamboat, arriving at Lakeland, Minnesota Territory, on Lake St. Croix in 1852. As modern as the convenience was, the steamboat experience had its limitations. Many of the captains oversold the human capacity of the ship. Crowded conditions became unsanitary, and disease could spread

Part IV

rapidly on the craft. "Plague ships" were known to arise, and this was the tragic case with the Secrest family.

The Secrest family became ill on the ship shortly before it reached Lakeland's shore. The large family group was relieved to be off of the craft, but they had little amenities available to them at the young settlement of Lakeland. Ambrose Secrest's family began to die, one by one, starting with his wife.

Cholera is a dreaded bacterial disease that is highly contagious, spreading swiftly during the high temperatures of summer. People feared the heat of summer when the disease was most virulent; someone becoming affected in the morning could be dead by evening. The Secrest family had contracted cholera.

People afflicted with cholera suffer from extreme dehydration due to severe diarrhea and vomiting. Hope seems lost when the cholera victim is unable to drink or maintain any fluids in his or her system. The heat of summer accelerates the spread of the bacteria and inhibits one's ability to retain life-preserving water. Ambrose Secrest's mother was the next to die.

As disaster struck the family, Ambrose lost two of his brothers and a sister to the plague. He lost a daughter next and, finally, his father, too. It is difficult to comprehend such human loss and a mystery how the survivors coped with

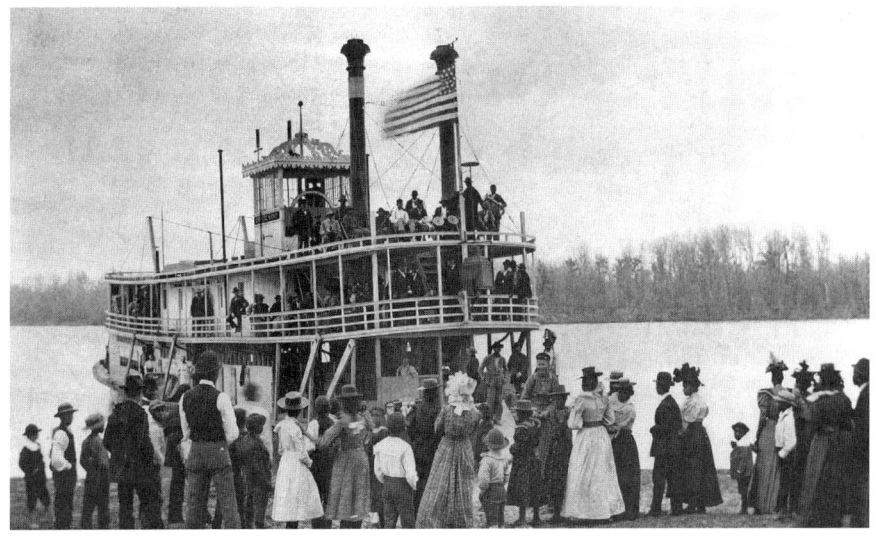

Steamboat the *Gracie Kent* was constructed in Stillwater by Muller Boat works. Captain William Kent of Osceola, Wisconsin, named this craft after his daughter Gracie. *Photo courtesy Washington County Historical Society.*

the tragedy. Ambrose could have given up on the frontier, but he did not. He proceeded with farming the prairie and milling flour, which was his trade. Ambrose had a younger sister, a brother and five motherless children to take care of. He eventually remarried, making a fine example of a successful pioneer life on the frontier.

The Wreck of the *Equator*: Captain Asa B. Green

Asa B. Green was a unique frontier man with a variety of talents. He was an auctioneer, lawyer, county sheriff, probate judge and steamboat captain. Green wished to reap some of the harvest generated by the river traffic on the St. Croix River by purchasing part interest in a luxury craft, the

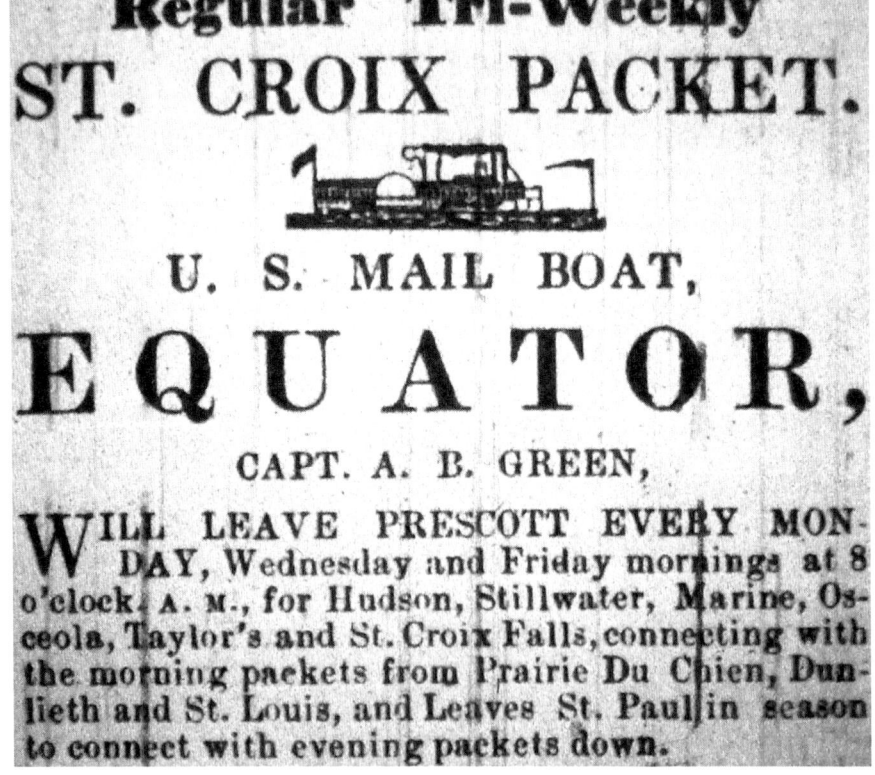

Advertising was essential to steamboat companies due to the heavy competition for goods, passengers and mail. Packet boats carried all three types of river commerce.

Part IV

steamboat *Equator*. As versatile as he was, he felt confident in piloting the *Equator* himself. Tragically, Green's steamboat career was cut short almost as soon as it began.

The steamboat *Equator* was a common sight on the St. Croix, making trips from Prescott, at the mouth of the river, to Stillwater three times a week. The first journey the *Equator* made in the spring of 1859 took place on March 29, the ice having broken up early. After a winter in storage, the *Equator* attempted to deliver Stillwater passengers to St. Croix Falls, but a deckhand fell overboard shortly after the departure. Captain Asa B. Green spent a good hour circling the large craft in an effort to locate the man. He could not be found.

Continuing the trip north, minus one deckhand, the *Equator*'s steam engine broke down at Marine Mills. About one hundred passengers were stranded out on the icy waters for an entire day. Many people on board worried about running out of food and contemplated a way off the ship. Fortunately, another steamboat, the *H.S. Allen*, arrived and collected most of the stranded travelers. Eventually, the *Equator* was restarted and limped back to the port of Stillwater.

Minnesota was a very good place to live when it wasn't cold or stormy out. Weather could become quite severe without warning, and when this happened, there was very little anyone could do about it except find a low place to huddle until it passed. Such an event occurred on May 21, 1859, as a large cloud, black as night, appeared on the western horizon of Lake St. Croix near Catfish Bar. Captain Asa B. Green had three hundred passengers aboard his packet ship on a pleasure cruise from Prescott to Taylors Falls.

A packet ship was a steamboat designed to carry supplies, materials, the mail and passengers. Green's *Equator* was a fast and elegant packet, but on this stormy day, it was heading into a forty-mile-per-hour windstorm with horizontal rains. On land, the pioneer farmers and townspeople had taken shelter in homes that were being shaken by the winds below a dark and angry sky. There was nothing the helpless people could do for the steamboat, whose whistle was heard shrieking over the storm, demanding rescue from shore.

The water on Lake St. Croix had turned into swells topped by whitecaps. The great waves washed onto the deck of the *Equator*, flooding the ship and putting out the fires in the steam boilers. Power to control the *Equator* was gone as the great craft was violently driven into the Wisconsin bank of the St. Croix, stern first. The paddle wheel was crushed, as was the aft end of the vessel. Terrified passengers, soaked by cold rain, were helped off the *Equator* by Captain Green and his crew in several feet of water.

The Perilous St. Croix River Valley Frontier

Three hundred traumatized passengers had been rescued from certain death and a watery grave while the storm raged on. A great gust of wind came, ripping off the pilothouse from atop the ship and smashing it down on the shore. Miraculously, no one drowned, and no injuries were reported.

It might have been hundreds of prayers said during the storm that were answered that day. Asa B. Green lost everything but his life that day and did not go back to the river. Instead, he enrolled in a Baptist seminary and became an ordained minister. Asa. B. Green served God as a missionary, chaplain and minister for the rest of his life.

How to Survive a Steamboat Wreck: Never Learn to Swim

Steamboats were the chief form of transportation in America for decades until railroads overwhelmed the nation. The steamboat era lasted over one hundred years, as river travel was a beautiful and romantic way of life, more so than many might imagine. But there is risk in almost anything; traveling by steamboat increased it.

Steamboats had their limitations, often experiencing fires and boiler explosions that were terminal in nature. Unforeseen storms were often the cause of damage and destruction. Invisible sandbars and tree snags ruptured hulls, as shallow waters dominated many parts of the rivers. Even bridges had become obstacles to reckless captains. And if that weren't enough, collisions with other river traffic occurred, destroying two crafts at once.

If someone were a regular traveler on America's rivers and had a mindset for personal safety, the recommendation was: never learn to swim. It had come to the attention of a few that when a steamboat disaster occurred, it was the healthy swimmers who were the first to drown. For those educated in swimming, the shore seemed an attainable goal once they found themselves in the water following the sinking of their craft. Swimmers who attempted to make it to shore became exhausted, drowning because the distance to shore was farther than imagined. As a general rule, having learned to swim became the cause of the steamboat victim's death.

If you were to travel by steamboat, never learn to swim was the wisest advice preached from many pulpits across America. If your steamboat were wrecked and you were struggling for life, it was recommended that you find some flotsam to cling to and patiently wait for rescue. As long as you could

Part IV

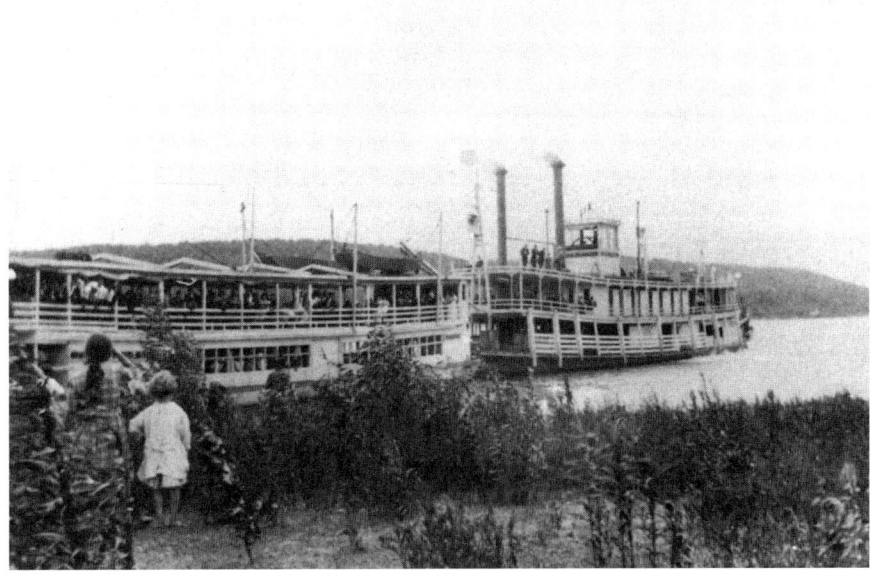

A steamboat tied to an excursion barge more than triples the capacity of the craft. The excursion ship is shown at Afton, Minnesota's landing. *Photo courtesy Afton Historical Museum.*

hang on to a piece of buoyant wreckage, you had an excellent chance of being rescued. Compassionate preachers who felt compelled to save their flocks from tragedy and despair, in this life and the next, taught this principle: "Be patient, wait on God and you shall be rescued."

"This Trail Is Mine," Road Rage Frontier Style: Chief Pinichon versus the Trader

An early trade-era tale was committed to the faint memory of a witness, who preserved the event for future reference. During the days of Fort Snelling, the post reserve and Dakota landholdings, native trails became congested with an increase in foot trade. Native people who traveled their trails to and fro, from camp to camp, now frequented the fort as well. Traders had entered the landscape, effecting change by delivering calico cloth, needles, thread, tin ware and cast iron to villages, which traded hides for the goods.

Chief Pinichon's village was across the St. Peters River, above Fort Snelling, on a well-traveled trail. Chief Pinichon had been at the fort with

The Perilous St. Croix River Valley Frontier

many of his warriors but was now traveling the trail, returning to the village. A group of traders was on the same trail, having left the village laden with heavy packs of hides destined for Fort Snelling. The lead trader could see the Dakota band of men on the trail in the distance and realized that his crew could not deviate from the path with the heavy packs.

The great chief also was aware that traders were ahead on the trail, approaching at a rapid pace. Pinichon and his warriors maintained a speedy pace, as the natives were used to covering many miles in a day. Wasting time on a native trail was to break a cardinal rule, and these men weren't breaking it. Chief Pinichon was an important man, with a band of courageous warriors following close behind. This meant that he would maintain his place on the trail. Both parties approached each other at an increased rate, and neither was about to divert for the other.

Neither the chief nor the lead trader had any thought of sharing the trail, and neither would acknowledge the other. Both men avoided direct eye contact of any sort; they each tucked their chins in attempts to force the other to sidestep the trail. Both leaders, now with heads to the ground, determined not to be the one to break pace or acknowledge the other's approach.

Both the warriors and the packmen were aware of what was about to take place but said nothing. The crucial moment was imminent—either the lead packer or the chief would step aside. But neither did. With heads down and eyes to the ground, the two stubborn men bashed heads at full force, sending both sprawling to the trail, one beside the other.

It was a skin-splitting collision, with both leaders stunned and bleeding on the ground. As if in tandem, the two dazed men struggled to their feet, sidestepped each other and continued on the trail as though nothing had happened. There was a total lack of acknowledgement of the crash and the injuries; silently, both men, covered in blood, resumed their previous pace.

This incident is not an unusual example of the mindset of the frontier people. Life was a challenge, and if one were weak-minded, he might not last long on the unsettled prairie. Wisdom is a good quality required for survival in an untamed land, but often a lack of wisdom is what it takes to make the frontier bend to one's will. Tragically, luck ran out for many small-minded people who arrived on the raw frontier.

Part IV

Road Rage, Horse and Buggy Style: Elias McKean versus Dr. Stone

Elias McKean came to the St. Croix Valley in 1841, immediately becoming involved in logging, sawmill operations, claiming land and plowing fields and participating in early government. He was a shrewd man, actively taming the frontier. Meekness was certainly not one of Elias McKean's qualities. He had been established for many years in the lower St. Croix Valley below Stillwater, near Ambrose Secrest. An old Indian path there had been slightly improved by adding a crown to the road but with only two ruts worn into it.

The road from McKean's farm to Stillwater was termed a turnpike. All that was meant by "turnpike" at the time was that there was no place to turn off it until you reached a town or village. An indignity occurred on the turnpike when Elias McKean was delivering a plow to Stillwater with his team of horses and freight wagon. At the same time, Dr. Stone was heading south on the trail, going from Stillwater to Afton. Stone was in his doctor's buggy and was in a hurry to make an urgent house call.

Both of the men were established in the community, one as a medical man and one as a great contributor to the government and economy. Elias McKean was not about to divert his heavy freight wagon from the turnpike into the field, and Dr. Stone was not about to redirect his lightweight rig into the prairie grass, risking broken buggy wheels. The two horse-drawn vehicles plowed toward each other, maintaining their dutiful pace.

It was the man with the strongest will who would win the challenge for the road; the other would pass on the prairie grass. The horses approached each other at a traveler's clip without hesitation until lathered horseflesh met horseflesh with brutal force, entangling harnesses, followed by the crash of wagon and buggy into shards and splinters of wood. The maimed horses screamed, collapsed and breathed their last. Both of the headstrong men were bloody, dazed and in serious condition. But this was the exaggerated version of the story—it did not happen quite that way.

The two drivers failed to yield, threatening an imminent crash of historic proportion, but common sense prevailed and both applied the brakes hard, the horses meeting nose to nose. An irate Dr. Stone jumped from his doctor's buggy as a furious Elias McKean was about to pounce on the well-dressed medical man.

An irate Dr. Stone shouted, "Get out of my way!"

"By what right do you presume to order an American from the public highway?" McKean growled.

"Turn out instantly!" yelled the man of pills. "I have a very sick patient down in Afton, and I must get to their bedside at once!"

"I contend that the longer I detain you here, the better your patient will be!" snapped Elias.

That remark sent rage through Dr. Stone. He raised his buggy whip and roared, "Get out of my way, turn out of the road, or I will drive over your infernal apple cart!"

McKean responded coolly, "Dr. Stone, take a single step more at your peril, and if you don't immediately drive out of this road, I will proceed to pulverize your whole damned outfit and pave this boulevard with your remains."

Dr. Stone had no choice but to pull out into the tall prairie grass to make a successful pass.

Road Rage, in a One-Horse Open Sleigh: Accident or Manslaughter

An incident of note happened just outside the Mississippi River town of Hastings, south of Point Douglas. Roads were buried in snow about three out of every four winters. If winter roads were clear of snow, people called it "dry wheeling." Dry wheeling on frozen ground was considered the best frontier life had to offer. Generally, winter did not go past without two or three snowfalls of good depth, requiring a change from horse and wagon to horse and sleigh.

Heading out of Hastings one sunny, cold January day was a merry traveler driving his sleigh. While gliding through the tracks of the sparkling white powder, the happy man noticed an approaching sleigh on the crest of a hill in the distance. There were but two ruts cut into the snowy road, and he was not about to blaze new ones on the prairie. The oncoming sleigh driver's thoughts were exactly the same. They were both in the snowy trail, and they weren't about to divert from it.

The snow ponies were clipping along as the sleigh rails slid gloriously through the slick and rutted snow. Each of the drivers imagined that the other would turn out into the unbroken depth of prairie, allowing for the two to safely pass. This did not happen. Instead, the mindless drivers destroyed their rigs in a massive collision of horse, wood and steel. The sleighs' wooden tongues, fastened to the horses by leather harnesses, acted like spears, piercing both vehicles. The driver who was traveling down the slope toward Hastings was killed, as was his horse. The driver from Hastings survived with injuries to himself and his horse, as well as a damaged sleigh.

The bloody survivor loaded the dead man into the front seat of his twisted rig and collected a few broken parts of the wrecked sleigh as evidence of the accident. He then made a turn in the deep prairie snow, returning to Hastings to report the incident. Limping into town with his injured horse, he made his report of the driver's death and informed authorities of the mangled horse and wrecked sleigh that lay on the trail outside town.

Many spectators were drawn to the gruesome scene, and a certain question was raised: why was there so much blood on the broken sleigh rail collected by the injured driver? After some scrutiny of the evidence, it was concluded that the dead driver had survived the wreck, only to be beaten to death with his own sleigh rail. The accident report was amended to include the charge of murder.

Wagon versus Road Builder and a Wild Man!: Constable Able Cudd Is Overturned

Abel and Martha Cudd were married in Illinois just a few miles from the river city of St. Louis, Missouri, near the end of winter in 1850. The springtime honeymoon was to be on a steamboat bound for Marine Mills in the recently formed Minnesota Territory. The newlywed couple was, respectively, twenty-one and eighteen when they left civilized life for a primitive one on the frontier. Abel Cudd worked at hard labor in Marine Mills, collected his pay and settled on farmland at Trimbelle, east of Prescott, Wisconsin.

Over time, Cudd became well known enough to be elected as local constable of Pierce County. Also, roadwork was progressing from Prescott through Trimbelle and Ellsworth and continuing on farther east. The need for road improvements was obvious, as the path through the prairie made travel difficult, becoming extremely muddy when wet. An early system of horse-drawn-grader-carved ditches on either side of the roadway effectively elevated the center of the path. The result created a crown on the road that shed rainwater into the ditch, thus shortening the drying time of the mud.

Abel Cudd was traveling by wagon with a team of horses on the road east of Ellsworth that was being graded and improved. The construction

THE PERILOUS ST. CROIX RIVER VALLEY FRONTIER

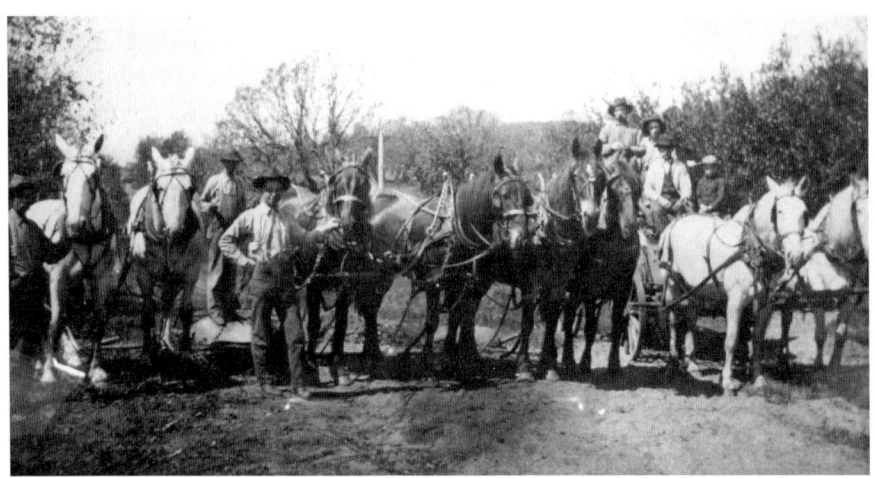

A road-building crew with its horse teams reshaped the trails with scrapers and drags that improved early travel on the frontier. *Photo courtesy Afton Historical Museum.*

of the road was in progress as he rumbled along, heading toward Ellsworth, when a wild rider overtook him in a thunderous hurry. The galloping galoot unexpectedly shot past Constable Cudd, spooking his horses into a wild and fearful rage. Cudd's team reacted by wrenching the entire wagon through the rough ditch, overturning the rig, driver and all.

Abel Cudd was furious at having been overrun and wrecked by the wild man speeding down the unfinished roadbed. The culprit was long out of sight, but Cudd would take action in Madison, the capital of Wisconsin. There, Cudd testified before the House of Representatives about the nature of legislation that needed to be enacted regarding road construction and traffic safety.

DEAD ON ARRIVAL:
THE THREE DEATHS OF DR. CARMIN GARLICK

Dr. Carmin Garlick had served with the Ohio infantry during the war with Mexico and then adventurously traveled to the west to the gold fields of California. As a doctor, he knew there would be great demand for medical care among the prospectors and miners. The gold rush made a few men wealthy but eventually went bust. Dr. Garlick, having done well, came out better than most of the unlucky miners.

Part IV

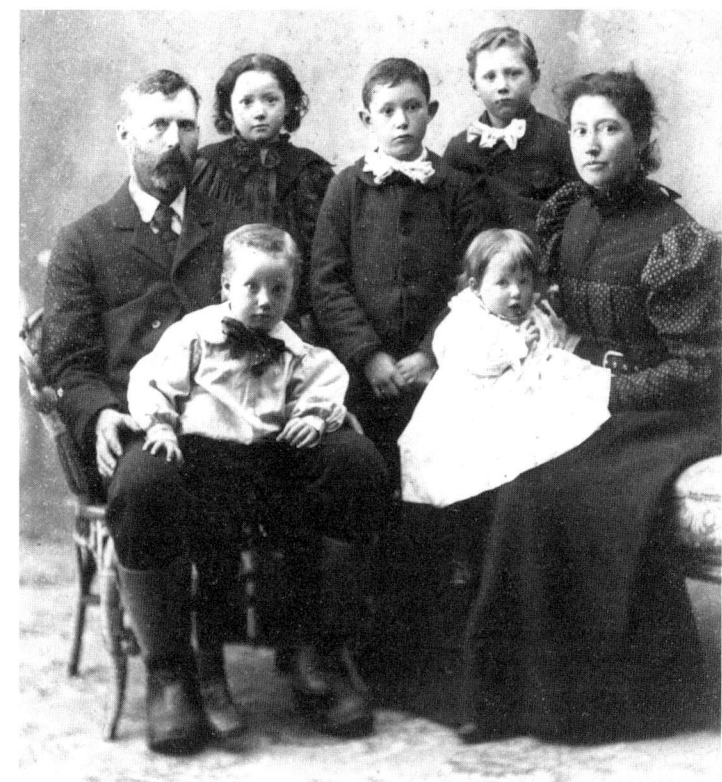

This 1854 Garlick family photo was taken prior to their departure for the St. Croix River Valley. *Photo courtesy of Ted Stout.*

The new opportunity for fortune was located in the St. Croix Valley, where prairie farmland was $1.25 an acre. There was a growing industry of pine logging to the north and a destitute population of Ojibwe, both of which presented "Carmi" Garlick with dreams of success. Dr. Garlick arrived with his wife and little children to a bend on the river of the upper St. Croix that he named Amador.

Born in Pennsylvania, Carmi was married young, at age twenty-one, to Mary Lane, but she died less than four months after the wedding. Two years later, Carmi married Elizabeth Thompson, and they made a life together in Ohio through the Mexican War until their expedition to the gold fields, after which they proceeded to Minnesota's frontier territory on the St. Croix River.

In 1854, Dr. Carmin Garlick and his young family came to the upper St. Croix, choosing to settle on a bend of the river near a tributary called Sunrise. Two fur trade posts frequented by the Ojibwe had recently folded up and faded from existence. The logging industry had replaced trading, and the Ojibwe had sold their hunting lands for annuity payments, food and clothing that arrived by steamboat. Dr. Garlick was a rare man who realized that the Ojibwe had gotten a raw deal. His desire was to provide medical care to the loggers and the Ojibwe, who were impoverished by late annuity payments and food deliveries.

Other opportunities presented themselves in 1857 when Carmi platted a town site on his land purchase, naming it Amador, after the California gold rush town where he had previously sought fortune. Carmi constructed a sawmill on the northern edge of town and built a wing dam out to the center of the St. Croix to collect the pine logs for his mill. He also applied for and received a license for a ferry operation to cross the river at the south end of Amador, and a newspaper was planned for the new community.

Pioneers began to settle the area in and around town. The steam ferry was in operation, as was the steam-driven sawmill, and a two-story hotel was constructed for Amador. A few homes were built in Amador during the summer of 1857, but the little boomtown was doomed by an unforeseen economic crisis of national proportion.

America's economy had flourished during the Mexican War and through the California gold rush, but the additional gold served to devalue the dollar, which began a recessive but not serious slide. Tragically, an oceanic ship, the SS *Central America*, carrying $2 million in gold sank to the bottom of the Atlantic during a hurricane on September 11, 1857. Hundreds of lives were lost to a watery grave, but the financial loss was the proverbial nail in the coffin of a weak economy. The dollar lost 75 percent of its value within a week's time.

Suddenly, Carmi did not see any return from sawing logs, which dropped from nine dollars to two dollars. People in town were so poor that they didn't have three cents to by stamps; the newspaper never launched, and the new hotel burned to the ground. Carmin Garlick submitted a plat of Amador to the (new) state of Minnesota, which was recorded in 1858, but the town failed to materialize.

The plat of Amador had eleven streets and 251 building lots. Amador was located adjacent to the Military Road that had been completed from Point Douglas, Minnesota, to Superior, Wisconsin. There was every dream of success on the St. Croix River, but Carmi walked away from the sawmill and ferry operation, which were costing more money to run than he had.

Tragedy struck the Henry Bush family (who had been running the hotel) when one of their young sons wandered away, disappearing for a year before only a skeleton of the lad was discovered. Likely suffering

PART IV

from hunger and exposure, he was found lying next to a log in the woods. Amador's cemetery was located near the banks of the St. Croix River, just beyond the south end of town. It wasn't long before the dead of Amador outnumbered the living.

Isaac Reese was one of the 1857 settlers of Amador who remained to raise his family there. It's probable that Isaac was too poor to move anywhere else to make a fresh start. Intending to stay, Isaac Reese married Johanna Johnson in 1858. Their son Henry was born nine months later; twins Albert and Alma arrived in 1865. When the Civil War began, Reese kept farming until late in the war when Chisago County offered married men a bounty of five dollars a month (paid to the wives) if they volunteered for war. Leaving a wife who was carrying twins, Isaac Reese served in Minnesota's First Battalion of Infantry for the last months of the war and then returned home.

Johanna gave birth to twins merely days after Isaac's return. Albert survived life on the frontier, but daughter Alma passed away from dysentery in 1873. She was buried in the Amador Cemetery in an unmarked grave. As many as fifty burials took place in the forgotten cemetery, none having been marked.

Ironically, Amador Cemetery was placed on an Ojibwe campsite and dancing grounds. The Ojibwe traveled there every spring and fall, spending quite a few days at a time in ceremonial dance. Many happy times were known to occur on the flats next to the banks of the St. Croix.

Dr. Carmin Garlick relocated south of St. Croix Falls to the Wisconsin river town of Osceola. There was need for a medical doctor in the growing town that was building steamboats. Carmi's old sawmill steam engine was built into one of the new steamboats constructed at Osceola. Lumber and boards from his sawmill were reused in frontier homes and barns. Nothing went to waste. Then the Civil War interrupted the lives of the pioneers, who were compelled to volunteer lest they lose the liberty they had struggled so hard to gain.

Carmi and Johanna had been living in Osceola for five years when their oldest child, Minerva, died. Even a medical man like Dr. Garlick could not save his nineteen-year-old daughter. Hardly over the grief of his loss, a call to serve Wisconsin came from the governor.

The governor of Wisconsin had heard of Dr. Carmin Garlick and his willingness to treat the Ojibwe of the St. Croix. The Fourteenth Wisconsin Infantry was enlisting volunteers who included full- and mixed-blood Menomonee men who desired to fight and be fed—and to be paid to do it. The Menomonee soldiers were quiet in that they kept to themselves,

The Perilous St. Croix River Valley Frontier

but they were voracious warriors on the field of battle. During lulls of camp life, the Menomonee hunted squirrels in the woods, returning with armloads at a time. Seventy-five squirrels were counted during a single hunt. The incredible part of the event was that the Menomonee men had been issued relic Belgian muskets that were so poor a typical soldier would consider them junk.

The trouble with having native volunteers in the infantry was that most medical men treated only white people. Carmi Garlick was the exception—a medical man who served everyone equally—and the wise governor knew it. Dr. Garlick was commissioned a captain and appointed to the Fourteenth Wisconsin Infantry on April 25, 1863. Carmi joined his regiment in time for the Siege of Vicksburg, directly down the Mississippi River.

The Menomonee soldiers, during a terrible assault of Vicksburg on May 22, captured and disabled two Rebel cannons on the elevated crest of the massive fortification. It was the farthest that any soldiers of the Union army were able to reach on that bloody, unsuccessful day. The Confederate fort was impenetrable, so the tactic changed to a siege in effort to starve the Rebels out. The new plan worked, and on July 4, 1863, the Rebels surrendered the city to the Yankees. The Fourteenth Wisconsin Volunteers were given the honor of being the first victors to march into the city.

As an assistant surgeon, Carmi Garlick was tending to the recovery of the wounded from the assault of May 22 and treating the sick, who suffered from malaria, yellow fever and consumption. Unfortunately for Carmi, he had contracted pneumonia, which eventually led to consumption, a chronic wasting disease that originates in the lungs. His advanced age of forty-five was a contributing factor.

There was no cure for the terminal disease Carmi suffered from, and the news that reached home in the St. Croix Valley was bad. Dr. Carmi Garlick, considered a great friend in Stillwater, Minnesota, was reported dead, having died of his Civil War illness on January 12, 1864. That wasn't exactly what happened; rather, Carmi had been discharged due to ill health from the Fourteenth Regiment on the twelfth. He was not dead.

Carmi was discharged and reassigned to the Thirty-fifth Wisconsin Infantry after thirty days' furlough. Service with the Thirty-fifth was lighter duty, but Carmi's health continued to fail. A year later, he was permanently discharged due to his debilitating illness. He traveled from his regiment in Arkansas to his old home in Ohio to visit family, who assisted in his recovery. After three months with relatives, Carmi left Ohio for Osceola to reunite with his wife and children.

Part IV

Carmi Garlick made it to Milwaukee, Wisconsin, where he passed away from consumption, commonly referred to as tuberculosis. The date reported was June 30, 1865, and the obituaries were written with affection.

Milwaukee is located on Lake Michigan, and for certain health conditions, the air there helps mitigate the symptoms. Carmi was actually recovering from his Civil War disease in Port Washington, which was twenty miles north of Milwaukee. He was using every known cure to prolong his life, but he passed away in Port Washington on September 30, 1865, as recorded by the surviving family.

According to military regulations, the bodies of officers who served in the Civil War were to be sent home for interment. Much confusion surrounds Carmi's death, which was reported several times. Only one thing can be certain: Captain Carmin Garlick was buried with full Masonic honors in Osceola's Mount Hope Cemetery.

The Last Ojibwe Fight with the Dakota, Murphy's Landing

Minnesota became a state on May 11, 1858, with the expectation of a great influx of pioneers to settle what had been native-owned land. A treaty document had been presented to the Dakota leaders who were living along the old St. Peters River, now named the Minnesota. The new treaty altered the language of the prior agreement made in 1851, cutting their reservation's area by half. This meant that reservation villages would have to be moved to the southern bank of the upper Minnesota River, above New Ulm. Pioneer farms would rapidly take the place of Dakota hunting lands.

For the Ojibwe, this seemed to be the end of their tribal conflict with the Dakota, as their blood enemy was being pushed nearly beyond a warrior's reach. A plan was speedily formed to attack Chief Shakopee's Dakota village at Major Murphy's ferry crossing, located near the village site. This was the closest Dakota site within Ojibwe reach. So many pioneers, farmers and city folk now occupied their former lands and battlefields that intertribal warfare had become more of a challenge.

Mille Lacs band of Ojibwe warriors journeyed to Shakopee's village down the Rum River to the Mississippi and then into the valley of the Minnesota River. Likewise, the St. Croix band of Chippewa came from Turtle Lake,

The Perilous St. Croix River Valley Frontier

Wisconsin, pausing on Star Prairie's main street for a terrific war dance that alarmed the small town's residents, who looked on in restrained fear.

Accelerating their pace, the warriors reached Hudson, Wisconsin, where a spectacular war dance was repeated downtown on Main. Townspeople were taken by surprise, thinking the world might end at any moment, when the St. Croix bolted for the waters of the St. Croix River, dividing into two groups, some swimming to the Minnesota side and others taking flight in canoes, beaching them four miles farther south in Afton.

In Afton, the townspeople witnessed the warriors' arrival by canoe and then their charge on the village as if the feared attack had finally come. Painted warriors, stripped to the breach cloth, went streaming through the town as the helpless folk cowered indoors and peeped through windows, expecting to be killed at the very next instance. As fast as the warriors entered Afton, they exited it west on the trail in a great marathon of war whoops and hollers. Eight miles over the prairie was the Mississippi, which they crossed, taking them to Chief Shakopee's village.

Chief Shakopee was camped with about 150 of his people at Major Murphy's because the major was their Indian agent, for whom they had respect. Shakopee's people had previously been on the narrow strip of reservation land on the upper Minnesota River, according to the 1851 treaty agreement. No one complained that the Dakota villagers had returned to their traditional home, as they much preferred it there. The Treaty of 1858 had recently dictated to the Dakota that they would reside on the southern half of the reservation land along the upper Minnesota River.

The Ojibwe warriors collected on the northern banks of the Minnesota River—at least 150 of them combined for an assault on the Dakota village. A hostile shot fired by the Ojibwe alerted the Dakota warriors to action. The Dakota women operated Murphy's rope ferry, transporting their outnumbered warriors into battle. The battle took place near a narrow strip of bottomland that was bordered by lakes on both sides, Rice Lake and Grass Lake. The Ojibwe repeatedly attacked the Dakota warriors in waves, but they would not enter the "narrows," as certain destruction awaited them once inside that trap.

"Rifles cracked and bullets whizzed" in the heat of battle. Battle cries sounded while Dakota women shouted encouragement to their warriors amidst the riotous noise of barking dogs. Warriors crawled and stalked one another through the grass and then attacked with war clubs flying. Valiant charges were made across the river and then repulsed again and again by bloodied combatants.

Part IV

The frontier town of Shakopee, built by pioneers from an 1851 trading post, neighbored the chief's village. When the gunfire began, curious citizens of the town ran for the river, by horse, buggy or foot, to witness the commotion and spectacle of native warfare. As many as three hundred frontier citizens gazed on the native conflict as if it were a death match between two hundred club-wielding gladiators.

Pioneer accounts of the Battle of Shakopee were thrilling and exaggerated. Claims of dozens of warriors killed were elevated to fifty and ultimately one hundred. The truth of the battle was that a typical number of casualties were suffered on both sides. There were four Ojibwe killed by the Dakota, and one Dakota warrior was killed.

A single death in battle is cause for mournful cries and wailing. The death of four warriors is a taxing number of losses on a population that lives by survival tactics. Who would feed and protect the families of the courageous? After the deaths of four warriors, the Ojibwe withdrew from the battle. The Battle of Shakopee was the last pitched battle between the Dakota and Ojibwe.

Black Pioneers in Afton: London and Jane Peters

Early in Afton, Minnesota's territorial history there lived an African American couple, London and Jane Peters. London Peters was born in the free state of Ohio about 1810. London never knew slavery, and barring indentured service, he lived life as a free black man. Jane Peters was born in the free state of New York about 1815. Their birth years are not culturally recorded, as it wasn't known whether they would survive infancy to reach adulthood. What mattered most was, if you lived, you lived.

London Peters was a frontier pioneer to the St. Croix Valley in the mid-1840s. He owned land but sold his claim to work as a cook in a boardinghouse with Jane at Point Douglas in 1849.

London also had forty acres in Pierce County, near Prescott, Wisconsin, which he sold late in 1855. It was after this time that London and Jane could be found in Afton, living in a cramped eight- by ten-foot cabin on Hay Creek. Jane, also known affectionately as Jenny, worked as a laundress washing clothes in Hay Creek for the farm laborers and sawmill workers in town.

One cultural dilemma presented to the Peterses in Afton was their neighbor Albert Martin. Albert Martin was a Virginian who had settled in

Afton and whose sobriety had come into question. Also, the fact that slavery was still permitted in Virginia might have influenced Martin's attitude toward his black neighbors. London Peters mysteriously vacated Afton, and the unstable Virginian was likely the cause. Jane, alone and aging, was taken in by the Edwin Hedderly family of Minneapolis as part of their wealthy household, but she remained there for only a short time.

London Peters went to Ontario, Canada, during America's Civil War years and lived there through his sixties. Jane Peters returned to the simple town of Afton as a guest of Asa Tracy. Jane was not able to be alone at her age. Asa and Flora shared their house and looked after Jane during her last years of life. An unmarked grave is likely her burial place in Mount Hope's pioneer burial ground.

William Bartlett's Journey to an Icy Demise

For many frontiersmen who came to the St. Croix Valley, there came big dreams of success, as if there were gold to be discovered on the frontier. Many of the river valley's pioneers had been out to the gold fields of California and had some small success until the gold run went bust. They were encouraged by advertisement to come to St. Croix. William Bartlett was one of the many gold seekers from Massachusetts who ventured across the expansive continent to seek his fortune in California.

The craze for yellow metal went bust for many seekers, and Bartlett left California for Missouri, an easier place to live. Health trouble arose for Bartlett—so severe that he was no longer able to work. Advertisements from the St. Croix frontier lured many frustrated Americans to settle at Stillwater and at Hudson, Wisconsin, on the St. Croix, noting that the climate was healthier than any other. Bartlett left Missouri for his health's sake and retired near Hudson, spending his able hours outdoors hunting and fishing.

The claims made in the advertisements must have been true because William's health steadily improved. After several months of recovery, Bartlett began operating a restaurant on Hudson's main street in the spring of 1860. Life returned to normal for William Bartlett, who made his acquaintance with many of Hudson's citizens, developing a warm circle of friends.

The restaurant business was doing well, requiring William to make trips to St. Paul and Stillwater for certain supplies, crossing the St. Croix on Captain John Oliver's ferry. Difficulty in attaining certain supplies was created during

Part IV

the time the river freezes over. Steamboat traffic ends, and ferry operations cease or resort to skiffs pulled by rope until the river's ice sheet becomes thick enough to trust on foot. Yet there is always a risk to travel by ice.

William Bartlett rented a team of horses and a carriage from Taylors Stables on the south end of Hudson and proceeded to cross the newly formed sheet of ice that stretched over the St. Croix. His "brave" buggy errand to Stillwater was made on the last day of November, extremely early for solid ice to have glazed over the river. Weather had been briskly cold, with temperatures dipping below zero, allowing for the precarious and slippery half-mile crossing of the river.

William completed his shopping chores, returning most of the way but stopping before reaching the river to stay the night at D.H. Boyden's, about two miles below Stillwater. Saturday morning came, and William was on his way to the Baytown landing, embarking on the last leg of his slick journey to Hudson's north end and home.

William Bartlett had successfully crossed on Friday, so Saturday's crossing seemed a sure thing. But the ice broke, sending the team of horses plunging straight down into the icy water and the carriage following soon after. The entire rig, supplies and animals sank to the bottom of the river.

William might have had a moment's notice of the tragedy and leapt from the carriage just as it sank, but heavy winter clothing prevented him from drawing himself from the bitterly cold water. Unfortunately, he was found with a severe forehead wound, likely caused from striking his head on a slab of ice.

William's body was discovered with only the top of his head showing. He struggled but failed to climb out of the icy hole, where he was frozen by his hair to the ledge. He was found an hour after the accident. The buggy, in fifteen feet of water, was recovered. This was the worst tragedy to occur at Hudson, Wisconsin, up to the time. William Bartlett was eulogized for his strict integrity and amiability by Reverend Speer, who had known him in California. His funeral was the largest attended in Hudson.

Winter Couldn't Be Worse, 1860–1861

Hudson, Wisconsin residents were shocked to receive news of the December 22, 1860 death of Cottage Grove's schoolteacher, who was found frozen about two miles south of Stillwater. The man had been walking at three o'clock in the cold of morning, intoxicated after patronizing the saloons of Stillwater. It appeared he had lain down on the road, quickly succumbing to subzero temperatures. "Stupidity" due to the severe cold was ruled the likely cause of death.

The news of the frozen schoolteacher was falsely reported in Hudson, contributed by an unreliable source. It wasn't true—no schoolteacher was drunk or frozen, stated the folks in Stillwater.

Edwin Holcomb of Lakeland was hunting deer on the Apple River in March 1861 but was caught in his own trap and shot through the thigh. The exiting projectile struck Edwin's other thigh, leaving a severe bruise. He had to be carried home, where Dr. Hoyt of Hudson treated him successfully, expecting a complete recovery. This was the third incident in as many years where a hunter set up a trick gun in the woods for hunting deer only to himself become the hunted. It was hoped that after a few more lessons such as this, men would desist from the barbarous practice.

A wedding party outside Hudson was thrown in joyous merriment. A young man reported to his loyal friends that he was married and that a reception was in order. Many partiers arrived in a condition implying that they had been partaking of spirits intended as wedding gifts. The wildness of the revelry intensified at the reception, which came to a crashing halt the instant they discovered a male bride under the matrimonial veil. The wedding announcement was nothing more than a cruel joke, made with the intention of consuming free gifts of liquor from the (formerly) loyal friends of the groom.

Temperance meetings were planned by Reverend Lewis at the Methodist church on Friday nights. Hope of a general interest in the topic would lead to creating a Society of Good Templars.

An Old Pioneer, Now a Ghost

Hudson, Wisconsin's early pioneer the "old mule" was found dead, having lived past the age of forty years. The mule had twice been across the plains to the Pacific Ocean and back. The mule had worked the streets of Hudson since its first days in 1849. Every man, woman and child knew of the famous old pioneer that labored on the streets of Hudson. The old mule would be remembered in the thoughts and minds of the early townspeople and then fade beyond their feeble memories, only to become a ghost.

PART V

ACCIDENTAL AND CRUEL NEWS

Richard Barron was brought into Stillwater from the woods, where he had fallen out of a tree. The branch Richard was on broke, sending him to the ground, where it struck him on the head. He suffered a serious concussion that was assumed to be fatal. Dr. Noyes stated that his condition was very critical.

A duck hunter boating on the St. Croix rested his shotgun between his knees for a moment's respite. The gun accidentally discharged with a painful bang, the barrel having been pointed directly at the hunter. The shot passed through the man, just missing his spine. He was taken to Stillwater in serious condition, but thoughts were that he would recover.

A young man named Addison, serving on the farm of James Mann, was killed when a loaded gun in the corner of the home accidentally discharged, the round passing through the boy's head. Dr. Hoyt was called to the home from Hudson, but his service was to no avail. Addison was dead.

The son of L.M. Makin, barely the age of six, fell into a vessel of boiling water and was severely scalded. It's unfortunate to say that he's not likely to recover, reported Dr. Hoyt.

Two women, a mother and daughter living twenty miles south of Hudson, were viciously attacked by a bull. The mother was seriously injured, and the daughter was killed when she was gored by the bull.

Charlie Curtis, just three years old, was scalded by boiling water. Little Charlie did not live. It was a sad and tragic blow to Stillwater's most popular citizens, attorney Gold T. Curtis and his wife, Mary.

A man named Tom McDonald fell from a second-story window at Stillwater's Wilson House on Saturday night, being seriously "mangled." He was still alive the next Monday morning, but no hope of his recovery was offered.

Lorenzo Cornman had his horse and buggy stolen in Stillwater. It was a bold theft to steal the animal and the rig, which were stored in the carriage house next to the Washington County attorney's home.

Runaway Team of Gray Horses

A loud morning commotion was created on Hudson's Second Street by a runaway team of horses. Charging in a thunderous rage of hooves and wagon wheels, Mr. Hall's gray horses had gone wild with no end in sight. With much hooting and hollering at the animals, the men of the city grabbed what debris they could find, heaving boards and throwing sticks into the path of the runaways. The wild team of lathered grays was finally stopped by the men of Taylors Stables at the south end of town. The horses weren't injured too badly, and the wagon wasn't damaged much either.

Runaways Gone Missing

Stillwater was the site chosen to construct the Minnesota Territorial Prison in 1851. The prison was located inside Battle Hollow, where the 1839 Dakota attack on the Ojibwe occurred. The natural geology of the hollow's three high walls formed a natural confinement space for the inmates. A single wall with a guard gate and guard towers built along Stillwater's north Main Street created the fourth wall of the prison.

Downtown in Stillwater, a team of horses had been spooked and stampeded, drawing a wagon wildly through the length of the city. The last anyone saw of the team, it was "going like a blue streak" toward the penitentiary.

Part V

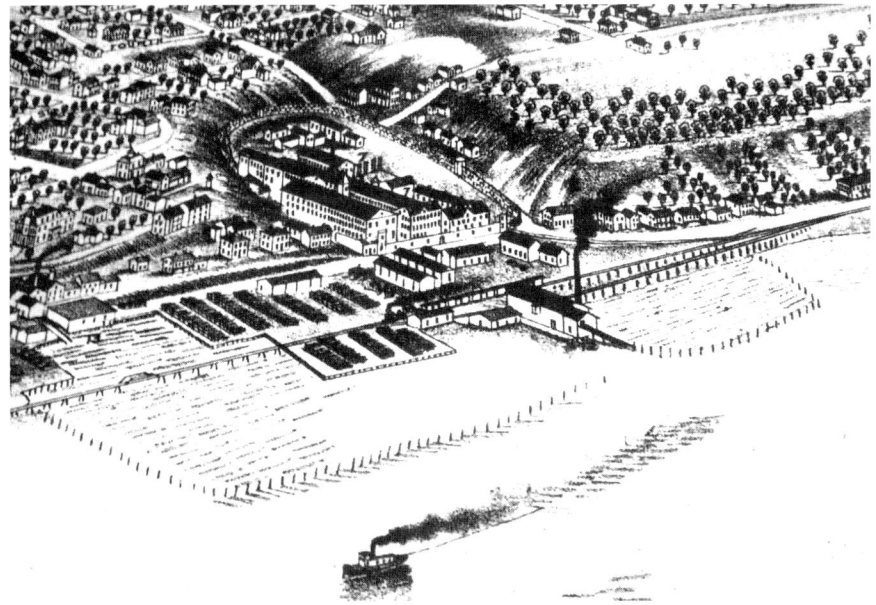

The Minnesota Territorial Prison was located at Stillwater in Battle Hollow, site of the 1839 Dakota massacre. Seymour Sabin's sawmill is across Main Street, in front of the prison.

The Spring of 1861 Arrives with Serious Events

Seven-year-old Willie Van Vleck of Stillwater went fishing in the St. Croix River at the foot of Chestnut Street. He failed to return home, and the next day his hat and fishing pole were found on the riverbank. After extensive dragging of the river, Willie's body was recovered in twenty-five feet of water. Judge Isaac Van Vleck, a resident of Stillwater's Sawyer House Hotel, chose the most beautiful place he could think to place Willie in eternal rest: Mount Hope Cemetery in Afton.

James Jackman was traveling down Stillwater's Third Street from Zion Hill when his buggy team accelerated beyond his control. Unable to slow the runaways, James leapt from the carriage to avoid the crash but landed on a stone wall and then bounced over a ledge. Jackman dropped (head first) ten more feet to the ground, breaking his ribs and sustaining other bodily injuries. He was expected to recover.

The Perilous St. Croix River Valley Frontier

A Virginia Wildcat with a Gun!

Hewitt Thomas brought his sons and their young families from Indiana to settle in and organize Afton in Minnesota's territory. Thomas bought Tilton's struggling sawmill to make his own attempt in the lumber business, then sold it off after a few years. He became a justice of the peace and a Republican delegate to the Minnesota Constitutional Convention of 1857. Son Meredith Thomas ran a store, William was the town blacksmith and son Minor T. Thomas was Afton's first clerk, also serving as a Washington County sheriff.

A strange event befell the Thomas family in May 1861, when Meredith's store at the blacksmith's shop was broken into. It wasn't discovered until

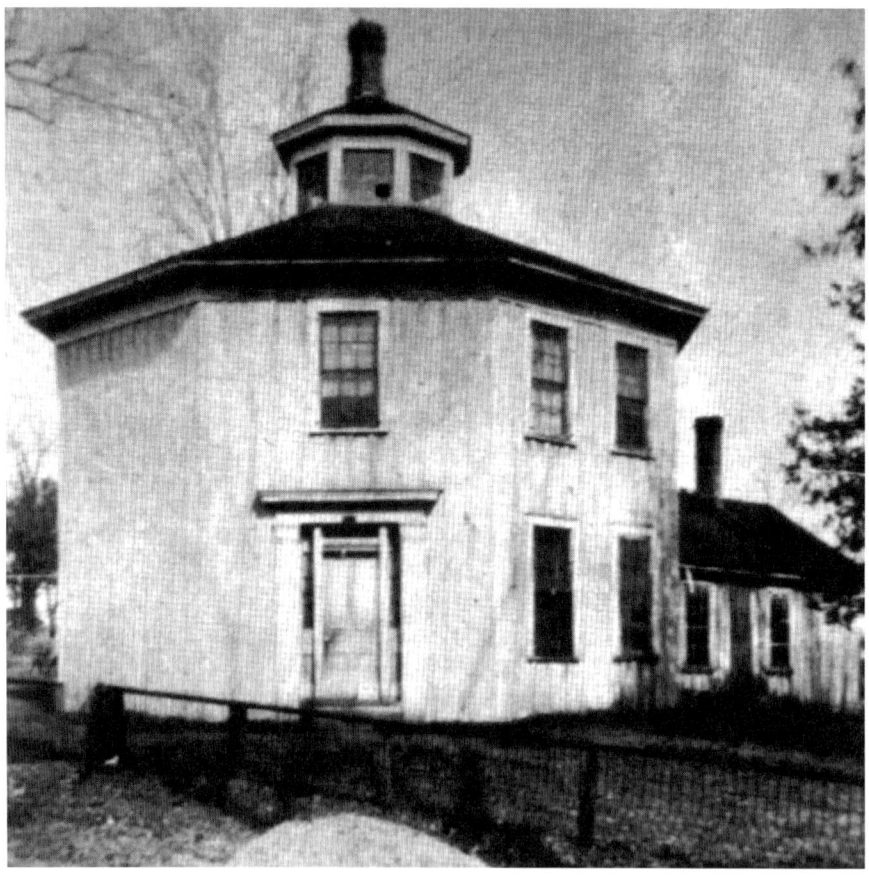

The 1855 Octagon, built by Meredith Thomas in Afton. Virginian Albert Martin invaded the home after midnight in 1861. *Photo courtesy Afton Historical Museum.*

Part V

after Meredith's wife, Helen, was awakened at two o'clock in the morning by the vision of a tall and silent figure hovering over her while lying in bed. Resembling nothing more than a spooky shape, it was actually a man holding a gun.

Helen jumped with fright and shouted, "Meredith, shoot him!" She sounded the alarm of impending crisis to Meredith, who sprang from his dreams and landed on his feet. He turned to see the hazy figure in the room. He didn't have a gun, but the mysterious invader didn't know that in the dark. The intruder fled out of the room, down the stairs and out to the street, with Meredith in his nightshirt following in hot pursuit.

It was a moonlit night, and Meredith pursued the silhouette of a large man running down the street, calling out for help every step of the way. It was two culprits, realized Meredith, to whom he was giving chase when one of them turned and fired a shot at him. When they reached a fence at Sam Paterson's hotel, the pair halted and instructed Meredith to stop. "Do not take one step further," they ordered, or they would shoot him. The felonious pair then jumped the fence.

Meredith woke up his brother Will for help. The young men's father, Hewitt Thomas, was awake, having heard the commotion out on the street. Albert Martin's Virginian voice was recognized by both Meredith and (Judge) Hewitt. Albert Martin was eventually apprehended, a culprit in both break-ins; Meredith's watch was taken from his bedroom, and the store had been rifled through. Albert Martin was jailed and expected to serve four years, though as many as twelve could be handed down. The Virginia "wildcat" Albert Martin never returned to Afton.

Civil War Troubles in Afton

Afton, a small Minnesota sawmill town on the lower St. Croix, was struggling with growing pains. The sawmills tried to make a go of it but would catch fire and burn. The operations would be sold off, rebuilt, run for a short time and fail to turn a profit. Tilton's Mill changed hands and became Thomas and Sons. The 1857 financial crisis caused it to run at a deficit, and no business could function for very long that way. The Getchell Mill survived with its store to carry the lumber business through the toughest years.

If that weren't enough, Sam Paterson's hotel in the center of town caught fire in a great conflagration and burned to the ground. Paterson, along with his wife and children, survived, as did fifteen residents occupying the hotel. Everyone in the quaint village was deeply affected by the thick smoke and intense heat of the fire. Why there weren't any deaths or injuries from it was a mystery.

And if that still weren't enough, the Southern states succeeded from the Union, and war was declared that spring of 1861. The destroyed hotel was a total loss; other families took in the homeless, an action that contributed to a growing number of boardinghouses in town.

Sam Paterson was a businessman out of a job, so volunteering for Civil War service with the Quartermaster's Department became a solution to the problem. Similarly, widower Charles Getchell served during the Civil War as a quartermaster to supplement his store, providing for its long-term success. Running the army store facilitated one's ability to make money on the side, and all quartermasters did that well.

The Fighting Reverend: Reverend Simon Putnam

Afton's Reverend Simon Putnam busied himself holding "war meetings" in churches, town halls and schoolhouses for the purpose of raising volunteers to fight in the War of Secession. Southern states rebelled against the election of a Republican president by seceding from the union. The United States, as the patriots knew it, had come to an end. Frontier pioneers who had just struggled to settle the raw frontier feared their hard-won liberty would be lost with the dissolution of the Union.

Reverend Putnam sternly encouraged young men and mature boys to enlist in the army to fight the "Godless Rebels" for dissolving the thirty-four states of America. Adding to that, the reverend fervently prayed, "May the devilish slaveholders be struck with a bolt of electric current!"

Reverend Simon Putnam was instrumental in adding to the ranks of the first volunteers who were tendered in the fight and would likely die to preserve the broken nation. A persistent man, Putnam encouraged the enlistment of companies of the first three Minnesota regiments of infantry before volunteering himself and his sixteen-year-old son, Myron, for the Third Minnesota Regiment. Myron Putnam was under eighteen years of age and too young to be issued a military musket like his thirty-eight-year-old father. Myron was enlisted as a musician and issued a drum.

Part V

A year later, during the summer of 1862, the Third Minnesota Infantry found itself surrounded by Nathan Bedford Forrest's Rebel cavalry at Murfreesboro, Tennessee. The regiment's commander, Colonel Henry Lester, sought terms of surrender, while the soldiers desired to "shoot their way out." A Pennsylvania regiment was captured in their camp, the Ninth Michigan surrendered six companies and all but one company of the Third Minnesota was surrendered in disgrace by (the coward) Colonel Lester.

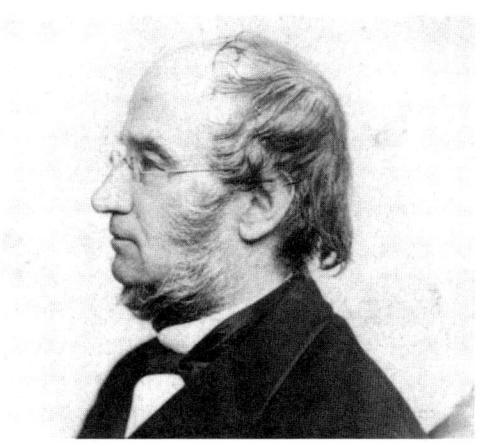

Simon Putnam was thirty-eight years old when he volunteered with his sixteen-year-old son, Myron. Simon was old and of ill health, so he was soon discharged, but he followed his spiritual conviction. *Photo courtesy Afton Historical Museum.*

It was revealed, following the humiliating surrender, that General Forrest was outnumbered by Union forces. The Yankees were merely outwitted by the Rebel commander's tactic of illusion. Forrest had cycled his cavalry in circles past the Third Minnesota Infantry, allowing them to see only the advancing horsemen, who then retreated in stealth only to make their advance again from the rear. The illusion was that of a continual reinforcement of enemy forming a front line of battle. It was a Rebel trick, and Colonel Lester fell for it. The Minnesotans returned home humiliated and disgraced.

Both Simon and Myron Putnam returned to Minnesota on terms of their Confederate parole. The Third Minnesota soldiers were soon permitted, on the condition of Confederates having been equally "exchanged," to return to active service. Simon had become too ill to serve and was discharged from the regiment. Drummer boy Myron continued on to Wood Lake, Minnesota, participating in the battle with Dakota warriors led by Chief Little Crow, the grandson of the Great Crow, Le Petit Corbeau.

The Dakota War had begun as a result of the tension that developed between the Dakota people and the Indian agencies, which were slow to administer annuity payments agreed to by treaty. Added to that, Indian agents withheld Dakota food supplies from the storehouses on the reservation. To complicate matters, a general crop failure had occurred across Minnesota in the fall of 1861 and 1862. Herds of deer had left the state for better pastures, resulting in a general state of starvation among the Dakota people.

Chief Little Crow once stated that the Dakota had never killed a white person and, with exception given to mixed-blood people, he was likely correct. One incident in 1851 can be pointed to in which a war party of Dakota stole a keg of whiskey from a lone Ojibwe. The resulting drunken war party fired on a team of horses, killing the driver, Andrew Swartz. The name Dakota translates to "allies," and with the entry of the new culture on the frontier, it could be said that the Dakota were living up to their name. That changed drastically on Sunday, August 17, 1862, when four hungry Dakota hunters (returning from a fruitless hunt) killed five settlers at Acton, in central Minnesota.

A rapid decision was made by a few bands of Dakota, who followed Little Crow, to attack the lower agency on the Minnesota River. The Little Crow war began on August 18 with the agency's residents all being killed. Hundreds upon hundreds of Minnesota pioneers were killed in Dakota raids across the central and southwest portion of the state. Untrained recruits of the Sixth and Seventh Regiments, led by Henry H. Sibley, were sent from Fort Snelling to track down the warring bands of Dakota. Sibley sent messages to six peaceful bands of Dakota to remain in their camps, for their movements might be erroneously identified as hostile.

It was the experienced Civil War soldiers of the Third Minnesota who, attempting to prove their bravery (having been labeled cowards), defeated Dakota warriors at the Battle of Wood Lake. Myron Putnam became chronically ill after the September 23 battle. After long-term care in Fort Snelling's hospital, Myron was discharged from service on July 9, 1863. Simon had recovered from his contracted illness well enough to be promoted to chaplain of the Third Minnesota Infantry. Two months later, Simon departed for some of the worst service of the Civil War.

While Chaplain Simon Putnam attempted to minister to the suffering soldiers in Arkansas, Myron died in bed at home. Myron was buried on a cold day by his mother, Julia, and his little sister, Mary, on Mount Hope, the old burial ground on Afton's bluff. It was December 8, 1864, and drummer boy Myron, a veteran of the Civil War, was only eighteen.

In Arkansas, the Third Minnesota soldiers were dying of dysentery, consumption and malaria. Virtually one-quarter of the men of Minnesota's Third Regiment died of disease. Chaplain Simon Putnam wrote letters describing their situation to General Thomas in Washington, D.C., requesting aid. Generally, a regiment that serves three years received thirty

Part V

days' furlough, but the Third was graciously awarded sixty days' rest and recovery. Simon was very ill when he walked in the door of his Afton home in the first week of September 1864. He greeted Julia and Mary, knowing that his son was buried on the bluff above their home.

Severely ill and failing, Reverend Simon Putnam would have been taken to visit Myron's grave in the cemetery, where he had performed many pioneer funerals before. Lilies of the valley decorated Myron's grave—flowers that Julia and Mary would have planted on their knees together. Simon lived only a few more days and passed away of the disease he contracted in the war.

Consumption was a contagious disease of the lungs that caused the sufferer to physically waste away. Early in the Civil War, it was virulent and terminal, running its course in about a year. Later, soldiers would live many years, even decades, seeking cures that sometimes helped extend their lives. Tragically, Chaplain Simon Putnam, having done so much for the Union cause and for the soldiers, did not live to see the war's end. Both father and son had been taken by a war that was not yet over.

Stillwater's Panic and Fear of Dakota Attack

The Dakota people had been forced into a state of starvation by living on a mismanaged reservation. Dakota warriors led by Little Crow attacked two Indian agencies on the Minnesota River, the city of New Ulm and Fort Ridgley on the prairie. Hundreds of settlers were killed across south-central Minnesota, several hundred were held captive and hundreds more were refugees. It was as if Minnesota had been set on fire in the middle of August 1862.

Many of Minnesota's men had left the state to serve in the Civil War—so many that it seemed as if little defense could be made of the state. This was surely something Little Crow had considered when choosing to lead the war. The Dakota War could have been much worse, but two-thirds of the available Dakota warriors chose not to participate.

News of the great calamity struck Stillwater like a lightning bolt late at night on August 19. Frank Ellis was awakened by his wife, who thought she heard Indians outside their farmhouse. Both husband and wife panicked, gathering their children and depositing them for safe keeping in the hog pen, then fled in their bedclothes toward Stillwater, running and screaming every inch of the way. Frank turned back to see his farmhouse in flames, set ablaze by raiding warriors, who were, in fact, nothing more than an electrical storm rolling into town.

    D.H. Boyden departed the saloons of downtown Stillwater when he was informed that Dakota raids had taken place over one hundred miles to the west of Stillwater. The swaggering Boyden jumped on his horse and bolted up Second Street like the famed Patriot Paul Revere to warn the residential neighborhood of the impending attack. Sleeping folks were awakened from their 2:00 a.m. slumbers by Boyden's screams of Indians and bloody murder. Scared half to death, folks raced outdoors to form a militia with their guns, whether they were good guns or broken ones. After more than an hour of organizing, it was determined that the (Indian) alarm was false. A severe storm had thundered loudly into Stillwater with incessant lightning flashes illuminating the sky. Whether it was the severe storm or nervous alarm, no one was able to sleep.

    A few months after the "Indian scare," a man clad only in a shirt was seen running down the boardwalks of Stillwater, yelling out, "I'll give any man ten dollars if he can tread on my shirttail!" The man was Frank Ellis, and he was blazing drunk—again.

Fun, Frolics and Fiascos: Ice-Skating on the St. Croix

During the Civil War, the winter fad of ice-skating swept the lower St. Croix Valley. Ice-skating allowed the hardiest of people to block the war from their thoughts for an hour or so of chilly fun. Skaters could not wait until the first glaze of ice covered the St. Croix River. The border river generally froze the last week of November during an arid blast of bitter cold. Boys were out there the earliest, testing the sheet of glass with their thin blades of steel. The moment that one could cross the entire river on skates was one of sheer glory.

    Skating clubs formed due to the vast interest in the sport. Four ladies and three men skated from Stillwater, Minnesota, to Hudson, Wisconsin, on the ice one evening in January 1863. The Stillwater gals challenged the Hudson ladies to attempt the same jaunt to Stillwater.

    Humorous commentary of the "slippery" sport reported, "Saints and sinners and angelic females alike find a common level." One of the young men of Stillwater had a special lady friend whom he desired to see, and skating to her city was the fastest way to get there. The trouble was that the young lover found a hole in the ice to fall through. The chilling experience cooled off his desire, and he returned home encased in a frozen suit.

Ladies and men enjoyed the splendid nature of skating even if the ice was thin. Ed Staples of Stillwater fell through and nearly drowned but got out, only to fall through again. The second time, Joe Carli laid down, threw Ed his coat to grab on to and pulled him out. Schoolteacher Evaline Smith skated two days in a row in November 1863, all the while fearing a cold bath from breaking through the ice.

Ed Armstrong of Hudson was well known to friends in Stillwater. He skated to Osceola to meet Jennie Kent. The young couple skated hand in hand under a moonlit St. Croix River until they fell through a hole and were lost. Mr. Webb laid out boards to rescue the pair, but it was too late. Edward tried desperately to save Jennie when he could have saved himself. Jennie's shawl was found held tight in Edward's death grip.

Edward Armstrong had wanted to be a soldier in the Civil War; he was twenty and of age to serve. His father, David Armstrong, denied him, saying he was too young. Edward was buried in Willow River Cemetery at Hudson, and Jennie was buried in Osceola's Mount Hope Cemetery. Jennie was fifteen.

A Confederate in Stillwater: John Colby

Early Stillwater resident John Colby came from Alabama to pioneer the St. Croix Valley. Many of the men in town met in the fraternal lodges during the evenings. As Stillwater grew in population, there were more places to socialize. Men were pretty much able to choose any night of the week to go out.

The Masonic lodge was dominant in the town, but the Odd Fellows had formed a year prior, their goal being the betterment and care of orphans. A secret lodge called the Sons of Malta sprang up and then disappeared. The Wide Awakes served Republicans as personal guards, as Democrats hated them so much that they would attack and beat Republicans into the ground. There was a group of thespian players, a Bible Society and a Mite Society. The ladies of the Mite Society charged twenty-five cents when they met for sandwich luncheons and then decided how to contribute their funds philanthropically.

It was the Knights of the Golden Circle that were the most secretive of all the organizations. Their meetings were announced with the words "Meeting Tonight" in Stillwater's Tuesday paper. Only the members knew what that meant, as the time, location and topic of the meetings were well-kept secrets. The Knights of the Golden Circle were staunch Democrats who believed in the U.S. Constitution "without interpretation," understanding that Southern states had a right to own human property under the Fifth Amendment and also supporting the unwritten rule of succession of states if they so desired.

The Knights of the Golden Circle also desired the U.S. annexation of Mexico. After that goal was achieved, Canada would virtually volunteer to become a state in the United States. If Stillwater's John Colby was a member of the Knights of the Golden Circle, he kept the secret well.

When the Civil War began, John Colby made a choice to fight for his home state of Alabama. John said his pleasant Southern farewells to his friends in Stillwater, headed downstream to the South and volunteered with the Twenty-first Alabama Infantry. His service to Alabama didn't last long due to his capture while defending Fort Morgan in 1864.

John Colby swore an oath not to raise weapons against the Union or face punishment by hanging. He was then placed on a prisoner's parole and allowed to return to civilian life. Colby was out of the Civil War. What he did next was return to Stillwater to pick up where he had left off. Unfortunately, he was not well received. His friends had been angered by the war, which was taking the lives of their fathers, sons and brothers; they blamed the Rebels for the deaths of many and for the maimed who struggled to get home.

Stillwater's community was so upset by John Colby's presence that it passed a resolution that John Colby be banned from the city indefinitely. John moved to Afton, but that town board passed the same resolution, banning Colby from its midst. News soon spread that John Colby was in Fort Snelling's jail, being held on charges of spying for the Confederacy.

John Colby's luck seemed to have played out. After his tormenters relinquished their vendetta, he quietly settled near a lake (that retained his name) in Red Rock Township, which he renamed Woodbury.

The Grief of War: John F. Peterson

John F. Peterson was the second Swede to arrive in the lower St. Croix Valley near Lake St. Croix. He lived near old Jacob Fahlstrom, who had earned recognition as the first Swede to arrive in Minnesota. Over forty years had elapsed since Jacob Fahlstrom had spoken his native language with another Swedish person, but now he enjoyed speaking it with John F. Peterson.

Peterson was a forty-three-year-old father of eight and husband to Christina on a farm in Afton when he volunteered for the Civil War. Farming was tough after both the economic crisis of 1857 and the crop failure of 1861. John volunteered after being offered a bounty of $200 to join; $200 to a dirt farmer was equivalent to a year's wages. How could that be turned down with a hungry family to feed during tough economic times? John Peterson's family would never see him again.

Sadly, after two years in the infantry, Peterson's life ended with illness, suffering and death brought on by serving as a soldier in the Civil War. His tragic death, at age forty-five, should not have happened. Yet in the scope of the war, his story was only one among hundreds of thousands.

The Civil War ended with the assassination of President Lincoln, as if Americans, who lost fathers, sons and brothers to battle and disease, had not suffered enough. The residents of the St. Croix Valley had sacrificed too many young men to the cause of preserving liberty. A benefit of preserving the Union was that the enslaved would now experience a newfound liberty, having been set free from title papers and ownership.

For a year following Lincoln's death, people wore black armbands (of mourning) over their black clothing. The black was worn out of respect for the president, but who could tell that from the grief of personal loss that befell the entire St. Croix Valley. The question in the valley was: would they ever recover from their grief?

Baseball Amusements in the St. Croix Valley

Baseball was becoming so popular during the territorial days of Minnesota that the organization of teams was announced in St. Paul in 1857. Stillwater, Afton and Hudson, Wisconsin, along with River Falls, had teams that would contest one another and the teams in St. Paul. One of the earliest games (of record) to occur in the St. Croix Valley was played late in the 1850s on a sand bar of the St. Croix River at Hudson.

Score keeping of the early games was of the players' own making, as evidenced by an 1861 game in which River Falls beat Hudson's team by seventeen points. Baseball continued its popularity beyond the dark days of the Civil War by maintaining its entertainment value. In the first week of September 1867, newspapers confirmed the victory of the Stillwater boys in "a hard contested match by 12 runs."

On Thursday, September 13, an incredible double header was played in Stillwater between the Afton Club and the home team, the St. Croix Club. The score of the first game was not reported, but the score of the second game was 67–46, with the St. Croix Club besting Afton. The elevated score was most likely caused by the depth of the grass, resulting in many lost balls. A large number of ladies and gentlemen witnessed the spectacle and then attended the dance that followed. There was hope that the grand affair would be repeated.

Freedom with a Bang: An African American Community Celebrates at Prescott, Wisconsin

London Peters, the African American pioneer who was born free in Ohio, purchased forty acres of land ten miles east of Prescott in 1855. London was noted for being the only one of his race in the area at the time. London's forty acres were on a hill above a well-traveled road. The place was dubbed Negro Hill for the first settler of his race in the area.

London Peters wasn't the only African American or black pioneer to settle in the St. Croix Valley. A small community of African Americans formed around Prescott, Wisconsin, in Oak Grove and Trembelle Townships. One black settler was counted in Prescott in 1855, but the numbers had grown to several dozen African American families by 1870. Two of Prescott's black residents were Civil War veterans, and after the war, emancipation was celebrated when it became a permanent reality. As they were termed in their era, the "colored" people of Prescott's community requested that the area's residents commemorate their freedom at Dunbar's Hall in July 1866.

In 1869, the grand event of celebrating freedom was repeated, with both races in attendance. Sidney Suydam offered to fire Prescott's Civil War cannon with a traditional three-volley salute to the black community's freedom. Sidney's thoughtful gesture was well meaning, but he was unable to complete the task. Acting alone without a gun crew on the cannon was Sidney's mistake.

While reloading the gun after the initial blast, Sidney rammed the second gunpowder charge onto red-hot embers that were still glowing down inside

Part V

the cannon's breach. The result was a premature explosion that blasted the ramrod through Sidney's hands. He could have been killed, but he survived severely mangled. During Civil War times, Sidney Suydam's hands would have been amputated, and most thought that this would be the case for him. The black community was so concerned for Sidney, a carpenter, that they immediately took up a collection to assist in his recovery.

Beaten to Death by Accident: RIP James Clegg, Saloon Keeper

A drunken brawl occurred on October 1, 1869, at Afton's Wolf Saloon, disgracing the fair name of the village when an argument began over the misplacement of a smoking pipe. The confused customer accused several others of taking the missing pipe, something of which the customer was quite fond. The argument intensified into a scuffle; with no resolution in sight, the fight was taken into the street in front of the saloon. The saloon keeper, James Clegg, grew tired of the protracted dispute and went after the men with a club, threatening to knock their damned heads off if they did not cease.

One of the combatants, Evans, came at Clegg with his fists, but Clegg clubbed him down. Clegg had had enough of the fight and was heading into the saloon when James Ackerman grabbed his club and smacked him on the side of his head. Clegg dropped to the ground unconscious while Ackerman struck twice more. Clegg suffered blows to his side and again to his head. He was rescued from the ground by friends and taken to his home, where his painful suffering continued.

After passing in and out of consciousness for two weeks, James Clegg died, thus ending his agony. Evans and Ackerman were arrested for murder. They were taken before Justice Isaac Van Vleck and held six weeks for a trial. Evans was not tried in the case, but James Ackerman was. Somehow, James Ackerman retained the esteemed defense attorney Willis A. Gorman.

Gorman began his career in Indiana as a U.S. representative and then served as a major in the war with Mexico, soon moving on to serve as Minnesota's second territorial governor. During the Civil War, Gorman was colonel of Minnesota's First Regiment of Volunteers, which fought many deadly battles without retreating. He was promoted to general and given a brigade to command, leading his men to the furthest point of Union

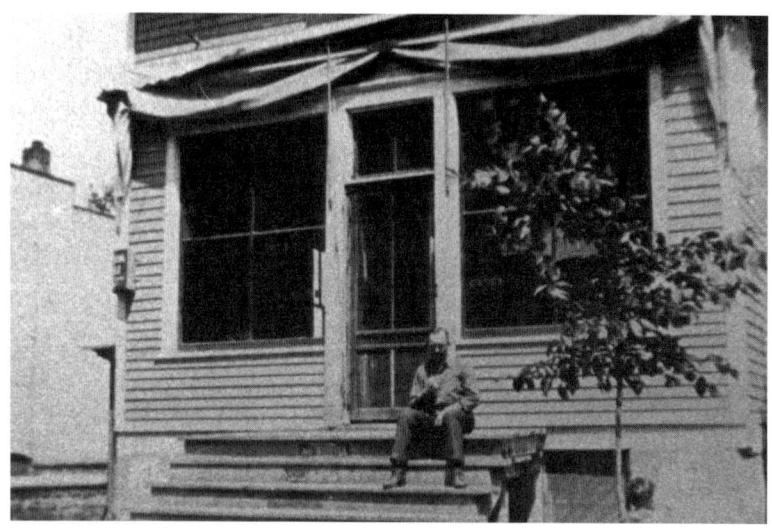

The old Wolf Saloon after it was converted to a confectionary store during Prohibition. It became Lerk's Bar after Prohibition's repeal. Harold "Lerk" Lind is seated on the steps of the bar. *Photo courtesy Afton Historical Museum.*

advance on the battlefield at Antietam, which is also known as America's bloodiest day in history.

The trial went well for James B. Ackerman. Attorney Gorman won his acquittal. James Bernard Ackerman had an extensive Civil War record with the Thirteenth U.S. Volunteers, Seventh Wisconsin Infantry and Twenty-seventh Wisconsin. James Clegg, a lowly Irishman serving grog, had no service record of which to speak. Certain documents mention James Clegg as "Killed." The medical record initially documented death due to "Concussion of the Brain" but was later altered to "Dis. (disease) of the Brain" after the acquittal. James Clegg's Evergreen Cemetery death record merely states, "Accidental."

James Bernard Ackerman was misidentified by the court reporter as John B. Ackerman, adding to the historic confusion of the event. James B. Ackerman married Mary Lowenzy Young the next year in Baytown, Minnesota, and then moved east across the St. Croix to farm at St. Joseph, Wisconsin, where he and Mary raised a family of girls. They hid in plain sight from the disgrace of the 1869 murder by adopting usage of their middle names—Birney and Louesa Ackerman. Birney Ackerman died in western Montana in 1928. He was a police officer.

Part V

The Postmaster's Dead Tree

The summer of 1876 was dry to the extent that drought had caused the St. Croix River to drop low enough at Stillwater to be walked across on foot. It wasn't the first such drought. People had learned by living in the valley that these ecological events happened—or at least most of them had learned.

A tragic accident occurred in Stillwater when a runaway horse and buggy tore down Third Street from Zion Hill and crashed into a tree that stood on the corner of Chestnut Street. The horse was killed and so was the driver. Postmaster Cutler lived in the corner house, and it was his tree that was damaged by the wreck of the horse and buggy. Postmaster Cutler claimed that the tree was killed in the accident and that the deceased party's estate should pay ten dollars in reparations.

Stillwater's townspeople were appalled at their postmaster for charging the dead man's family ten dollars for the tree. People also knew, due to the drought, that the little shade tree was nearly dead already. Striking the tree with horse and buggy did little to damage it, and furthermore, the poor driver deserved a little sympathy.

It was soon learned that the bereaved family was selling magazine subscriptions, at ten cents each, to raise the ten dollars demanded by the

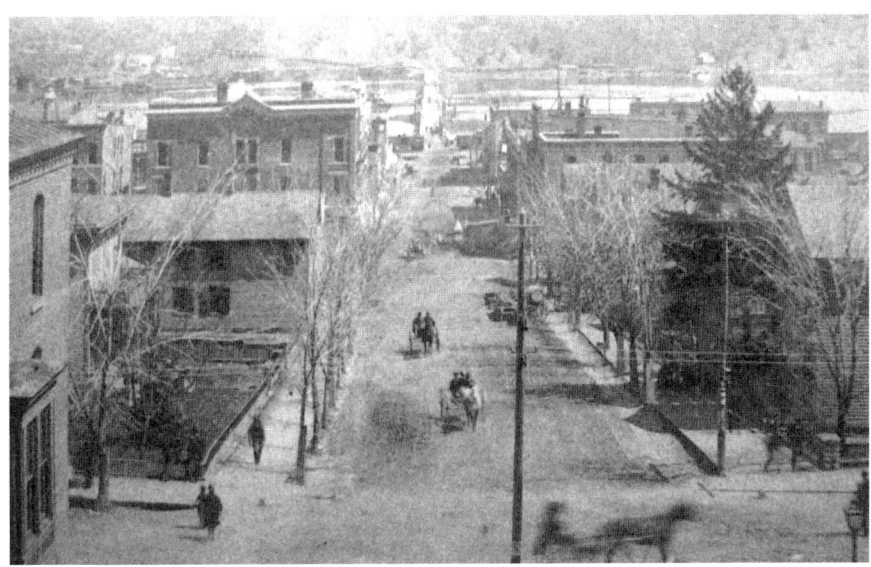

A view of Stillwater with Third Street in the foreground and Chestnut Street leading down to the St. Croix River. Postmaster Cutler's trees can be seen on the left. *Photo courtesy Washington County Historical Society.*

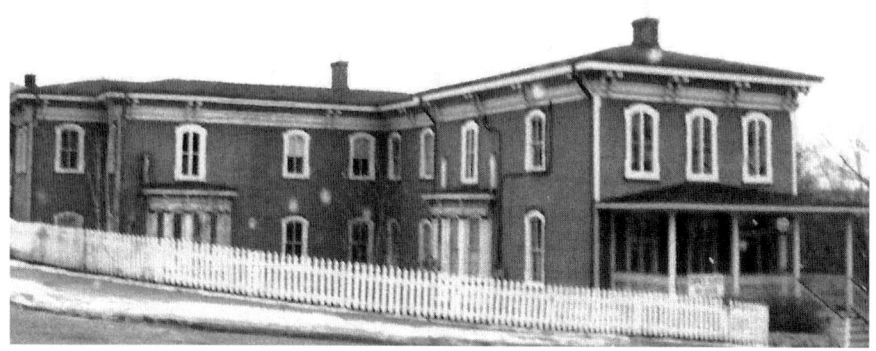

Postmaster Cutler's residence on Chestnut and Third in Stillwater. The trees are no longer growing in the boulevard. *Photo courtesy Washington County Historical Society.*

postmaster. There was speculation about what the charge would have been if the tree had actually been alive at the time of the accident—$100 or even $1,000? What if the horse and buggy had run over the postmaster instead and killed him? No money would have been collected then, proving that a dead tree is worth more than a live postmaster.

A similar incident repeated itself on Third Street, this time beginning at Myrtle Street. A Jewish peddler was driving his mattress wagon when a thrashing machine struck fear in the horse, causing it to charge out of control toward Postmaster Cutler's corner. The insane horse rounded the corner at Cutler's, missing all of the postmaster's trees and gaining speed down Chestnut. Some thought the horse controlled himself well at Cutler's, having read the accounts in the *Stillwater Messenger.*

Speeding around the corner and heading down Main Street, the poor peddler was ejected from his rumbling rig. A horse and buggy on Main Street carrying Miss Butler and Miss Orff was overturned by the maniacal animal, which then turned up Nelson's Alley. Fortunately, the charming ladies were unharmed. The peddler's rig, piloted by the mad horse, stormed up the length of the dead-end alley and halted at a stone wall without further disaster. No dead trees were injured.

Part V

"I Danced with Jesse James": Widow Eliza Ross

Frank and Jesse James were outlaw brothers who had gained fame by robbing wealthy barons, who, to some frontier-minded people, had more money than they knew what to do with. Well, that was the popular myth of their mayhem, anyway.

When the Civil War came to Clay County, Missouri, Yankee raiders came through, making certain that the resident farmers were loyal to the Union. Rebel-minded folk would be punished severely for dividing the nation into two.

Union raiders came to the James farm, assaulting sixteen-year-old Jesse and his stepfather, Rueben Samuels. Jesse's mother and Rueben owned slaves—a family with two sons. The adult couple had their own private slave quarters, but their two sons slept in the (James) cabin loft with Frank and Jesse. For the perceived infraction, the Yankee militia abused Jesse with a whip and hung Rueben from a tree. Rueben, though injured (as was Jesse), inspired Jesse to sign up with a band of partisan rangers, or loosely organized rebels, who were fighting the damn Yankees during the Civil War.

The Civil War ended, but not for Frank and Jesse James, who sought out wealthy Yankee targets in retribution for winning the war. Banks were robbed if they had Northern states connections. Railroads were also targeted but as part of a vendetta for their attempts to buy up the James farm (and others), which was not for sale. Jesse's mother, Zerelda James Samuels, was physically maimed and his half brother killed in a firebombing of their home. Pinkerton Agency detectives seeking the outlaws attempted to burn down the Jameses' house, but their incendiary device exploded by mistake.

Publicity had turned against the Yankee influence that sought destruction of the James family. Frank and Jesse, who focused on stealing from the damned Yankees, became popular with the general population of the country. In 1876, Frank and Jesse combined efforts with the Cole Younger Gang to raid a Yankee bank in Northfield, Minnesota. The robbery failed, with a temporary bank clerk being killed and no money taken from the vault. A shootout took place on the main street, and the Younger Gang was shot up pretty bad.

The bleeding Youngers escaped town, as did Frank and Jesse, but the James brothers split off from the soon-to-be-captured gang, heading west to Granite Falls, Minnesota. Then the Jameses resorted to an old Rebel trick: doubling back through central Minnesota via St. Cloud and then circling toward Anoka and Stillwater. The outlaws thought they might be recognized

The Perilous St. Croix River Valley Frontier

in a busy little city like Stillwater, so they headed south toward the sleepy little river town of Afton. The notorious Younger brothers, having been wounded and captured, received convictions for which they would serve twenty-five years in the Minnesota State Prison at Stillwater.

No one expected to see the famous James outlaws in Afton, nor would the townsfolk be likely to recognize them. The most popular place to find lodging among Afton's boardinghouses was at the well-established Cushing House. The Jameses came in on horseback and boarded the horses with William Cran at his livery stable, just a few doors down from the Cushing House Hotel.

The Wolf Saloon was farther south down Afton's dusty main street, next to Hay Creek. The two outlaws certainly would not miss a stop at the saloon. It was there where the brothers were informed of the upcoming dance, right next door at the Wolf Dance Hall.

Back at the Cushing House, news of the dance spread. Visitors being in town would make it even more splendid. It took only one fiddler to make music at the social event. Sometimes two fiddlers or three made the party even more jubilant. These events did not happen often, as socializing on the frontier had its limitations. Everyone would have taken three or four turns dancing with one another, being certain to make acquaintance with all who were there. Frank and Jesse attended, and one can be sure that this made their stay in Afton a pleasurable one.

When Frank and Jesse James decided to leave Afton, they enacted the final move of their getaway plan. Returning to the livery stable where their two horses were boarded, they offered both animals and saddles to William Cran if he wished to buy them. The travelers explained that they planned to buy steamboat tickets, with a destination of St.

The Civil War–era image of Jesse James that widow Eliza Ross's grandson Orville displayed in his home honoring the family's history that Eliza Ross had danced with the famous outlaw in Afton. Library of Congress image, 2005682818.

Part V

Louis, Missouri. William Cran said he would pay $75 for each complete outfit. A total price of $150 was agreed to, and the brothers walked away toward the landing to board a riverboat heading downstream.

All was quiet in town when William Cran paused with a halt, as if the air had been knocked out of him. He had just bought horses from the famous outlaw Jesse James and his brother Frank! It was a special connection with notorious fame that William Cran never forgot. No alarm was given.

The dance had been well attended, but most Afton folk knew nothing of the pair of notorious strangers. Eliza Ross was a widow who danced at the hall the night that Jesse was there. Eliza was thirty-two at the time; the youthful and experienced traveler she favored would have been twenty-nine. William Cran must have confirmed with Eliza that Jesse James was the man she had danced with at Wolf's Dance Hall.

The Questionable Death of Captain Emil Munch

Emil Munch was an experienced Prussian blacksmith who went to the pineries of Chengwatana. Forging hardware, chains and shoes for the oxen, mules and horses was never-ending work that paid well. Munch soon became heavily involved in the construction and milling operations that took place along the Snake River. The enterprising and popular Munch was then elected to Minnesota's first state legislature in 1858. When the Civil War came, Munch, a man with leadership ability and knowledge of iron and bronze, joined Minnesota's First Battery of Light Artillery

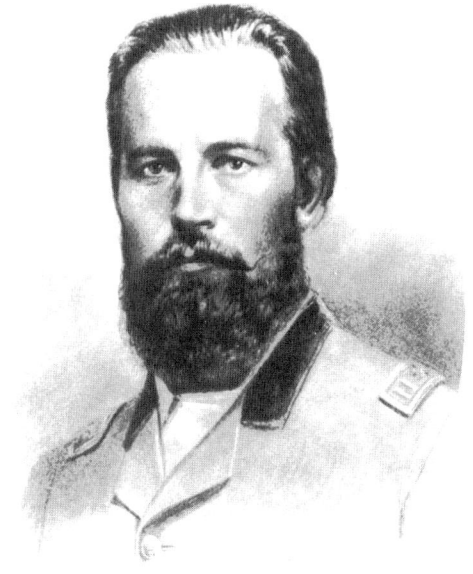

Captain Emil Munch's enlistment photo at the youthful age of twenty-nine wearing his new non–U.S. regulation gray Minnesota militia uniform. *Photo courtesy Afton Historical Society.*

at Fort Snelling. He wanted control of the regiment and manipulated his stature to the command position of the First Battery of Light Artillery.

A great Civil War event that Captain Emil Munch experienced was the Battle of Shiloh in Tennessee. The April 1862 battle was of immense proportion, eclipsing any of America's battles up until that time. The worst place to be on April 6 was at the Hornet's Nest, and Minnesota's First Battery was centered there. Flying projectiles filled the battlefield's air. Bullets whizzed like angry hornets with a deadly sting. Union soldiers fighting on the right of the Minnesota artillery were captured by aggressive Confederates. During the course of the hellacious day, shots seemed to come at Emil Munch's battery from nearly every direction. It was not a good day for the Yankees.

Cannons roared like thunder, spitting their bolts with fire and lightning. Smoke obscured the air, reeking of sulfur from the bowels of the earth. Thirsty artillery horses stood at nervous attention, helpless in battle other than to take their wounds and die. Captain Munch's command horse was killed when it was shot out from under him. Emil's thoughts were to save the saddle for the next horse he could locate when he was stung by a Rebel's hornet, shot in the thigh. Munch, unable to move, passed his command to Lieutenant Pfaender. Somehow, the Minnesotans evaded capture on that infernal day.

On Christmas Day 1862, Captain Emil Munch, after much suffering, resigned his command and returned to Minnesota. Back home, he was given a new command—the Minnesota State Militia—and put in charge of the Indian war in the state if it were to occur again. Munch continued to rotate through numerous leadership positions until the end of the Civil War.

After the war, Munch was elected Minnesota state treasurer; after serving his term, he settled in Lakeland. He purchased Lemuel Bolles's old flour mill in Afton's Valley Creek community and rebuilt it as the Reliance Mill, which he successfully operated for nearly fifteen years. On August 30, 1887, Emil's death from a heart attack was reported across the state of Minnesota. An active builder, leader and protector of the state, Emil Munch was well honored.

The report of Munch's death by heart attack was the most respectful way to explain how such a great pioneer had passed from the earth. Many people had been told of the fire that Munch fought in his home, which was the cause of his heart attack. Some folks were aware that Munch was burned in the house fire that caused the heart attack but kept that a secret out of deep respect for the man. A small number of people held it in close confidence

Part V

that Munch had accidentally started the fire by breaking a kerosene lamp after midnight in his home. A select few folks knew the truth—that Captain Munch had burned himself severely. It seemed such a shame to lose a brave veteran of the war that saved the Union to an accidental death by fatal burns caused by a household kerosene lamp.

Woman of Mystery: Mary Traveler

Many plagues visited the river sites of the St. Croix. Illness arrived by steamboat and now by railroad as well. Stillwater was a destination of many who sought work in the sawmills and millwork shops. Window sash manufacturing had become well established at Stillwater, including two (clam shell) button factories. Boardinghouses were everywhere, hosting the influx of labor. Opportunity in Stillwater was drawing many to the maturing frontier city.

In 1888, a young woman was merrily traveling on a steam engine train with her toddler son, destined for Stillwater. Folks on the train noticed the decline of

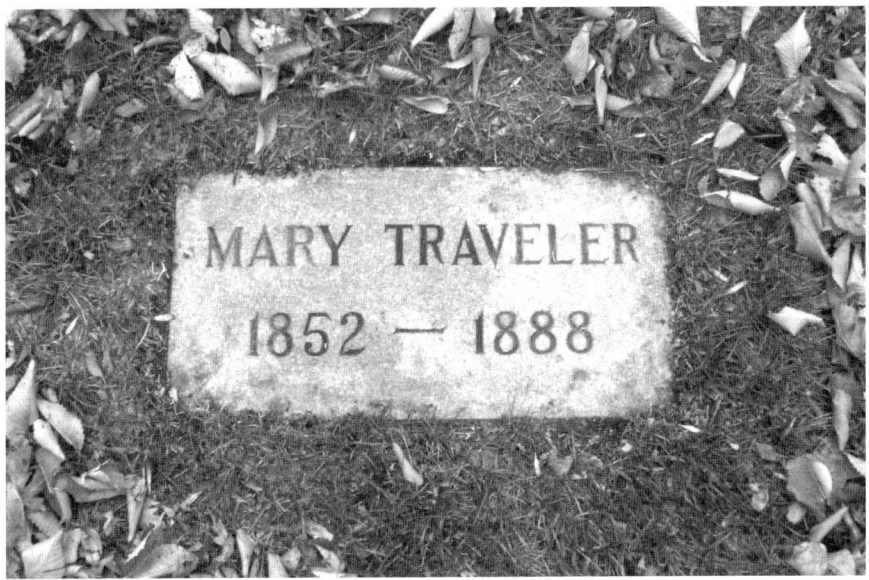

Mary Traveler's fictional name was given to her after her burial. Her birth year was an estimation. Her renamed son, Eddie Traveler, spent his life searching for anyone who knew who he was.

the woman's health as the train approached Stillwater's railroad depot. As the people departed the train, the young mother passed into unconsciousness. The desperately ill woman and her child had to be removed from the train.

Treatment was given to the comatose woman, but her condition worsened. There was a search of her possessions for any sort of identification. Nothing was found. Her son was about one year old, not old enough to speak or reveal anything about his mother. Notices were placed around Stillwater in an effort to locate her husband or family who might be expecting her arrival. No one was found.

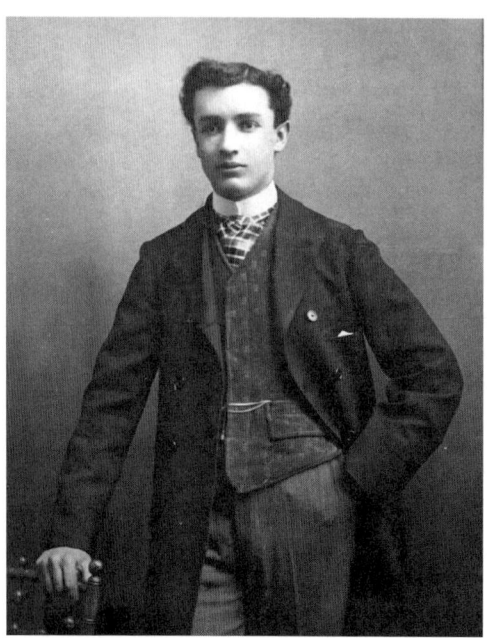

Eddie Traveler, a respectable young gentleman, was eternally plagued by the unsolved mystery of who he really was. *Photo courtesy Washington County Historical Society.*

The woman, whose identity a complete mystery, did not live. She was given a proper burial in a county-donated grave plot adjacent to St. Michaels Cemetery. It was a sad and lonely burial of "Mary Doe," as concerned folks dubbed her. Her son was taken in by a generous family and given a new name, Eddie.

There were compassionate people in Stillwater who felt sadness for the mystery woman and chose to donate a gravestone to her plot. The sterile-sounding name of Mary Doe did not sit well with them, so her name was altered to Mary Traveler. Edward Traveler was raised in Stillwater but left his adopted family when he was of age. Edward lived a respectable, successful life and settled in Canada, yet he continuously searched for who he was.

EPILOGUE

The End of an Era

Ferdinand Bahneman farmed his father's land at the small village of Valley Creek in Afton Township. Spring arrived once again, and Ferdinand took the hay wagon out for a pleasure ride to entertain his children. While following a bluff line above the creek, he halted the wagon and instructed the kids to wait until he returned from checking in on some friends. The children knew that a family of Dakota had secretly returned to the area and located a small cave for their winter quarters.

Ferdinand returned from below the bluff as if he had seen a ghost. The kids stared at him because his face was long and white. Ferdinand did not speak of what he had seen. Even at dinner, Ferdinand was acting strange. He had changed, and something over the edge of the bluff had traumatized him. The children could only imagine that something terrible had happened to the cave dwellers during the winter. Ferdinand never spoke of the incident or of the native family. He was never the same.

Charles Getchell, who was widowed in 1857 when his wife, Electa, died in Afton, married Julia Putnam, Reverend Simon Putnam's war widow. The couple worked the Getchell Store together for ten years after the war and then moved on to homestead North Dakota in 1875. Charles Getchell regained his pioneer spirit there by organizing Getchell Township north of Valley City. The family farmed the land and raised their blended family on the prairie.

Epilogue

Charles Gethcell died in 1890 after making daughter Electa "Ada" Getchell Hills the executor of his estate. Little Ada had lived when her mother, Electa, died, and now Ada used her rightful name, Electa. Electa brought her father's body to Afton and buried him in Mount Hope's pioneer cemetery next to the mother she never knew. Today, the rolling hills of the North Dakota prairie on the Getchell farm retain the name Electa Hills for Charles's first love.

Not long after Charles Getchell was buried, pioneer David Berry would be buried, too. Soon, the old pioneer cemetery of Mount Hope went neglected, the old pioneers having come to the end of their time. Andrew Mackey, the first settler at Catfish, was the oldest man in Washington County when he died at age ninety-eight in 1892. Elias McKean died on July 5, 1894. McKean's death was attributed to a heat wave of temperatures approaching one hundred degrees. He was seventy-seven.

Jake Fisher, one of the most eccentric men of the St. Croix Valley, had staked the original land claim that became Stillwater. He dabbled in just about every enterprise the valley had to offer. When the Civil War interrupted the pioneering of the valley, Jake volunteered at age forty-four as a wagoner with Minnesota's Second Company of Sharpshooters. At the end of his term, Jake reenlisted. His smoking pipe was shot from his mouth during one battle; he was wounded at Cold Harbor but survived and then was captured later at Reams Station, resulting in his imprisonment at Andersonville Prison. Jake Fisher's eccentricity was somewhat more than folks could tolerate, and he was committed to an insane asylum in 1889. Jake Fisher died in the asylum five days later.

Lissete Carli, the first full-blood white pioneer child to be born in the St. Croix Valley, grew up in the frontier town of Stillwater and married David Grout. Lissete died in 1864 at the age of twenty-one. Her mother, Lydia, was a local (pioneer) celebrity until her death in Stillwater in 1905.

In 1896, Pete Roselle was delivering a wagonload of bricks from Stillwater up the frozen St. Croix River to Hay Lake School near Scandia, but he didn't make it. Pete's load of bricks crashed through the ice, horses and all. Pete tried desperately to save the horses from an icy grave by releasing them from the wagon's leather harness. Unfortunately, Pete himself became entangled in the harness. Together, all of them froze in the river. Nothing ever seemed to change in the St. Croix River Valley.

Coal fuel came to use in steam trains and sawmills. Coal burners replaced wood fuel in nearly every household in the cities of the lower St. Croix. Coal smoke, with its acrid, sulfuric odor, burned the eyes and nostrils. Black

Epilogue

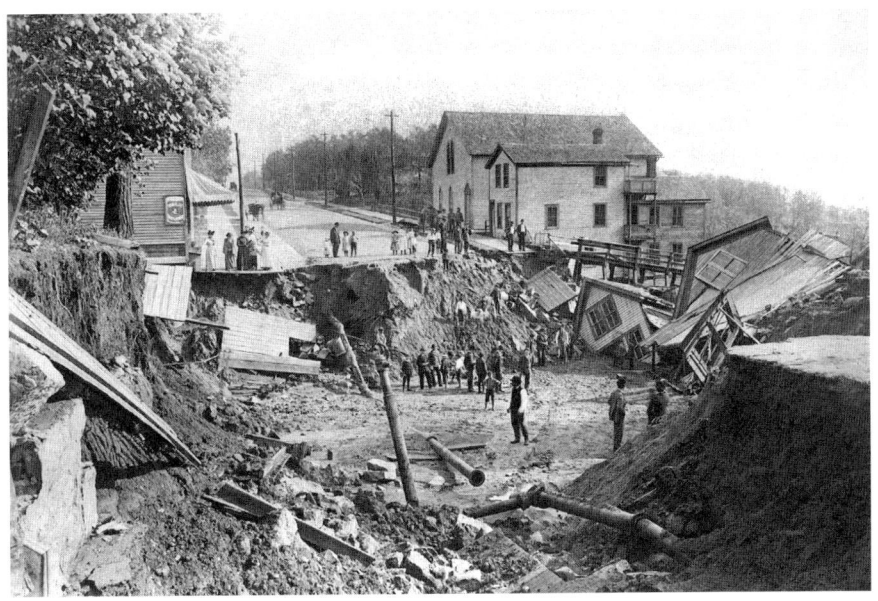

Natural disasters continued to take place in the St. Croix Valley. Cloudbursts of cataclysmic proportion that occurred in 1826 and 1852 struck again in 1885, 1894 and 1926. Stillwater, 1894. *Photo courtesy Washington County Historical Society.*

ash fell from the sky, turning snow-covered ground into a dusty dark gray. Beautiful American flags that were patriotically flown turned from gray to black, requiring replacement once or twice each winter.

Gasoline fuel came to the frontier as a modern convenience. Candles had already been replaced by kerosene oil lamps. In 1899, gasoline was used for fuel by Ferdinand Richert in an upstairs bedroom lamp. The gasoline lamp exploded, burning his wife, Martha, who died from her injuries.

Enter the Modern Era, or "Locked Inside the Bank's Vault"

The Cosmopolitan Bank was built in Afton in 1913. America's banking system had been recently overhauled by an act of Congress, resulting in modern banks being established across the country. In 1921, a bandit with a gun walked into Afton's bank and robbed it of $2,000. Afton was a small town, and there was no protection in the area to speak of. Inside the bank

Epilogue

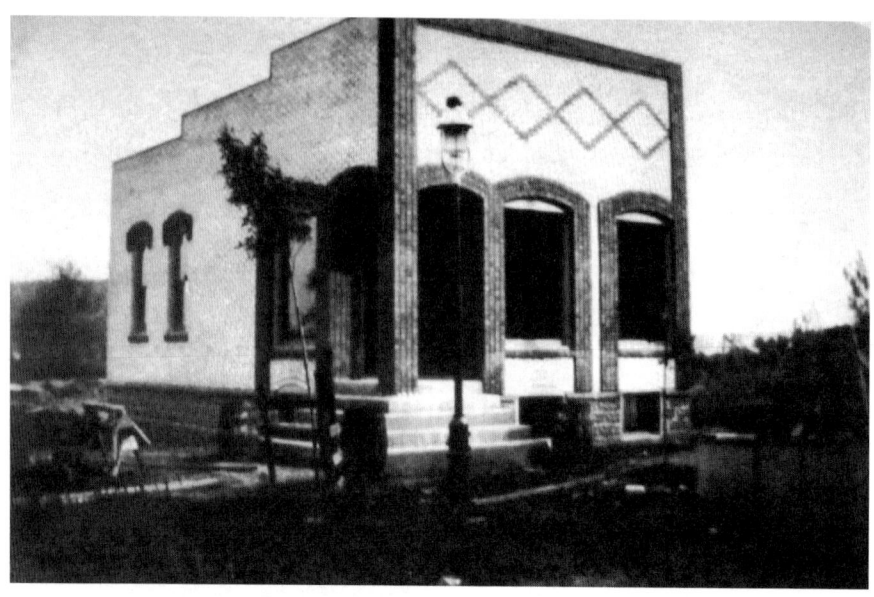

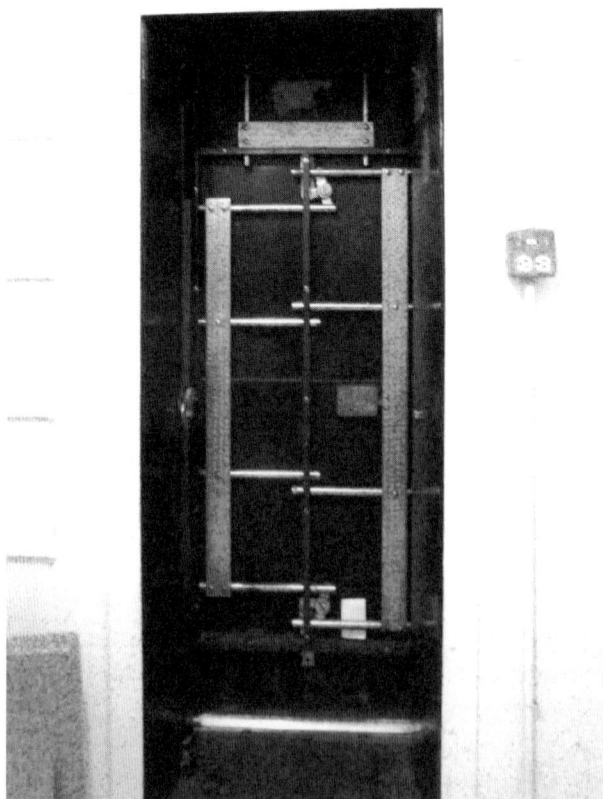

Above: The Cosmopolitan Bank building is shown under construction and nearing completion in 1913. *Photo courtesy Afton Historical Society.*

Left: Inside the Cosmopolitan Bank's vault, where the bank's cashier and teller were trapped after the 1913 robbery.

Epilogue

was a sturdy vault that was unlocked. The armed thief, J.P. Beltz, forced cashier Harry Swenson and the teller, Ester Schultz, into the bank vault and slammed its door shut. The bank robber continued his spree at Stockholm, Wisconsin, thirty-five miles away, holding up a bank there. This time, luck ran out for the hapless bandit, and he was captured nearby in Red Wing, Minnesota, with $2,000 in his possession. Harry Swenson and Ester Schultz found a screwdriver inside the vault and worked with it for hours until they found a way to remove the lock and force open the door's heavy latch pins. The bank closed permanently due to embezzlement eight years later.

The native people who canoed the St. Croix River are missing from its waters now. The prairies they once maintained with fire have been turned over by plow or have been planted with Austrian, Norway or Scotch pine and spruce. St. Croix Valley sawmills went silent in 1914, the pineries having been depleted of first-growth white pine. Arbor Day came to the St. Croix Valley in 1873, and every sort of tree has been planted, except for the slow-growing oak of the prairie savannah. The natural white pines that were cut down will not grow back because roving deer continue to eat their tender sprigs before they have a chance to grow. Invasive plant species of Siberian buckthorn, Russian

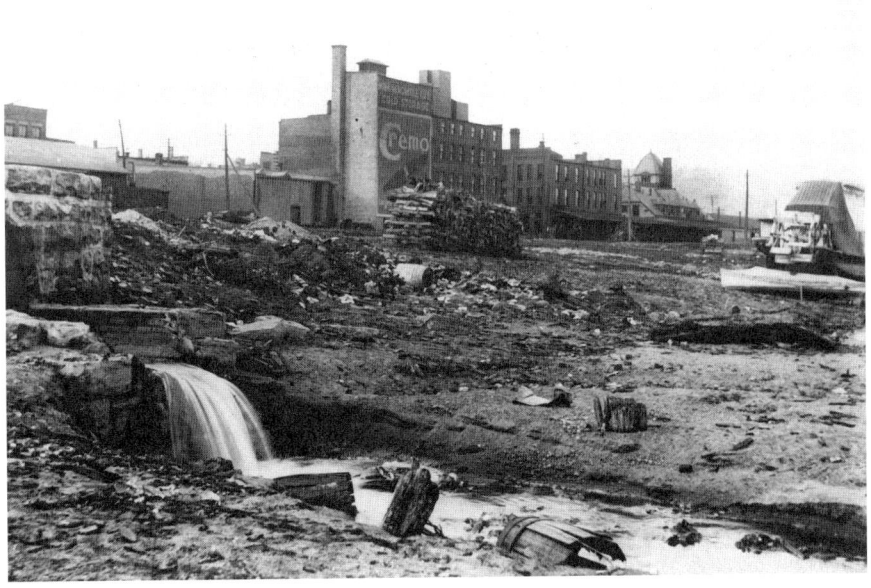

The 1911 drought lowered the St. Croix, exposing the dump that it had once been. Concerned for the river, people cleaned up the mess and built Lowell Park in place of the dump. *Photo courtesy Washington County Historical Society.*

Epilogue

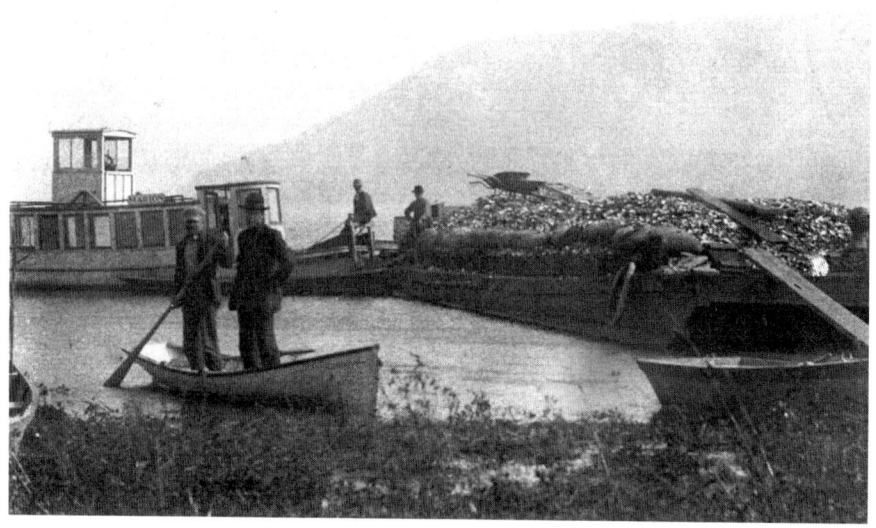

For several decades, clam harvesting was done by the barge load. Fortunately, clam populations are resilient, having made a complete recovery. *Photo courtesy Afton Historical Museum.*

thistle and Mediterranean mustard seed cannot be halted from spreading across the formerly glorious prairie. First-growth forests (that were once prairie) are impassable today, choked with fallen branches and dead trunks. The original prairie and white pine forests are only a memory that is written of in books.

For decades, St. Croix River clams were harvested by the barge load for their shells, but that ended in the 1930s. Bakelite and plastic replaced clamshells for button-making material, and clam populations, once thought to be at risk, are flourishing throughout the river.

Hybrid corn that is now planted on the once arid prairie aspirates as much as two gallons of water per stalk per day, altering the mild climate into a humid one. The area's annual average precipitation, which was merely twenty inches per year (one hundred years ago), is double that today.

In 1939, representatives of the Dakota and Ojibwe people were invited to Stillwater for the centennial dedication of the monument to the historic battle they engaged in at Battle Hollow. Peace had finally been achieved between the two great nations.

The natural element of phosphorus flows through the waters of the St. Croix River. Essential for healthy life, an excess of phosphorus causes the growth of algae, which, in an overabundance, can kill fish. Phosphorus is

Epilogue

found in limestone, which is the bedrock of the lower St. Croix, and there is no way to clean the phosphorous from it.

Vibrio cholera is a natural intestinal bacteria essential for life, but too much of a good thing can be terminal to humans, and there is no way to live without it. Fortunately, sewage treatment plants mitigate the potential health risks for us today.

E. coli is a bacterium, essential to life, that lives in the intestines of humans and animals. It's the same natural, potentially deadly bacteria that grows in your kitchen sink drain and countertop washcloth. E. coli has been tested for and found in watershed creeks that flow into the St. Croix. There is E. coli in the St. Croix River, and there is no way to clean it out. The essence of the river is imperfect in the midst of its natural beauty.

Mount Hope Cemetery, burial place of frontier people and pioneers, has been vandalized numerous times over the last one hundred years. Other St. Croix Valley pioneer burial grounds have suffered similar abuse. Much of the St. Croix Valley's historic record has been lost. Restoration efforts are attempted, but the permanent solution of preservation remains elusive.

Steamboat traffic on the St. Croix ended, having been replaced by railroads. Railroads were replaced by an extensive highway system. Riverboats have made their reappearance on the St. Croix, allowing one to experience a romantic cruise on the historic river. A private railroad has reopened at Osceola, Wisconsin. People and families now find it an entertaining experience to travel the rails.

Prairie restoration projects have taken place in a few areas of the St. Croix Valley. In Minnesota, Wild River State Park, Afton State Park, Belwin Conservancy and Carpenter Nature Center have restored prairie so that one might appreciate it. Bison have recently been reintroduced to Belwin's prairie; their presence there are key to returning the grass to its former glory. In Wisconsin, KinnicKinnic State Park has restored its prairie, and at Crex Meadows Wildlife Area, the Department of Natural Resources has thirty thousand acres of natural marsh, prairie and forest in permanent preservation. Today, one is able to step out into the prairie grass and regain a sense of what the lost era might have been like.

Retired Stillwater schoolteacher Marian Williams Glynn was raised on a farm on the hill above Lilly Lake in Stillwater. As a young woman, she was aware of the native burial mounds on Benson's farmland that lined the bluff overlooking the lake. One burial there was different from the others, with a stone pile and an old grave marker that stated:

Epilogue

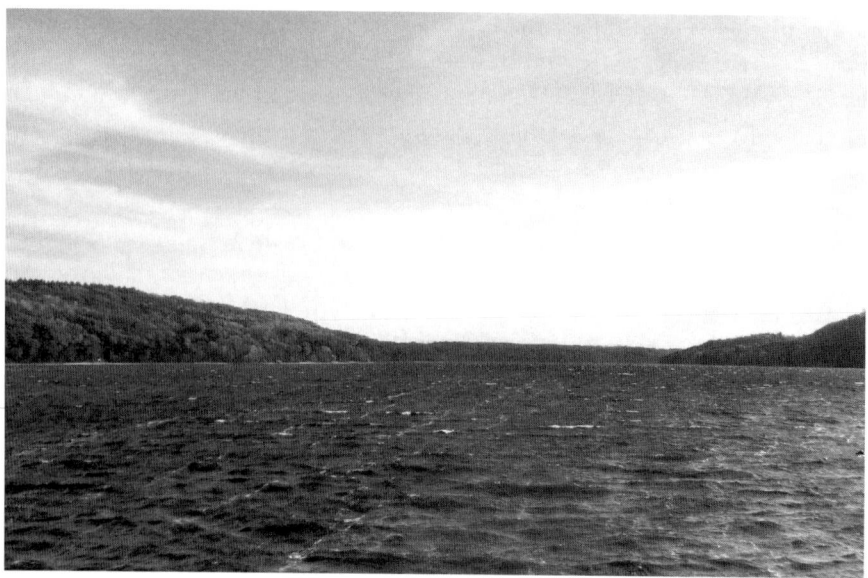

The Wild and Scenic border river of Wisconsin and Minnesota—the St. Croix River.

*A Sioux Chief
Who was
Killed in Battle.*

Marion's research led her to believe that the marked grave was the Dakota (Sioux) chief who died from wounds at the Battle of Zion Hill. Marian spent the rest of her life on the land, passionate about the history of the St. Croix Valley. In later years, Marian discovered that the stones from the chief's grave had sunk below the sod and were lost. Other mounds have disappeared from the land as well, as modern development replaced Benson's old farm. If Marian Williams Glynn were here today, she might be heard to say, "Search for the chief's lost grave, it's right out there."

BIBLIOGRAPHY

Alghren, Dorothy Eaton, and Mary Cotter Beeler. *A History of Prescott, Wisconsin: A River City and Farming Community on the St. Croix and Mississippi.* Prescott, WI: Prescott Area Historical Society, 1996.

Anderson, Gary Clayton. *Little Crow, Spokesman for the Sioux.* St. Paul: Minnesota Historical Society Press, 1986.

Blair, Emma Helen. *The Indian Tribes of the Upper Mississippi Valley and Region of the Great Lakes: As Described by Nicolas Perrot, French Commandant in the Northwest; Bacquevile de la Potherie, French Royal Commissioner to Canada; Morrell Marston, American Army Officer; and Thomas Forsyth, United States Agent at Fort Armstrong.* Cleveland, OH: Arthur H. Clark Co., 1911.

Brown, William R., and Mitchell Y. Jackson. *Minnesota Farmers' Diaries.* St. Paul: Minnesota Historical Society, 1939.

Buck, Anita Albrecht. *Steamboats on the St. Croix.* St. Cloud, MN: North Star Press, 1990.

Cordes, Jim. *Reflections of Amador.* 1976. Reprint, North Branch, MN: Jim Cordes, 1987.

Bibliography

Daniels, Dr. Asa W. "Reminiscences of Little Crow." *Minnesota Historical Society Collections* 12 (1905–08).

Dunn, James Taylor. *The St. Croix, Midwest Border River*. St. Paul: Minnesota Historical Society Press, 1965.

Easton, Augustus B. *History of the St. Croix Valley*. Chicago: H.C. Cooper Jr. and Co., 1909.

Folsom, W.H.C. *Fifty Years in the Northwest*. 1888. Reprint, Taylors Falls, MN: Taylors Falls Historical Society, 1999.

Goodman, Nancy, and Robert Goodman. *Joseph R. Brown, Adventurer on the Minnesota Frontier, 1820–1849*. Rochester, MN: Lone Oak Press, 1996.

Hartsough, Mildred L. *From Canoe to Steel Barge on the Upper Mississippi*. Minneapolis: University of Minnesota Press, 1934.

Hubbard, Lucius F., William Pitt Murray, James H. Baker, Warren Upham, Return I. Holcombe and Frank R. Holmes. *Minnesota in Three Centuries, 1655–1908*. New York: Publishing Society of Minnesota, 1908.

Koblas, John. *Jesse James Ate Here*. St. Cloud, MN: North Star Press, 2001.

McMahon, Eileen M, and Theodore J. Karamanski. *Time and the River; A History of the Saint Croix, A Historic Resource Study of the Saint Croix National Scenic Riverway*. Madison: University of Wisconsin Press, 2002.

Neill, Rev. Edward D. *History of Washington County and the St. Croix Valley*. Minneapolis, MN: North Star Publishing Co., 1881.

Park Genealogical Books. *Minnesota Adjutant General's Report of 1866*. Roseville, MN: Park Genealogical Books, 1997.

Pond, Samuel L. *The Dakota or Sioux in Minnesota as They Were in 1834*. 1908. Reprint, St. Paul: Minnesota Historical Society Press, 1986.

Bibliography

Schoolcraft, Henry Rowe. *Personal Memoirs of a Residence of Thirty Years with the Indian Tribes on the American Frontiers, 1812–1842*. Philadelphia: Lippincott, Grambo and Co., 1851.

Treuer, Anton. *Ojibwe in Minnesota*. St. Paul: Minnesota Historical Society Press, 2010.

Turner, Frederick Jackson. *The Character and Influence of the Indian Trade in Wisconsin: A Study of the Trading Post as an Institution*. Norman: University of Oklahoma Press, 1977.

Warren, William W. *History of the Ojibway People*. St. Paul: Minnesota Historical Society, 1984.

Washington County Historical Society. *Minnesota Beginnings, Records of St. Croix County Wisconsin Territory, 1840–1849*. Stillwater, MN: Washington County Historical Society, 1999.

Williams, J. Fletcher. *Outlines of the History of Minnesota*. Minneapolis, MN: North Star Publishing Co., 1881.

Winchell, N.H. *The Aborigines of Minnesota: A Report Based on the Collections of Jacob V. Brower and the Field Surveys and Notes of Alfred J. Hill and Theodore H. Lewis*. St. Paul: Minnesota Historical Society Press, 1911.

Newspapers

Hastings Democrat
Hudson North Star
Hudson Star Observer
Stillwater Democrat
Stillwater Messenger
Washington County Post

INDEX

A

Abel 13
Ackerman, James 157
Acton, Minnesota 150
Addison
   accidental discharge death 143
African American community 156
Afton, Minnesota 9, 24, 25, 27, 107, 129,
       130, 138, 139, 140, 145, 146, 147,
       148, 150, 151, 154, 155, 156, 157,
       162, 163, 164, 167, 168, 169, 173
   war party 138
Afton State Park 24, 173
Amador Cemetery 135
Amador, town of 134
Arbor Day 171
Armstrong, Ed 153
Atkinson, Martin
   drowning of 104
Aztalan, Wisconsin 24
Aztecs 25

B

Bahneman, Ferdinand 167
Barron, Richard
   fatal fall from tree 143

Bartlett, William
   drowned in Lake St. Croix 140
baseball 155
Battle Hollow 55, 59, 70, 79, 144, 172
Battle of Shakopee 139
battles 34, 38, 53, 55, 56, 59, 70, 79,
       81, 144, 150, 164, 172, 174
Bayport, Minnesota 21
Belwin Conservancy 173
Benz, Augustus 115
Berry, David 101, 168
Big Stone Lake 16
bison 56, 57, 59, 60, 173
Bissell, Elijah 81
Bissell's Mounds 81
   Afton, MN, geology 81
"blood for blood" 34
Bolles, Lemuel
   flour miller 65
Bonga, Jean
   a slave 78
Boyden, D.H. 141, 152
British 32, 38, 44, 50, 52, 76, 78
Brown, Joseph R. 69, 72, 78, 93, 176
Brown's Valley 16
Buffalo River
   site of bison hunting 59

INDEX

Burns, Robert
  poetry 107
Bush, Henry
  Amador Hotel owner 134

C

Cahokia, Illinois 9, 18, 21
Cain 13
calendar mounds 21
Carli, Joe 153
Carli, Lissete 72, 168
Carli, Lydia
  first white pioneer woman at Stillwater 68
Carli, Paul
  drowned 72
Carpenter Nature Center 173
Carver, Jonathan
  Caver's Cave named for the explorer 75
catfish
  a small community on the west bank of the St. Croix 37, 38, 65, 72, 73, 74, 85, 101, 107, 125
Catfish Bar 37, 38, 65, 74, 85, 125
Chengwatana
  site where the White Pines were logged 99, 163
Cheyenne 31
Chippewa 31, 34, 61, 137
cholera 27, 123, 173
Christian Indians 78
Civil War 88, 114, 135, 136, 137, 140, 147, 148, 150, 151, 152, 153, 154, 155, 156, 157, 158, 161, 163, 164, 168
clam shells 172
clans 32
Clegg, James 157, 158
coal smoke 168
Colby, John (Confederate) 153
  Resident of Stillwater and Woodbury 153
Cole Younger Gang 161
Columbus, Christopher 11

Connor, Thomas
  trader 56
consumption 151
Cornman, Lorenzo
  horse and buggy stolen 144
Cosmopolitan Bank
  robbed in 1913 169
Cottage Grove 104, 141
Cran, William 162, 163
Crex Meadows Wildlife Area 173
Cudd, Abel 131
  road construction accident 131
Curtis, Charlie
  scalded 144
Cushing House 162
Cutler, Postmaster 159

D

Dakota
  hunters 33, 106, 150
  man, always hungry 70
  people 18, 31, 32, 38, 47, 60, 62, 76, 78, 80, 83, 98, 149, 151
  warriors 34, 35, 39, 40, 42, 62, 79, 96, 138, 149, 150, 151
Dakota War 149, 151
Dalles (dallas) 14, 17, 39, 41
Davies, Gorham
  daughter taken 103
Davis, Johnathan 82
Deering plow 65, 101
  the sod breaking plow 65
Dibble, William, and Eliza McCauslin
  the mixed race wedding of 84
Dick, black pioneer 94
Dickson, Robert 57
  trader 57
diphtheria 105
Douglas, Senator Stephen A. 91
drought 23, 28, 116, 118, 159
drumlin 19
duck hunter
  shot himself 143

Index

E

E. coli 173
economic crisis of 1857 134, 155
1857 Financial Crisis 147
Electa Hills 168
Ellis, Frank 151
Equator (steamboat) 125

F

Fahlstrom, Jacob 75, 76, 77, 78, 81, 154
Fahlstrom, Marguarite
  mixed blood Ojibwe/African 78
Fairview Cemetery 19
fall harvest 82
Falls of St. Croix 17, 53, 56, 59, 62, 67, 68, 86, 87, 116
ferry 68, 91, 109, 110, 111, 112, 114, 134, 138, 140
  operations on the rivers 114
first frontier deaths
  recorded in the St. Croix Valley 72
Fisher, Jake 70, 72, 168
Fitz Randolph, Taylor 80
fluvial erosion 24
Folsom, William 84, 87
Forrest, Nathan Bedford 149
Fort Snelling's jail 95, 96, 154
Foster, Joel 94
Fourteenth Wisconsin Infantry 135
Fox
  people 38
  warriors 39
Frazer, Jack
  trader 44
French 30, 32, 33, 38, 42, 43, 44, 45, 59, 74, 100, 175

G

Gamelle, François 79
Garlick, Carmi 13, 132, 133, 136, 137
gasoline lamp
  explosion of 169
Getchell, Charles 107, 148, 167, 168
Getchell, Electa 107, 108, 167, 168
Getchell, Electa Ada 168
ghost
  Hudson's famous mule 142
Glynn, Marian Williams 173
gold fields
  of California 132, 133, 140
Gorman, Willis A. 157
Grave Marker River 38, 41
Great Monkey Circus 118
Great Spirit 23, 55
Green, Asa B.
  steamboat pilot 124
Greysolon, Daniel, Sieur du Lhut 30
Guernsey, William H. 101

H

Haskell, Joseph 64, 67, 81, 93, 104, 105, 107
Haskell, Ralzaman 107
Hastings, Minnesota 130
Hedderly (Edwin) family 140
Hennepin, Father Louis 30, 49
Holcomb, Edwin
  shot himself hunting 142
Hole in the Day, Chief 12
Hone, David and Mary 68
Hone, Mary
  first white pioneer woman 68
Hopewell 18
horses
  falling through ice 83, 141, 168
Hoyt, Dr. 142, 143
Hudson Bay Company 34, 77
Hudson, Wisconsin 138
  war dance 138

I

indentured servant 89, 94, 122
invasive plant species 171

J

Jackman, James 145
James, Jesse 161, 162, 163

Index

K

Kaposia (Dakota village) 68, 96, 98
Kenny, John and Mary Jane
   the mixed race wedding of 84
Kent, Jennie 153
killed by being gored 143
Kinnickinnic (lower St. Croix tributary) 20, 94
KinnicKinnic State Park 173
Knights of the Golden Circle 154

L

Lake Agassiz 16
Lake Calhoun 62
Lake Superior 15, 17, 30, 39, 76
landform 24
landslide
   disasters 97, 98
Le Petit Corbeau
   Dakota chief 46, 47, 48, 49, 50, 51, 149
Lester, Colonel Henry 149
Lewis and Clark 43
lightning
   injuries and death caused by 98
Little Crow 45, 46, 149, 150, 151, 175, 176
log rafts 100
Lord Selkirk's Canadian fur trade colony 77
lower St. Croix 187
lumber rafts 100

M

maintaining the prairies 27
Makin, L.M.
   son was scalded 143
Marine Mills 61, 68, 72, 84, 100, 117, 125, 131
Martin, Albert 139, 147
Masonic Lodge 153
Massey, Louis
   Willow River pioneer 75
McDonald, Ann 113
   burial place 113
McDonald, Edith O. 109
McDonald, Thomas and Anne 109
McDonald, Tom 144
   fell from a window 144
McKean, Elias 129
McKusick, John 70, 71, 72, 91, 93
McKusick, Johnathan E. 83, 93, 97
Menomonee soldiers
   Indian assault at Vicksburg 136
Minnesota Department of Conservation 28
Minnesota State Board of Health 28
Minnesota Territorial Prison 144
missionairies 30, 62, 72, 78
Mississippian culture 18
Mississippi River 12, 15, 17, 29, 30, 34, 35, 37, 38, 42, 43, 44, 47, 49, 50, 59, 61, 68, 77, 83, 91, 96, 104, 111, 112, 114, 121, 130, 136
Mite Society 153
Morrison, William and Allan
   discoverer's of the source of the Mississippi 52
mound-building people 12, 18, 31
mounds 9, 12, 18, 19, 20, 21, 24, 25, 81, 84, 173, 174
   Monks Mound 18, 21
   Moon Mounds 21
Mount Hope 102, 106, 107, 137, 140, 145, 150, 153, 168, 173
Mount Hope Cemetery 137, 145, 173
Munch, Captain Emil 163, 164, 165
murder 86, 87
Murphy, Major
   Indian agent 138

N

National Scenic Riverway 29, 176
Native Americans 22
   made sick by butter 103
Negro Hill
   named for London Peters 156
Negro suffrage 89
Ne-she-ke-o-ge-ma
   accused of murder 87

Index

Nodin (Indian)
   accused of murder 87
Norris, James 60, 64, 65, 93, 104
Norris, Sophia and James
   adopted daughter killed 104
Northern Divide 17
Northfield, Minnesota 161
Northrop, Anson
   hotel owner 92
North West Company 34, 77

O

oak marker trees 27
Odd Fellows 153
Ojibwe 12, 31, 32, 33, 34, 35, 36, 37, 38, 39, 40, 41, 42, 45, 47, 49, 50, 51, 53, 54, 55, 56, 59, 60, 61, 62, 64, 66, 67, 69, 77, 78, 79, 80, 84, 87, 88, 92, 93, 94, 95, 96, 97, 103, 104, 106, 133, 135, 137, 139, 144, 150, 172, 177
   warriors 34, 35, 37, 138
O'-ki-zu Wa-kpa' 34, 36, 45, 50, 60, 68
Old Cave settlement 75
Omigaundib 36, 37
Oneota 18, 31
Osceola, Wisconsin 116, 173
Otis, Benjamin, and Ann Little Wolf
   the mixed race wedding of 84
Outard Blanche, Chief 48

P

Page, Captain John
   logging on the Willow River 85
Painted Rock 188
Palmyra (steamboat) 103, 117
Paterson, Sam 147, 148
Perro, Big Joe
   steamboat pilot 101
Perrot, Nicholas 38
Peters, Jane 139, 140
Peters, London 89, 139, 140, 156
Peterson, John F. 154

phosphorus 172
   in the St. Croix River 172
Pike, Zebulon 42, 43, 44, 45, 46, 47, 49, 50, 51, 52, 61, 68, 91
Pine Glen 79, 80, 81
pineries
   where White Pines were cut 65, 99, 101, 117, 171
Pinichon, Chief 127
plague 27, 78, 106, 122, 123
   1842 78
Point Douglas 91, 109, 110, 111, 112, 113, 114, 130, 134, 139
prairie grass 26, 57, 62, 79, 90, 129, 130, 173
Prescott, Philander 68, 114
Prescott's Landing 68, 91
Prescott, Wisconsin 10, 139, 156
Putnam, Chaplain Simon 150, 151
Putnam, Myron 148, 149, 150
Putnam, Reverend Simon 105, 106, 148, 151, 167

R

Ramsden, Thomas 121
Ramsey, Alexander
   Territorial Governor 96
Randolph, Elizabeth Campbell 80
Rattler, Mrs.
   killed 79
rattlesnake effigy 25
Red Medicine Stone
   see Red Rock 46
Red Rock 60, 78, 79, 81, 154
Reese, Isaac
   Amador Pioneer 135
Richert, Martha
   gasoline explosion 169
River Warren 16
road rage 127, 129, 130
Roselle, Pete
   froze in the river 168
Rosseau (interpreter) 45
Ross, Eliza 161, 163

Index

Rust, Henry
  murdered 86

S

Sac and Fox Nation 41
Sam Paterson's Hotel 147
savannah 101, 171
Schoolcraft, Henry 77
  discoverer of the source of the Mississippi 52
Schultz, Ester
  locked inside the vault 171
Secrest, Ambrose 122
Seventh Wisconsin Infantry 158
sewage 27, 28, 173
Shakopee, Chief 137, 138
Shakopee's village 137, 138
Shakopee, town of 139
Sibley, Henry 80
Sioux 31, 45, 174, 175, 176
skiff 110, 111, 112, 115, 116
slavery 94
sleigh accident
  or manslaughter 130
smallpox 78
Smith, Evaline 153
Snake River 61, 99, 163
Snell, Silas
  employed by Capt. Page 85
Solon Springs 29
Son's of Malta 153
SS Central America 134
  sunk Sept. 11, 1857 134
Star Prairie
  war dance 138
St. Croix County 69, 72, 78, 89, 92, 177
St. Croix Falls 10, 17, 64, 65, 70, 87, 93, 116, 125, 135
St. Croix Ojibwe 61, 62
St. Croix River 12, 13, 14, 15, 17, 18, 19, 20, 21, 24, 28, 29, 30, 31, 32, 33, 34, 36, 39, 41, 45, 47, 50, 53, 54, 56, 59, 61, 62, 65, 67, 68, 73, 74, 76, 85, 87, 92, 98, 100, 103, 105, 106, 107, 114, 124, 133, 134, 135, 145, 152, 153, 155, 159, 171, 172, 173, 187, 188
St Croix River Valley 15
St. Croix Valley 12, 18, 20, 21, 25, 28, 31, 44, 55, 59, 60, 64, 65, 68, 74, 79, 81, 82, 83, 89, 91, 101, 105, 121, 129, 133, 136, 139, 140, 152, 153, 154, 155, 156, 168, 171, 173, 174, 176, 189
steamboats 117
  limitations of 126
Stillwater, Minnesota 19
St. Michaels Cemetery 166
Stone, Dr. 129
Stouffer, John and Hannah
  deaths of their children 105
St. Peters River 45, 47, 49, 50, 51, 60, 127, 137
Sunrise River 13, 106
surveyors 90
Suydam, Sidney 156
Swede Hollow 77
Swenson, Harry
  locked inside the vault 171

T

Taliaferro, Lawrence
  U.S. Indian Agent 59
Tamarack House 69
Taylors Falls 10, 17, 29, 91, 116, 125
terrace 24
Thirteenth U.S. Volunteers 158
Thirty-fifth Wisconsin Infantry 136
Thomas, Hewitt 146, 147
Thomas, Meredith 146
Thomas, Minor T. 146
Thunderbird
  killed by the Dakota 98
Tom the Cat 97
Tracy, Asa 140
traders 30, 33, 38, 49, 50, 51, 54, 57, 76, 77, 87, 128
Traveler, Mary 166
Traverse Continental Divide 16

Index

trial 86
Trimbelle (Pierce County, Wisconsin) 131
turkey buzzards 59
Turtle Lake, Wisconsin 138
Twenty-seventh Wisconsin Infantry 158

U

upper St. Croix 29, 188
U.S. Constitution 154

V

Van Vleck, Isaac 145, 157
Van Vleck, Willie 145

W

Wabasha, Chief 57
warriors 34, 35, 37, 39, 40, 41, 42, 47,
    48, 49, 50, 54, 64, 70, 79, 80, 95,
    96, 128, 136, 137, 138, 139, 152
Waub-o-jeeg, Chief 39
Welch, Mr. 110
  ferry operator drowned 112
Wheeler, Harry 116
whiskey 47, 83, 84, 86, 87, 88, 96,
    117, 150
Wide Awakes 153
Wild and Scenic River Act 29
Wild River State Park 173
Willow River 41, 42, 73, 75, 85, 94,
    98, 153
Wisconsin Board of Health 28
Wolf Saloon 157, 162
Woodland culture 18, 31

Y

yellow fever 78
Yellow Head (alias for Jacob
    Fahlstrom) 77

Z

zephyr (west wind) 27, 108
Zibi, Menominikeshi 41
Zion Hill 53, 54, 55, 56, 62, 145, 159, 174

ABOUT THE AUTHOR

I was very young, just four years old, when I was packed into a chubby, "warning orange"–colored life preserver to boat on the clear blue waters of the St. Croix River. The St. Croix was a recreational river and a pleasure boater's dream. The wooded river valley was emerald green, broken by a few yellow sandstone cliffs resembling mountains of gold.

People water-skied at high speeds around homemade houseboats that puttered amidst the tranquility of the lower St. Croix. Large cabin cruisers generated wave action that broke the routine with their huge rolling wakes.

While traveling the St. Croix, I was fascinated by

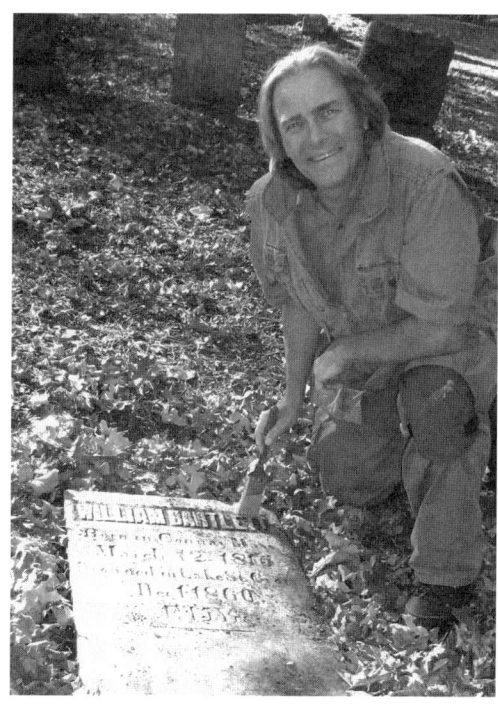

The author at Willow River Cemetery, Hudson, Wisconsin.

About the Author

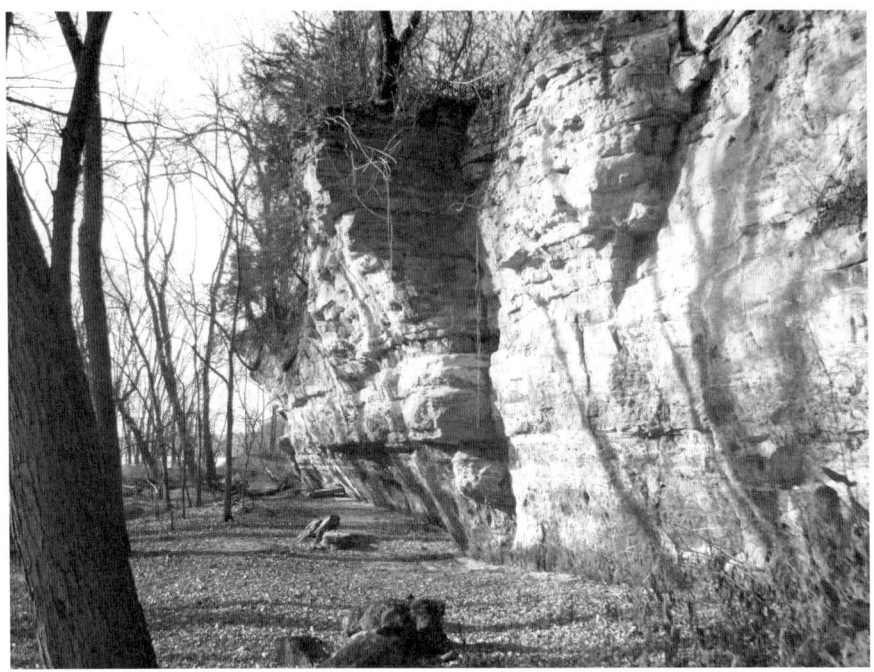

Limestone cliffs of the St. Croix River, located north of Stillwater. Part of the cliffs' walls were painted by native people over two hundred years ago.

a series of mysterious limestone columns that projected skyward from the waters, reminiscent of a Romanesque era of centuries past. My question was answered—the stone columns once supported a railroad bridge that carried steam trains over the valley more than a half century before. It was gone now, and to me it remained a mystery.

Our ski boat met canoeists paddling south while on the narrow, calm portion of the St. Croix. There was a fragile-looking old shack perched on the edge of the river, as if it might tumble off of its ledge, an old sawmill that had survived from a time long past.

A deep and dark cave to explore was cause for a young one's heart to race. A cave in the cliff that was dug to store cheese was the answer to my question. A few hundred feet from the old cheese cave was Painted Rock, a faded, nearly gone history of native life and warfare. The ones who painted the rock the colors of red, yellow and blue had vanished into history, and today their paint has vanished, too.

I have spent decades on the St. Croix River exploring the water, its sandbars, sandy beaches, lush ravines and a few craggy caves, continually

About the Author

aware of the people who once existed here. A personal river episode occurred when an unpredicted rainstorm arose with high-velocity winds and zero visibility. Fortunately, I was able to save the Chris Craft from being wrecked on jagged rocks. I was twelve. Familiar with the mighty Mississippi as well, I witnessed a collision of three boats, sinking two and sending people screaming into the water. I discovered that river life can become crazy, just as it did in history.

I come from a heritage of accomplished storytellers, my mother and her parents. Near the end of my grandmother's life, I asked, "How long has your side of the family been in America?" She thought for such a long while that I wondered if she had forgotten the question. But eventually, she replied, "We've been here a very long, long time."

Many people claim Cherokee roots as a portion of their heritage, but I have followed mine, which are documented on historic Cherokee Rolls and annuity payments. I have learned much about the Cherokee people and their heritage, discovering that I can identify with many other tribal people of this land. I have developed a fascination of history and an insatiable curiosity about the mysteries that native people and St. Croix Valley adventurers have left behind. I continue to live in the St. Croix Valley with the river, its history and native culture all flowing through my veins.

Visit us at
www.historypress.net

This title is also available as an e-book